THE KNITGRRL GUIDE TO PROFESSIONAL KNITWEAR DESIGN

THE KNITGRRL GUIDE TO PROFESSIONAL KNITWEAR DESIGN

HOW TO KEEP YOUR KNITS ABOUT YOU

Shannon Okey, knitgrrl.com

COOPERATIVE PRESS

Cleveland, Ohio

Library of Congress Control Number: 2010901893

ISBN 13: 978-0-9792017-1-4

First Edition
Published by Cooperative Press
http://www.cooperativepress.com

COOPERATIVE PRESS

Senior Editor: Shannon Okey
Cover Designer: Tamas Jakab
InDesign consultant: Stacie Ross

TO ALL THE KNITTERS, CROCHETERS AND OTHER CREATIVE PEOPLE IN OUR INDUSTRY WHO WANT TO TAKE IT TO THE NEXT LEVEL.

TABLE OF CONTENTS

INTRODUCTION

Hello! You may not already know me, so I'd like to tell you who I am, what my background is and just why I'm qualified to write about being (or becoming) a professional knitwear designer.

I started knitting much later than most designers I know – one of them learned when she was 4! However, being from a creative family, I've always made things, and according to my mother, I also have a long track record of setting up shop and selling them.

> *Age 5: I'm running a lemonade stand, and the gnarliest, leather-wearing-est Harley rider imaginable pulls up. Think ZZ Top on a bike. He gives me a whole dollar when I'm only charging 25 cents, and I carefully pour him barely half a glass. Fortunately, my mother came running out to work on my customer service skills! (I've learned a lot since then).*

Fast forward 20+ years: In the early 2000s, knitblogs and websites dedicated to nothing but knitting were fairly new inventions (Jenna at Girl From Auntie has owned up to being the first[1], in March 2001. Dangerous Chunky was another. Knitgrrl.com, my knitting blog, separated from my personal site in 2002. The Yarn Harlot came on the scene in 2004).

A friend I initially met online (Kathy Cano Murillo, aka the Crafty Chica) emailed to say her editor was looking for someone to write a knitting book for tweens, and suddenly, bam! I've quit my day job at a law firm to write *Knitgrrl* and *Knitgrrl 2*.

From the very beginning, I was walking through uncharted waters, even though I'd been hired to write books before. Knitty.com's first issue went online in the fall of 2002, and many of us looked to its publisher Amy Singer for guidance on how we should develop submissions, and write our patterns. The Knitty Submissions Guidelines[2] and stylesheet are, in my opinion, still the most user-friendly for new designers getting established.

Until Knitty, it was common practice in the magazine world to write a pattern in only one size and expect that the publication's tech editor would do the grading required to supply more than one size for the end user. Knitty not only encouraged new designers to learn how to do these formerly arcane skills for themselves, it later broke new ground by requiring larger sizing on all patterns, instead of just a handful, if any at all. Knitty was, and continues to be, an incredibly positive influence on the knit design world.

The first flood of book deals in the suddenly-hot knitting book market came rushing along in Knitty's wake. I wrote my Knitgrrl books, Amy published her first (*Knit Wit*), Vickie Howell sped straight from publishing a guitar strap pattern in Knitty to her first book, *New Knits On The Block*, and just kept on going, hosting Knitty Gritty (an entire TV show about knitting) for several

---

1   http://www.girlfromauntie.com/journal/index.php/2007/reduction-to-practice
2   http://www.knitty.com/subguide.php

seasons. And let's not forget Debbie Stoller's book *Stitch 'n Bitch*, published in 2004, which has since sold more than a quarter of a million copies, not counting its sequels. Suddenly every publisher wanted a knitting book and they didn't seem to care what it was actually about – *50 Easy Projects on Size 50 Needles*? OK! Here's a contract! Where do we sign?

Somewhere in the shuffle, something was lost. Those of us swept up in the knit-tsunami were learning on the job, so to speak. Book contracts, magazine contracts, television appearances, maintaining a website? WHAT? We quickly made friends with each other and emailed back and forth, trying to make sense of it all. I can still remember Jillian Moreno, currently the editor of Knittyspin (who had once worked at fiber arts publisher Interweave Press) asking me very bluntly about my book deal and taking me by the proverbial hand to make sure I didn't make any stupid mistakes. I call her my 'fairy knitmother' for a reason!

If you don't have a fairy knitmother like mine, then let me extend that same hand to you.

Or, to paraphrase a popular story about Picasso – he was once asked to draw something on a napkin in a bar. He did, in about 30 seconds. On handing it over, he said "That'll be a million dollars." The requester was shocked, exclaiming "But that only took you 30 seconds!" "Yes," said Picasso, "but it took me fifty years to learn how to do that in 30 seconds."

I'm not going to charge you a million dollars, and it's not going to take fifty years, but I do hope I can cut down your learning curve a bit!

In the years since Jillian first reached out to help with my initial book deal, I've gone on to write, co-author or edit a dozen books (*Knitgrrl, Knitgrrl 2, Spin to Knit, Felt Frenzy, Crochet Style, Just Gifts, Just Socks, AlterNation, The Pillow Book, How to Knit in the Woods, Alt Fiber* and the second edition of *Knitting For Dummies*). I've served as the editor in chief of a monthly print knitting magazine in the UK (Yarn Forward), written a regular column for knit.1 magazine, contributed articles to many others (including CRAFT, Adorn, Vogue Knitting, SpinOff, knit.1, Interweave Felt, Sew Hip, Inside Crochet, and Yarn Market News, the business magazine of the yarn industry), and appeared on television (Knitty Gritty, Uncommon Threads, Crafters Coast to Coast, and Knitting Daily TV, among others). I was named one of six "New Guard of Knitting" in Vogue Knitting's 25th anniversary issue. I've taught all over the US and Canada, not to mention to a worldwide audience via my Knitgrrl Studio virtual classes…and on a cruise ship, too!

In short, I've crammed an awful lot of knit- and design-related work into the past several years, and with my friends, some of whom you'll meet in these pages, I have quite a bit of information to pass along. This is not a profession with a clearly defined career path, and it is changing every day, but hopefully I can help you figure out where the signposts are. Thank you for reading.

Shannon Okey

p.s. A note to crochet and other designers: although the term "knitting" and related words are used throughout this text, the examples presented also apply to crochet designers, etc. To prevent some really unwieldy sentence structures, I've used "knitting designer" in place of "knitting and/or crochet designer," or other lengthy terms.

I hope you will not construe this as a slight on crochet, or on any other fiber or fabric-related art, and rather as an attempt to be concise! When something specifically applies to crochet itself, such as 'crochet stitch diagrams' or other concepts, I will note that the example is meant for crochet. No stabbing me with your hooks, ok? Ditto for the use of "her" instead of "his or her." My hope is that a wide variety of designers will be able to make use of the more general information in this book to improve and expand their professional skills.

CHAPTER 1

What does it mean to be a professional?

This may seem self-evident, but judging from the behavior I've witnessed by designers and free-lancers of all experience levels, it needs to be said: professional behavior is crucial if you want to get work *and keep on getting work* in the knit design business, or in any other creative venture.

What does this mean? Do you have to be deathly serious at all times? Should you put on a business suit before you type up your magazine submission? No. In fact, the professional sector of the knitting world is filled with wickedly funny people, and they're remarkably laid back, for the most part. My former intern Carrie said of the TNNA tradeshow (National Needle Arts Association – more on them later) that she'd never seen so many people hugging in her life!

Do not, however, let that fool you. This is still a business, and you need to treat it as such. My guidelines – with explanations to follow – can be boiled down to six major points:

✔ **Be professional in emails, phonecalls and all forms of communication.**

✔ **Deadlines are not negotiable.**

✔ **Negotiate in good faith.**

✔ **Your peers can offer advice, but you are responsible for your own business.**

✔ **Business is business. It is not personal.**

✔ **Follow through when you commit.**

Cut these out and paste them on your wall if you have to, they're some of the most important facts you should internalize from reading this book. You can't be perfect – no one is – but you can stand out from the vast majority of your competition simply by following them as best you can.

Be professional in emails, phonecalls and all kinds of communication

When you send an email or letter with a submission, consider it a job interview, because that's what it is! Editors and publishers get dozens upon dozens of submissions for every slot in their magazine or book lineup. I can tell you from personal experience that I have a hard time taking a submission seriously when it's full of spelling errors, doesn't include what's been asked for, or flat-out ignores other instructions. We'll look specifically at submissions later on, but remember – this might be the editor's first introduction to your work. Make it a positive one.

I also can't believe I need to bring this up, but it should be said, and it is not a hypothetical, this actually happened. (Not to me, but to the editor of another major knitting magazine). Never, *ever* call an editor and cry into her voicemail the night before a photo shoot because your garment isn't finished. First of all, the designer in question should have let the editor know sooner that there were problems getting it done so he or she could make alternate plans. Second, remember Tom Hanks in *A League of Their Own?* I like to call this guideline the "There's no crying in baseball!" rule.

Emails are another area where it's very easy to slip into unprofessional behavior. Don't abbreviate, don't use slang, or texting/internet-speak. Be sure to spell the person's name correctly; for all the "Sharons" I get instead of Shannon, I can't even begin to imagine what lands in Eunny Jang's (editor of Interweave Knits) inbox. If your email access is unreliable, give the person an alternative way to reach you. Once when waiting for a response from a designer, I had to dig up an email she'd inadvertently sent from her work address (with her work phone number on it) in order to reach her, since she wasn't checking her personal email.

Social media is something else altogether (see the Social Media chapter), but the same guidelines apply. If you're going to tweet on Twitter, post on Facebook, or maintain a blog, remember that editors and other people you'd like to work with are also online and could possibly see what you write. They might not care what you had for lunch, but unless your profile is set to private, think first before posting anything you wouldn't be comfortable with your own mother reading.

Deadlines are not negotiable

See above. Crying won't fix things if you're late. Don't take on more than you can reasonably handle unless you have a backup plan (such as sample knitting help). Let editors know as soon as you can if a problem develops, whether the yarn support is late, or the garment shrank when you blocked it…whatever the problem is, it's easier to fix if you're honest about it. You can be apologetic, but always be straightforward. Speaking as a former magazine editor, I would rather continue to work with someone who lets me know there's a problem and gives me possible solutions or alternatives than someone who doesn't respond to status queries and waits until the last minute.

Your contract or agreement should have deadline information in it, and if it doesn't – ask.

Negotiate in good faith

You need to understand what you are committing to do when you sign a contract. If you cannot agree with the substance of a contract or other agreement, don't sign it, and if you have to hire a lawyer, an agent or another professional to make yourself comfortable, do it!

It is not only OK to suggest changes to a proposed contract, it may be the only way to get what you want. If the other party to the contract says no, you need to decide whether to go forward or not. One size does not fit all when it comes to contracts, so you are responsible for making sure you understand and agree with what you sign.

Negotiate in good faith, though. If you can't sign a contract, tell the other person why. He or she may have suggestions for changes that will make it acceptable to you, or ask for yours. I have had success using the following approach:

1. Read the contract, in full, without distraction.
2. Narrow down what is objectionable to you. Many publishers now provide a digital copy of the contract first, which makes it easy to add highlighting or use "track changes" for comments.
3. If you have an alternative suggestion for the terms you don't like, write them down.
4. Take a moment to compose a response to the editor/publisher/contracts manager, but don't send it immediately! Give it an hour or so, then re-read.

For example:

In clause 3(b) of this contract, it states that you are allowed to republish this pattern in any format, indefinitely. Is this something we can discuss? I am not comfortable with [licensing the pattern for an indefinite time period / allowing electronic reproduction of the pattern after the magazine is published]. *Can we* [put a limit on the time period / clarify the formats in which it can be published]?

And so forth…

They may not agree to your changes, but they can't agree if you don't ask.

Your peers can offer advice, but you are responsible for your own business

Ravelry.com's Designers group and other online forums are an amazing resource for budding and experienced designers alike. Chances are extremely good that just about any question you have has already been tackled in some way on their VIP info page (http://www.ravelry.com/groups/designers/pages/VIP-Info-Copyright-Design-Patterns-Writing-etc).

With greater access to information comes the responsibility of sorting through it all. "IANYL" is an acronym you'll see on many message boards that means "I am not your lawyer" (in other words, the person in question may actually *be* a lawyer, but has no legal relationship with you). In that spirit, you should take information found online – or even in this book – with not only a grain of salt but also with the understanding that legal issues are often specific to a particular geographic location or set of circumstances. Other business-related items, such as how to register as a business or pay taxes, are also usually very specific to your state, province or country.

Stick to the internet and your peers online for advice on service-oriented issues instead, such as how to manage unhappy customers, find a good web developer, or make great-looking knit charts. If you need specific business guidance, hire a lawyer, accountant or other relevant professional. Don't risk your business on free advice.

Business is business, it is not personal

The internet seems to have exacerbated some designers' tendency to take even the smallest slight personally. Whether someone has insulted your pattern, or your business model, or just made a smart remark about you on a mailing list, you have to remember that *business is not personal*.

Not everyone will love every pattern you write. Not everyone will like you as a person. I was savaged more than once when I took on the editorship of Yarn Forward because I'm American and the magazine is based in the United Kingdom. It's difficult not to take something like this personally, but it's part of having your work out there in front of the public.

Don't react. If you must react, don't do it in haste. One small comment on a message board or mailing list can follow you for a very long time. Be the bigger person. Take a day to respond if you feel you must. Learn from this infamous 2004 Knitter's Review thread[3], it's a doozy.

When something *actually* threatens your business, respond appropriately. Did someone post one of your pattern PDFs to a mailing list? Send an email to your lawyer before you send one to the mailing list moderator. Did someone post on her blog that the directions for your Fabulous Sweater Pattern are not so fabulous, and all her friends are chiming in? Send an email offering pattern help, don't link to her blog from yours and call her an idiot!

Remember: most of your customers will likely never know *you*. If they have a customer service problem, address it cheerfully and professionally, asking for additional information if needed. If they say they don't like you, well, that's their loss.

3   http://www.knittersreview.com/Forum/topic.asp?ARCHIVE=true&TOPIC_ID=16053 – If you ever wondered why your LYS stopped stocking Noro and other yarns sold by KFI, here's your answer, on page 2 of this forum thread.

Follow through when you commit

I'm still shaking my head at this one – a designer practically bragged on an online forum that the yarn sent for a commissioned magazine design wasn't good enough, and had been sent back to the magazine. The editor in question confirmed to me this was indeed the case, and that the designer's actions caused a lot of scrambling to fill a sudden blank in the pattern lineup. Ask yourself: do you think this designer is ever going to get work at that magazine again? Or anywhere else the editor might work someday? Knit design and publishing is a very small world: the magazine editor you annoy today might be acquiring books for another publisher tomorrow, or working for a company you're asking for yarn support. Don't burn bridges.

These are not every possible example of professionalism (or lack thereof) in action, but they are specific to this industry and indicative of what many designers, editors and others have experienced. Keep them in mind and you'll form lasting relationships that will garner you work for years to come. Every editor has a designer or writer who can turn something great around on very little notice when the need arises – *be* that person! It's the perfect way to guarantee you'll get steady work and a solid reputation.

CHAPTER 2

Social Media

Blogs, Ravelry.com, Facebook, Etsy, Twitter, you name it – there are more ways to connect to your fellow designers (and your potential customers) than ever before. How can you use online media effectively? This chapter will show you how. Why so early in the book? Social media is an integral part of building a successful business in the twenty-first century, like it or not, and many of the examples that follow will make reference to it, so it's good to have terms defined and general uses for social media discussed here at the outset.

What is social media?

I like the current definition of social media on Wikipedia, namely:

> *Social media are media designed to be disseminated through social interaction, created using highly accessible and scalable publishing techniques. Social media supports the human need for social interaction, using Internet- and web-based technologies to transform broadcast media monologues (one to many) into social media dialogues (many to many). It supports the democratization of knowledge and information, transforming people from content consumers into content producers. Businesses also refer to social media as user-generated content (UGC) or consumer generated media (CGM).*

Shorter version: Social media brings human interaction online with easy-to-use technology.

Once you've signed up for a Twitter account, your only limit in reaching other Twitter users around the world is that of the 140-character "tweets" you post there.

Or, you can connect with over 700,000 other knitters and crocheters on Ravelry.com. Nearly everyone has a Facebook profile, there are thousands of blogs…where do you need to be, and what should you do once you're there? Let's take a look at the major social media options and what they offer you as a designer.

- **Blogs**
- **Ravelry**
- **Twitter**
- **Facebook**

Blogs

Blogs (a contraction of 'weblog') have only been around for a decade or so. Originally the province of techies who hand-coded their own websites, blogs were designed as a sort of easily-updated web diary, eventually developing lives of their own as communities evolved that linked among related sites. Whether thematic, such as a knitblog, or a more general collection of links and commentary, blogs have come quite a long way from their earliest incarnations.

I chose to separate my own knitblog at knitgrrl.com from my personal site when I realized I was boring all my non-knitting friends! Instead of carefully writing my own HTML, webpage by page, by the time knitgrrl.com was ready to stand on its own in 2002, there was software to automate new blog entry creation. Each individual entry is called a 'post.'

Now that we have some idea of what blogs are, let's take a look at options for creating your own. Blogging software, too, has come a very long way in the past 10 years. Your main choices include:

- **hosted software**, such as Blogger or LiveJournal, or WordPress' hosted version
- **standalone software** such as WordPress, Movable Type or Drupal

Hosted software is housed on someone else's computer servers and doesn't require as much technical aptitude as installing and running your own standalone blogging software, but truthfully, they're much the same once everything is up and running.

Several years ago, Google purchased Blogger (http://www.blogger.com), one of the first hosted blogging software options. Its [name].blogspot.com domain addresses are frequently used by knitalong creators and others looking for a quick and easy way to set up a site on which multiple users can post. You can use Blogger software inside your own website to create an easily-updatable blog.

LiveJournal is not a very professional choice if you're setting up a business-related blog. Its userbase skews more towards teenagers, much as MySpace now does, and it is often viewed in a negative light. Web-savvy users tend to avoid LiveJournal, MySpace and AOL-related web addresses because they are often misused by spammers.

Whenever possible, you should register your own domain name – yourcompanyname.com – even if you only use it for email and redirecting traffic to a site hosted elsewhere such as WordPress.com. It may seem unimportant, but it's all part of building your personal brand.

As for standalone options, Movable Type and Drupal are both heavy-duty software to use for blog- or entire website creation, and best installed by someone who is comfortable with maintaining their own software. That said, if you're interested in learning more about Drupal or hiring someone who has helped build several large online fiber arts communities online, check out http://emmajane.net. Emma Jane Hogbin is not only a techie, she's also a knitter! She is the co-author of *Front End Drupal* and offers teleclasses on building web pages, as well as managing e-commerce and email lists[4].

My recommendation?

For its ease of use, flexibility and large built-in development community, I usually recommend either the hosted version of WordPress (set up an account and free blog by going to http://www.wordpress.com) or its standalone version (available for free download at http://www.wordpress.org), installed on your own website.

There is obviously quite a bit more to this than the brief overview I've just given you, and I'll be expanding on it in my upcoming craft business book series. (If you'd like to know when they're released, join the mailing lists at knitgrrl.com or cooperativepress.com).

I've got a blog, now what?

Maybe you've just gone through WordPress' "Famous 5-Minute Installation," or you've set up your own blog at yourname.wordpress.com. What do you do next? Before you even reach this point, you need to take a cold, hard look at what you want to accomplish with your blog. Think of it as a business plan or a mission statement for your overall social media strategy.

If I sat down to create a brand new blog or website today for knitgrrl.com, here's what my plan would look like. Interview yourself, if you like this format and it helps you think things through!

☆   **What is knitgrrl.com going to be about?**

Knitgrrl.com is a website about knitting author Shannon Okey, her books and her patterns. It is a one-stop shop to find information about or links to Shannon-related content.

☆   **What kind of permanent pages will knitgrrl.com feature?**

There will be an About page, a page about Shannon's books, a shop to sell patterns and link to other places they are sold, an errata page for pattern problems, and a press page where people can

4   http://hicktech.com/services/classes

find links to articles about Shannon, or get in touch if they work for the media.

☆ **What kind of posts will knitgrrl.com feature?**

At least once or twice a week, Shannon will post about her current projects, with photos whenever possible, write about new books she likes or link to funny, knit-related items (that video with sheep performance art, for example).

☆ **What else will you find on the front page of knitgrrl.com?**

A mailing list signup form, a link to the knitgrrlstudio.com/shop page, my most recent tweet on Twitter, and a button to click through to the Knitgrrl & Friends pattern group on Ravelry.com.

You see that I've come up with a very specific list of must-haves, and if I were starting from scratch, this list would make it very easy to think through what I want and need, not to mention how to go about it (do I need to cut-and-paste some code to display my "most recent tweet" link? Do I need to make a "button" image for the Knitgrrl & Friends pattern group?)

Your business blog (and unless you've already got a huge following on your personal blog or website, I recommend keeping them separate) should be the nerve center of your overall strategy when it comes to getting out the message about what you do as a designer. Facebook posts and Twitter tweets are ephemeral by comparison: on your blog, you're the boss, and you control what displays, when, and how.

Making friends

When you write posts for your blog, link to related items. It seems almost too obvious to state this! The internet is, at its core, a large amount of specialized content joined together in relevant pathways by links. As your readership/fanbase grows, they'll be linking to you – so return the favor by linking to things you find interesting or relevant. Whether you're mentioning a useful knit technique video on YouTube, a specific pattern on Ravelry, or another designer's new book, you should link to them wherever feasible.

☆ **How do you create a link?**

Let's say I want to tell all of knitgrrl.com's readers about my new shop, Knitgrrl Studio. Inside my blog software, I write:

```
I just opened a new brick-and-mortar studio and learning
space called Knitgrrl Studio, and it has an online shop,
too.
```

Then I provide a link to the website. On knitgrrl.com, it will look like this (special formatting indicates there are clickable links, most often by displaying the text in a different color, or underlined):

> I just opened a new brick-and-mortar studio and learning space called <u>Knitgrrl Studio</u>, and it has an online shop, too.

Which, in HTML, looks like this when you type it:

```
I just opened a new brick-and-mortar studio and learning
space called <a href="http://www.knitgrrlstudio.
com">Knitgrrl Studio</a>, and it has an <a href="http://www.
knitgrrlstudio.com/shop">online shop</a>, too.
```

Many blogging software packages show who's been linking to your site when you log in. It's natural to want to see what people have said about you and your site! As an example, look at the "Incoming Links" section in the bottom right section of my WordPress 'dashboard' screen.

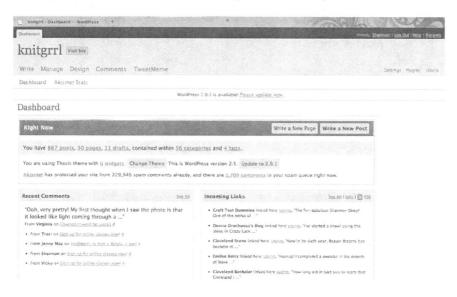

If you're writing good content, other bloggers and sites will start to link to yours, and you may discover a whole new audience for your work.

Write what you know

This has never been more true than it is when you are writing for a niche (specialty) site such as a knitblog. Are you a sock expert? Do you know everything there is to know about cables? Write about it!

Link to other places people can find you

In addition to linking other sites, books, etc, make your blog the single best place to find you online. Link to your Ravelry profile, your Twitter feed, your Etsy shop, the knitalong you started… anything that's relevant.

Get read

Whichever blog software solution you choose, make sure it has an RSS feed built in to make your posts accessible using feed readers and other services. The major software packages referenced above do this automatically. RSS stands for "really simple syndication," and it's an automated way to deliver your blog posts to your readers' chosen place to read them.

Feed readers can be browser-based (Bloglines, http://www.bloglines.com, is probably the single most popular one, at least among knitters. Looking at my site's readership statistics, more people read knitgrrl.com using Bloglines than by coming directly to knitgrrl.com), or desktop software such as Feedreader for Windows, or NetNewsWire or Vienna for Mac. No matter which you choose, all feed reader software pulls the titles and opening paragraphs of your blog posts into a single screen where the user can read through the most recent updates from blogs they choose to follow. Make your titles memorable, and the first paragraph or so interesting enough that they'll want to read the rest!

To see what a raw feed looks like, go to knitgrrl.com and click the orange megaphone-like symbol next to "Subscribe" in the upper right corner. (That symbol is universally used by most blog software to indicate a RSS feed). These short headlines are what many of your readers will encounter when they see you've updated your blog. Make them count!

In addition, you may want to include Share This (http://sharethis.com) or another similar plug-in for your blogging software that makes it very simple for your readers to share links back to your site with their Twitter/Facebook/blog/etc. I use Tweetmeme (http://tweetmeme.com) to encourage my readers to retweet the items I post on my blog. Read the Twitter section below for more on "retweeting" and other terminology.

Ravelry.com

I could probably write an entire book on using Ravelry.com effectively as a designer! It has so much to offer, from inspiration and market research (What are the most popular/active recently published patterns? Click over to the Patterns section – http://www.ravelry.com/patterns – and discover what they have in common!), to community with other designers, other sock knitters, other cable fans…you name it. With over 700,000 registered users (as of May 2010), Ravelry is the number one knitting and crochet community site online.

Take a look at their stats page: Ravelry users are unusually dedicated. These statistics change constantly, but as an example, see the image on the next page.

Can you afford NOT to be on Ravelry? As a designer, I cannot think of a more targeted place for you to find potential business, whether it's by selling pattern downloads, or advertising your work. Ravelry's ad prices are incredibly competitive, so much so that even large yarn companies such as South West Trading Company are switching over from advertising in print magazines.

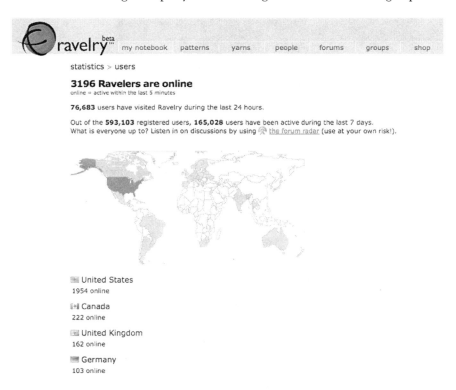

The SWTC is supported by an ongoing and strong presence on Ravelry. We firmly believe that this online community presents the greatest opportunity for connecting with and exciting knitters. While we continue to do some print, we've pulled back for 2 key reasons: Print media is expensive and we love the idea of paperless media. Over 3000 knitters are on Ravelry at any given moment providing instant and trackable results. We love it!

– Jonelle Beck, president, South West Trading Company

Ravelry is, bar none, the single place you need to be online if you'd like to do well as a knit and/or crochet designer. If you skip over all the other social media information I'm supplying here, *this* is the one thing to take away. You don't have to spend 10 hours per day on Ravelry, but at a bare minimum, you should:

1. Have a designer profile, and link your designs to it (full details and how-to are available at http://www.ravelry.com/wiki/pages/Designers)

2. Set up a group for you/your patterns by going to http://www.ravelry.com/groups/new

3. Invite members of your mailing list (if you have one) or readers of your blog/etc to join your group.

4. Participate in at least one other group that interests you, be it sock knitting or cables, the Ravelry Designers' group, or even a group on another non-knitting hobby you have. Get to know the community as a whole.

How can having a group dedicated to your patterns help? Take a look at designer Ysolda Teague's group as an example: http://www.ravelry.com/groups/ysolda

When members post examples of their finished Ysolda designs, it's the most powerful form of advertising she could have. Other people have demonstrated firsthand that the patterns are not only highly knittable, but also very wearable/pretty/etc, and over 4000 members (at the time this screenshot was taken) participate in the group. Remember this:

Endorsement from a third party is always more powerful.

What does that mean? It's all very well and good for *you* to say how wonderful your patterns are, but if someone else says it, people are more likely to believe it and pass it on. So much the better if they're also discussing how fun the pattern was to knit, or something else they liked about it on the group! It also gives you a chance to post any needed errata/updates, answer quick questions and get a sense of what your customers like and want. Let your customers and fans spread the word about your patterns!

Concerns about Ravelry

Some other online discussion groups' members have spent considerable amounts of time debating the Ravelry Terms of Service (abbreviated TOS). As with any other online service, you should carefully review their TOS and privacy policies.

Ravelry's TOS is here

http://www.ravelry.com/about/terms

and it is constantly updated (you can even read the revision history and see what's changed over time).

I personally feel that the benefits of having your name and patterns out in front of that many knitters outweigh concerns that have been raised elsewhere, and have been actively following Ravelry's response to them. However, as I stated above: you can gather advice from many different sources, but it's still up to you to decide what makes sense for your business, not to mention your comfort factor with doing business online in particular.

The Designers Group on Ravelry

This is the single best place on Ravelry for general designer conversation, and it is located at:

http://www.ravelry.com/groups/designers

The Designers group moderators created a VIP info page available here: http://www.ravelry.com/groups/designers/pages/VIP-Info-Copyright-Design-Patterns-Writing-etc. Topics include:

1. Being a designer on Ravelry
2. General copyright issues
3. Copyright infringement
4. Pattern originality
5. Designing: as a business
6. Designing: process, writing, and in general
7. Designing: sizing, shaping and yarn
8. Designing: other miscellaneous design topics
9. Publishing patterns
10. Pattern submissions

We'll delve into these topics also, but know that this resource is available to you, and is constantly being revised and updated.

Twitter

There are a lot of people out there who don't "get" Twitter. Why on earth would anyone want to read a bunch of 140-characters-or-less messages from random people? Twitter itself took on some of these questions with their Twitter For Business guide. A quick quote:

> *Every day, millions of people use Twitter to create, discover and share ideas with others. Now, people are turning to Twitter as an effective way to reach out to businesses, too. From local stores to big brands, and from brick-and-mortar to internet-based or service sector, people are finding great value in the connections they make with businesses on Twitter.*

Twitter's main feature is its immediacy. Or, as they say in the business guide:

> *The conversational nature of the medium lets you build relationships with customers, partners and other people important to your business. Beyond transactions, Twitter gives your constituents direct access to employees and a way to contribute to your company; as marketers say, it shrinks the emotional distance between your company and your customers.*

Knitters and crafters in general are sociable people. We like to create communities, be they online discussion lists or in-person knit nights. Twitter lets knitters 'talk' to their favorite designers, yarn stores and brands. In the 'getting started' section of the business guide (http://business.twitter.com/twitter101/starting), Twitter says:

> *You can meet several communication goals simultaneously by thinking about your Twitter account as a friendly information booth or coffee bar. It's a place for people to ask you spontaneous questions of all kinds.*

Do you need to be on Twitter 24-7 for this to work? No. Twitter is a form of asynchronous communication, which means that unlike chat, you don't have to be online at the same time as the other people you are speaking with or to – when you have a moment, you can check in, respond to any comments made, make some of your own, and be done.

Some knit and crochet designers and companies you can follow:

@knitgrrl (me!)
http://wefollow.com/twitter/knitting – a guide to the most influential knit-related Twitterers
http://wefollow.com/twitter/crocheting – ditto for crochet

Learn the lingo: Twitter vocabulary

☆   **Following**

To receive messages on Twitter, you 'follow' other people and companies that interest you. After you follow them (by clicking "Follow" on their Twitter page), you will see their messages as they are posted. Anyone who follows you will receive whatever you post.

If someone follows you, they can see what you post – but THEIR followers cannot see what you post unless you "retweet" it (see below). For further information on this, I direct you to a blog post by Kim Werker, founder of Crochet Me and former editor of Interweave Crochet:

http://www.kimwerker.com/2009/11/10/twitter-fail-or-how-not-to-lead-an-industry-online

☆   **Tweet**

An individual message is called a 'tweet' but you could also call it an 'update' if you think tweet is a silly word.

☆   **@username**

To send a message to or about someone, use this format:

```
@knitgrrl I love your patterns! [or]
I love @knitgrrl's patterns
```

If I am following your account, the message will appear on my Twitter home page, and if I'm not following you, it will appear in my @username folder on the right sidebar. People who are following both you and me will also see the message on their Twitter home page. Whenever you see an @username, you can click through to that person's Twitter page and see whether or not you want to follow them.

To find messages directed to you (those starting with your @username) or that mention you (those that include your @username elsewhere in the tweet), go to your Twitter home page. On the right side of the screen, click the tab labeled with your @username. It's a good idea to keep a close eye on @-mentions, because they're often sent by customers or potential customers you may not be following.

☆   **Direct messages/DMs**

These are Twitter's private messaging channel. They appear on your home page under the Direct Messages tab, and if you've got email notifications turned on, you'll also get an email when somebody DMs you. DMs don't appear in either person's public timeline, or in search results. No one but you can see your DMs. You can only send DMs to people who are following you.

☆   RT/retweet

Share cool things you find via Twitter or namecheck someone you like by reposting their tweets and giving them credit. This is called retweeting (or RT), and it looks like this: "RT @knitgrrl My new pattern is available on Ravelry!"

Retweeting is a form of conversation on Twitter. It's a fast and recognized way to spread messages and ideas across Twitter quickly, and like incoming links into your blog, it may help other potential fans find your Twitter feed.

☆   Trending Topics

On the right side of the Twitter search page, you'll see ten Trending Topics, which are the most-mentioned terms on Twitter at that moment. They update constantly.

☆   Hashtag (#)

The hashtag (which uses the # symbol followed by a term describing or naming a topic) is added to a tweet as a way of saying, "This tweet falls into this category." When somebody clicks on that hashtag, they'll get all of the related tweets.

For example, if you post, "My fave knit designers: @knitgrrl @stefaniejapel @modeknit. #Follow-Friday", your message would become part of Twitter search results for "#FollowFriday." If enough people use the same hashtag at once, the term will appear in Twitter's Trending Topics.

Follow Friday has become somewhat of a tradition for sharing your favorites each Friday, and helping your followers on Twitter find other interesting people to follow. For example, one Friday, I posted:

to help people find the Twitter feeds of Stitch Cooperative members, the pattern distribution co-operative I founded.

☆   Shortened URLs

Since you only have 140 characters to use when creating a tweet, if you include a link to something that's very long, Twitter sometimes automatically shortens the URL for you, but not usually. Head over to http://www.tinyurl.com or http://bit.ly and manually shorten the URL (web link) yourself before posting it.

What NOT to do

Here are some "best practices" from Twitter's own business user guide: http://business.twitter.com/twitter101/best_practices

Also, don't spam people. If you send a lot of unsolicited @messages or DMs with self-promoting links, people will not only "unfollow" you (if they're already a follower), they may even report you as spam!

For a case study that's more relevant to our professional world than it would be to most other businesses, see: http://business.twitter.com/twitter101/case_etsy

Etsy.com uses Twitter to connect with both Etsy sellers and shoppers. Far from being a boring, dry, 'corporate' account, you never know what you might find on their Twitter feed. (http://twitter.com/etsy)

For example, a recent tweet:

> RT @craft: Book Review: Yarn Bombing: The Art of Crochet and Knit Graffiti http://
> bit.ly/10d3Bi

Let's take this apart, shall we? You've caught up on the lingo, so you know 'RT @craft' means Etsy
is re-tweeting something Twitter user @craft (CRAFT magazine) already tweeted, in this case a
book review of *Yarn Bombing: The Art of Crochet and Knit Graffiti*. If you follow @etsy but not @craft,
you may not have seen the earlier posting. If their book review is interesting, you might want to follow @craft in the future to see what else they post.

OK, WHY SHOULD I CARE?

My, you're impatient. Let's see if I can do this in 140 characters or less, just like Twitter.

And with 15 characters to spare!

You may not always have the time to carefully craft a well-written blog post with exciting, relevant
links, but almost anyone can spare a minute to write something this short. (Not to mention – for
those of you with day jobs, or less than perfect online access – you can even post to Twitter from
your mobile phone).

Once upon a time "word of mouth" advertising, long held to be the most powerful form of advertising (since, as I mentioned above, third-party endorsement is always more effective than telling
someone how great you are), was limited to just that. Mouths. Moms talking in the grocery store
about peanut butter brands, business guys discussing golf clubs. (Insert your own imaginary 1970s
sitcom stereotypes talking about products here). Today social media is an integrated part of daily
life that you can use to your business advantage.

There is an excellent article I highly recommend called 'The Cult of Personality (part 1)'. You can
find it here: http://www.famefoundry.com/637/the-cult-of-personality-part-1

In part 2 of the series, Fame Foundry interviews Eliza Metz, aka Miss Violet of the popular knitting podcast Lime & Violet. You can read it here: http://www.famefoundry.com/1091/the-cult-
of-personality-part-2

It's a fascinating description of how, essentially, the social media aspects of podcasting helped Eliza develop her "empire."

Things to take away from both of those articles are:

- Mentions of you/your brand/your products spread immediately. You never know just how many people might retweet the link to your new pattern, or your blog post, or your company website.
- You can't control your marketing message 110%, but you have a much better chance of managing it if you are an active participant. Designers who respond to their customers in positive, public ways develop a solid online reputation that helps to bolster sales. No one wants to do business with a meany.
- Public relations should be – and now can be – just that. Developing relationships with the public about you, your brand, etc. Fame Foundry put it best in part one of their articles when they said: "People do not follow companies. People follow people."
- **You need to both participate and give in order to receive from social media.**

This last bullet point is something I want to discuss in detail. A short while ago, the internet was abuzz with links to 'Amanda Palmer made $19K in 10 hours on Twitter' as well as snippets from that post and others like it. You can read it here:

http://www.hypebot.com/hypebot/2009/06/amanda-palmer.html

Background info: Amanda Palmer is a musician with a large cult following. Palmer's band the Dresden Dolls and her solo efforts have gathered a large and devoted fanbase around her work. Recent problems with her record label have highlighted some of the issues surrounding traditional "top-down" media and marketing efforts, but Amanda has turned these around to her benefit with skillful use of social media.

She really did earn $19,000 in ten hours, and went into great detail on how she did it – $11,000 alone came from designing a t-shirt in collaboration with her Twitter followers one Friday night, and almost $2000 more from a Twitter-announced donations-only show.

Let's be brutally honest here. Knitting is a more "niche" activity than music fandom, and there are only a handful of knitting "rockstars" who could make something like this work. (After all, hasn't the Yarn Harlot raised over a million dollars for Médecins Sans Frontières / Doctors Without Borders through her Knitters Without Borders program?) But it doesn't mean we can't apply similar thinking to our own marketing efforts.

Read 'The Cult of Personality (part 1)' again after you've read how Amanda Palmer made $19,000 in ten hours. Can you see how she's applied many of the principles they recommend?

"Being a friend and building a relationship demand more involvement than merely being present. You must participate and give."

When's the last time you saw Metallica hanging out online on a Friday night answering questions from their fans, or writing a song[5] in response to recent media headlines, or…? What *do* those guys do on a Friday night? Probably count their piles of money or something.

Social media may not immediately result in direct sales. You are doing this to build a long-term relationship between your brand (you!) and the public. People like to recommend people they personally enjoy and trust (refer back to the Follow Friday Twitter phenomenon above). Be a person they can trust.

Facebook

Facebook is, at the end of the day, Twitter with a lot more bells and whistles…and time-wasters. In fact, you can even set up Facebook to repost what you write on Twitter, which is useful if you don't want to commit to updating multiple social media sites every day. Some people prefer one, some prefer the other – you might as well be there for both audiences. I put Facebook in the category of "can't hurt, might help," although at the time of writing, more and more knit designers are creating fan pages for their work on Facebook, so things are changing day to day. For a much more detailed overall analysis, Fame Foundry wrote another great piece called 'Two-Faced: The Promise and Pitfalls of Facebook'[6] that you may want to read).

You can have a personal profile page on Twitter, and a business page. Many knit designers and other small, single-owner businesses choose to keep their personal profile completely separate from their business one. I don't, but Facebook's new privacy settings allow you to be very particular about who can see what you post there.

Here's my personal profile on Facebook: http://www.facebook.com/knitgrrl

And here's my business page on Facebook: http://www.facebook.com/knitgrrlstudio

Go to http://www.facebook.com/twitter to link your Twitter and Facebook account pages if you'd like to have Twitter post automatically to your Facebook page.

To create 'fan pages,' go to: http://www.facebook.com/#!/pages/create.php

Here's the fan page for Lorna's Laces, as one example:
http://www.facebook.com/#!/pages/Chicago-IL/Lornas-Laces-Yarns/104146074282
Or Vogue Knitting's: http://www.facebook.com/#!/pages/Vogue-Knitting/91533205498

---

5   http://www.twentyfourbit.com/post/292769269/amanda-palmer-uploads-new-song-gaga-palmer-madonna-to
6   http://www.famefoundry.com/702/two-faced-the-promise-and-pitfalls-of-facebook

Social media: some numbers

In January 2009, I surveyed over knitgrrl.com 1200 readers about their social media choices. (Percentages can add up to more than 100% since those surveyed were allowed to choose more than one social media site they use regularly. Please note, this is not a truly scientific survey in that it polls a self-selected group of people who presumably already identify as knitters, otherwise they probably would not read knitgrrl.com). Here's the breakdown:

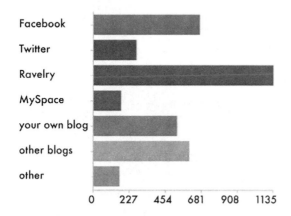

Facebook gets the lion's share of users after Ravelry. (93% of those polled use Ravelry, 55% use Facebook. Blogs are next in line – 43% have their own, and 49% read other people's blogs. Twitter represented a mere 22% at the time, but in the past year as more knitters, knit designers and companies have started using it, Twitter's userbase has expanded exponentially. MySpace only got 14%...again, probably not your best bet.

The downsides of social media

For all the good things social media can do, it is a notorious time-suck. I highly suggest reading Sonia Simone's post 'How to Get Any Work Done (When Connecting Is Your Job)'[7]. Many of her suggestions are especially applicable to the designing life:

I work in 50-minute chunks, followed by 10 minutes of goof time.

The goof time is really important when you're doing creative, difficult work. Your brain needs time to play and rest and have a good time, or it won't work for you when you need it. Sometimes I knit, sometimes I hang out with the cat, sometimes I just walk in circles. Under no circumstances do I do anything productive.

7   http://www.remarkable-communication.com/productivity-and-social-media/

My social media connection time is also on a timer. Twitter is confined to specific times of day, and no more than 10 minutes at a run. I usually answer email in 20-minute chunks.

If you're spending all day sitting and knitting (I know – laughable, right? Knit designers who get to knit all day are about as common as yarn shop owners who get to knit all day), you need to take periodic breaks or risk having your hands snap off at the wrist. Juggle Simone's suggestions to make this work for you business-wise. On a typical productive day, my schedule includes my own variants on "goof time," such as checking in over at Twitter, reading a handful of blogs I like (feed readers are great for getting this done quickly), making more coffee or swapping in a new DVD.

(It's a widely-known fact I get most of my knitting and design work done while watching my Buffy The Vampire Slayer box set).

Schedule social media time into your personal schedule alongside the "goof time" – both will pay off for you in the end.

☆   Dealing with negative feedback in social media

It's not all kittens and rainbows. Mashable.com (a great general social media news resource, by the way) published this recently: http://mashable.com/2010/02/21/deal-with-negative-feedback

Some facts to take away that are applicable to you, as a designer or creative business:

Analyze what kind of negative feedback you're getting before you act. Is it constructive criticism? A specific one-time problem that needs your attention? Did you do something wrong? Or is the complainer simply looking for attention ("trolling")?

You need to respond, but how? The first types of feedback above (constructive criticism, one-time problems, errors...) deserve and should get a response. How public your response is depends on the problem – if someone is telling everyone within virtual earshot about errors in your pattern, you can both say "Thanks for pointing that out, we're looking into it." or the like, then send a private email or message to the person for specifics.

If you've made an error, acknowledge it, fix the situation and move on. However, if the person is simply looking for attention / attacking you for no good reason ("designer X sucks" is a no-good-reason attack, while "designer X's pattern Y is so full of errors I couldn't knit it" is something that warrants a constructive reply), best to ignore it and move on.

☆   Disagree (1)

One of the most frustrating parts of Ravelry, in my opinion, is that you can't see who has marked 'disagree' on something you've written, so you can contact them directly to continue a discussion or find out more. Several designers I spoke with while writing this book told me they have a "phantom disagreer" who seems to follow them around the site marking 'disagree' on *anything* they write. It's frustrating, but it happens. The relative anonymity of the internet means that some people can be really petty and horrible, and write things they'd never say to your face in real life.

(Although, that said, there are a handful of people who hate me online that cause me to truly wonder what they would do if they ever met me in person. Hmm. Not so sure I want to know).

Your two options are to post again and ask for clarification, or simply ignore them. In the case of 'phantom disagreers,' the latter is preferable. I once made a statement that applied only to me and my reasons for doing something, only to garner many 'disagrees.' In that case, I thought it was beneficial to point out my statements applied only to me (as I'd said previously, but clearly needed to reiterate!), and then asked the other 'disagreers' to own their response and come forward to discuss their reason for clicking it. The important thing to remember is that if you're talking about business, treat it that way – business isn't personal, remember? – and not to fan the flames if at all possible.

CHAPTER 3

TCB, No PB&J Required, or: The Business Side of Things

Don't take this the wrong way, dear reader, if you only have designed one or two items, because **prolific does not necessarily equal professional**. One of my designer friends has a name for designers who act in an unprofessional way, particularly online where everyone can see them. And every time she says it, I laugh. (Cruel, I know).

We're not laughing at them because they've only designed three items and two of them are washcloths. (Heck, the Mason-Dixon ladies have created an entire empire out of washcloth love, and we adore them for it. Check out their interview in Chapter 12). We're laughing because they don't even know how much it is they don't know, **and** – this is very important – they don't seem to care too much about finding out.

Sometimes you have to be cruel to be kind. (Sorry, Nick Lowe).

So what *does* equal professional, you ask? We'll turn to Elvis on that one: **TCB**. Elvis believed in the power of TCB so much, he even had a ring made featuring the letters TCB and a lightning bolt.

TCB = taking care of business.

If you work hard and have a devoted following, money will start spilling in through your windows. People will throw it at you in the streets. *OK, slight exaggeration.* But you do need to be prepared for that day, and one way to start is by keeping excellent records. Get ready for success and it will eventually come to you! Have you ever heard someone complain in a yarn store – or any store, really – that they spend so much money there every year, they should really (get something for nothing, or a discount, or...)?

I know *exactly* how much I spent at my LYS and other craft supply stores last year, and the year before that. One of those years, it was $6000. That is no small amount of supplies being used in my business, and it needed to be written off on my taxes as a business expense. You should consult with your own tax expert when it comes to what can and cannot be written off (the home office deduction in US tax law is a notorious audit trigger).

However, before you get to that stage, you need to keep track of what's what. Here's how I've been doing it: I use my checking account's debit card for almost everything, and I keep my paper receipts in the proverbial shoebox, organized by month. At the end of the year, I download all the transactions from my checking account (and from my PayPal account, or any other means by which I have been paid throughout the year), and sort them by type. It takes a little time to do, but you'll be surprised how many things you will find that can be counted as a legitimate business expense. Believe me, that $6000 was a shock when I first added it up!

Accounting/bookkeeping software solutions include QuickBooks (both online hosted versions and standalone desktop software version) and MYOB.com, two of the most popular packages. However, recently I found a free online accounting package called Outright that has a lot of things going for it as a designer who sells patterns online. Since it runs in your web browser, it works on both PCs and Macs, and you can share information with your tax professional and bookkeeper if needed. (Talk to him or her first, if you already have someone – some tax professionals prefer getting a QuickBooks or other Intuit-formatted file from their customers).

What's great about Outright is that you can import, among other things, all the sales you've made through PayPal and other online payment solutions. Ravelry, E-junkie, Patternfish and most other sales venues for patterns use PayPal as a default payment processor (more on this later), which makes it a very convenient way to track these sales. Much easier than my old spreadsheet method, in fact!

I recommend reading through section 5 (Designing: As A Business) on the Ravelry Designer's group resource page for further suggestions and updated conversations on these topics. If nothing else, it will help you clarify what questions pertain to the level at which your business is currently operating so you can go to your tax professional armed with the right questions to ask.

From small streams mighty rivers flow: where to make money?

Five dollars here and there may not seem like much for a pattern that took 50 hours to create, but it adds up quickly! However, there are other methods for earning money as a designer that can both augment your pattern design business and create additional revenue streams that will build up over time into a regular, somewhat predictable source of income. (Note I say "somewhat" – nothing is ever certain in the wonderful world of self-employment).

Most knit designers who end up quitting their day jobs do so when the amount of money they are earning at one job is equaled by their design work (or becomes close to equal when paired with additional lifestyle changes, such as having children, that don't allow for a traditional 9-5 job).

Pattern sales themselves will be discussed elsewhere – how to format them, where to sell them, whether to wholesale or not. Let's first look at some other sources of income for the independent knit designer so you can determine what might work for your particular skills, build up your income, and plan your design business accordingly. I find that the self-interviewing technique I used in the blog section can be helpful here as well – ask yourself which of these income sources might be right for you, why they're right for you specifically, and how they'll help rather than hinder developing your business. Think of it as a more detailed pro/con list.

Teaching

Teaching is often the first additional revenue stream designers take on, whether it's teaching a regular class at their local yarn store or applying to teach at one of the larger fiber festivals. Good teachers build their reputation as someone with solid skills who is also talented in conveying those skills to other people. Knitting and its related disciplines are not always black and white, there is no one "right way" to do anything. Accordingly, there is a market for different forms of presentation in just about any subject.

For example, designer Annie Modesitt (interviewed on page 128) is a renowned teacher who, in additional to classes featuring her other skills, has taught thousands of knitters that they don't knit wrong, just differently. Combination knitting combines the motions of both western-style knitting and eastern uncrossed knitting, and as she says: "You are NOT knitting wrong! If you're getting the fabric you want, then you're knitting fine for YOU!" There is more than one way to make a knit stitch and a purl stitch in this world, and her related book *Confessions of a Knitting Heretic* has sold tens of thousands of copies since 2004 as a result.

Identify what knitting techniques and topics you are most knowledgeable in, or enjoy the most, and develop potential classes from there. This often happens organically – if you are a sock genius and the local yarn store owner isn't, chances are good you will either be asked (or have success when you ask) to teach a sock class.

One benefit to teaching a regular lineup of specific classes is that you can easily answer the question "so which classes do you teach?" Prepare a resume-style handout in PDF format (or post it on your website, if you prefer) so yarn store owners and festival organizers know what you have to offer. See Appendix A for a copy of mine so you can determine what you might want to include.

Writing books or articles

Writing can be a lot faster than knitting, and pay even better. Creating proposals for magazine articles is not much different from creating a design proposal (which we'll discuss later). Outline what it is you want to write about and why, what materials you have at your disposal and why you're the right person for that piece. Do you run an 8,000-head sheep ranch? OK, you've got a good shot at writing an article on practical sheep care, or sheep shearing, or packaging wool to send out for processing. What aspects of your knitting life are out of the ordinary and would be of interest to someone else? Do *not* send in something generic such as: "I want to write an article on cable knitting."

And?

Cable knitting and *what?*

Be specific – do you have a more efficient way to cable without a cable needle? Have you found a way to make 10 new cables fully reversible? That is what the editor wants to know, and it helps if you can send some sample photos or images, too, for clarification. Follow the general guidelines in the Chapter 7, or specific guidelines set out by the publication or publisher if they are available to you. (If they're not online – and most are these days – ask).

Books are proposed in much the same way, but the turnaround time is a lot longer! We'll talk a little more about contracts related to design and book work below as well.

Providing professional services

Are you an accountant by day, designer by night? A photographer? Graphic designer? You can use these superpowers to help other designers and augment your own income. Why not start a tax preparation service that caters to creative professionals? (My own tax guy does exactly that – he's got musicians, artists and me on the roster). Or advertise pattern layout and design services – not everyone is an Adobe Creative Suite whiz, but if you are, do it! It's college economics class all over again – use your comparative advantage.

I consider my writing skill to be a comparative advantage – I can write much faster than I can knit! For me, writing articles in knitting magazines makes more sense than designing items for them on tight deadlines since I'm much faster at one than the other. Find your own comparative advantage and use it. You may even discover you like blending your former "day job" with knit design more than design all by itself.

Yarn company sales reps fall under 'professional services,' in my opinion, and have the added benefit of keeping you on the front lines of the industry. Working for one or more yarn companies, you get to travel from shop to shop in the course of your work, which is also an excellent way to research regional trends and what's popular right now – great things to know as a designer! Payment is commission-based, and the job is flexible compared to most, making it excellent for those who love making sales and meeting new people.

Test knitting

Speed knitters, apply here. Other designers and companies are always looking for people who can knit samples for trunk shows, test a new knitting pattern, etc. Section 6 in the Ravelry Designer's group VIP information section (Designing: Process, Writing, and In General) has links to several discussions about the etiquette behind using or becoming test knitters, such as fair pay. If you're a fast knitter, you can often earn a fairly reasonable sum from the comfort of your couch. Ravelry's Testing Pool group is one possible place to find these opportunities, though if you're willing to test knit and have your own blog or website, it's not a bad idea to post your rates and availability there, too.

Editing

Skilled technical editors are in constant demand, and often have a waiting list a mile long. Part of this is a general lack of education – how *does* one become a technical editor, anyway? There is no one practical way to learn all the skills required other than on-the-job training. A solid foundation of all the major knitting skills is a must (if you don't know how to do something, how will you know if the directions for it are wrong?), as is a background in garment construction and sizing.

You'll find that most of the better knitting tech editors also know how to sew garments, or at least have a familiarity with how pattern pieces for a wide variety of styles fit together.

One of the most in-demand skills a tech editor can have is multisizing, or grading. The proportional relationships between pattern sizes are not always self-evident. See the Resources section at the back of the book for some general garment construction textbook recommendations. As you gain experience working with your own and others' patterns, you will be building up a skill set that can be quite lucrative.

Selling knitting-related products

Etsy.com and other online venues have made it easy to sell hand-dyed yarn, stitch markers and any number of knitting-related gadgets. (Too easy, some would say!) Quite a few designers sell yarn and write designs optimized for that yarn, leading to a double sale. It is easy to stand out as an online business person if you hold to the general principles in the rest of this book (professionalism, quality social media interaction, etc).

Kitchen Sink Dyeworks owner Mercedes Tarasovich-Clark (http://kitchensinkdyeworks.com) says:

"I was making hand dyed items for far longer than I was designing knitwear (going back 14 years), but quietly, in the background, and just for fun for most of the time. The hand dyed yarns took off for me because I was looking for a way to expand my market, and the easiest way I could see to do that was to market something unique. While some people love the daily ritual of a brick and mortar shop, I found it stifling, so I decided to rewrite my own options by making a new path, one that had more opportunities for designing, travel, and markets and communities outside of my four walls.

I think the best advice I could give to anyone looking to run a fiber related business is to sit down with yourself and look really hard at what makes you tick. If you're super-gregarious and thrive on personal interaction, running a hand dyed yarn company for 8 hours a day on your own will probably become pretty lonely, but if you're happier being more introverted and "in your own head", then a 5-6 days a week brick and mortar shop may drive you over the edge (*raises hand*). Think about what part of the community clicks with YOU and build your job around it. And never discount the huge amount of social stimulation and feedback you can get from online community: I may be happier working on my own, but even a loner needs a little conversation or some fresh ideas now and then. The fact that I can jump onto Twitter for a 15-minute coffee break and come away recharged with ideas is a lifesaver. And for those within a "real life" community, it still doesn't hurt to jump in and see what knitters and fiber folk in other parts of the world are doing, to keep a fresh perspective."

Jordana Paige, creator of The Knitter's Purse, began knitting in high school, and began developing patterns *after* her original knit-related product (the reverse of most other designer/creators). While in college working towards her business degree, with an emphasis in marketing, she had the idea for The Knitter's Purse (a bag that looked like a purse, but functioned as a knitting bag):

"About a year after starting the company I saw a submission call from Vogue Knitting for knitting patterns. I thought it would be a great way to promote my company. I submitted a sketch and was shocked when I got a call accepting my design. I'd never written a pattern before so I was a bit panicked. I quickly learned and began submitting patterns for magazines and books. With each design I learned more about garment construction and how to write a well-written pattern. The knitwear designs started out as a way to promote the handbags. It showed customers that the person designing the bags was truly a knitter. I know what knitters need in a knitting bag because I am a knitter. Offering both bags and patterns has created a nice pairing for the company. The patterns have given me many opportunities, such as teaching at retreats and appearing on Knitty Gritty, all the while promoting my handbags. The patterns and handbags really compliment each other."

CHAPTER 4

Send in the lawyers

I hope you'll never encounter a situation where a lawyer is *needed* rather than *recommended*, but it's best to be prepared in case you encounter a tricky copyright issue or even something pleasant, such as a contract to design for a magazine or book!

Please note: I am not an attorney. All information provided here, including external links, is for your information only. Laws change, situations differ from country to country (and sometimes even state to state). Seek the advice of a trained professional in your jurisdiction if needed.

Copyright

Copyright is one of the most contentious topics in the design world, hands down, but an essential part of taking care of business as someone who develops intellectual property for sale.

(Next time you're at a fancy cocktail party with people who don't appreciate knitting, don't say you write knitting patterns for a living, say you're an intellectual property developer in the textiles field. It's true, after all!)

Jenna Wilson, designer of the infamous Rogue sweater pattern and a lawyer herself (although not YOUR lawyer – as specified previously, all legal and other professional advice pertaining to your business should be obtained from someone licensed to practice in your state, province or country), has written some of the easiest to understand and frankly, best pieces available online about copyright as it pertains to knitters.

`http://girlfromauntie.com/copyright`

Part of the battle we fight as designers is educating the public on copyright issues. This is getting easier as time goes on, and as these issues are more broadly discussed in the media and online. As designers, we need to, at a minimum:

> • Make sure we use appropriate language on our patterns to explain the copyright in a simple, easy-to-understand way
> • Model good behavior for your customers. Don't infringe on other designers' rights, and speak up when others are.

For example, at the end of all my patterns, I include the following paragraph along with encouragement for the knitter to post his or her finished item to Ravelry.com:

This pattern is provided for your personal, non-commercial use and may not be resold or shared. Questions? Problems? Email admin@knitgrrl.com or check the knitgrrl.com errata page.

I also include "© 2010 Shannon Okey (admin@knitgrrl.com) All rights reserved." in the bottom footer of each page, with the correct year as appropriate (reflecting the date of creation).

Creative Commons (creativecommons.org) is another standardized way by which you can inform your pattern or e-book purchasers what they are, or are not allowed to do with your work. You can read the licenses online[8] and apply them to your work if you think they will work for you. Creative Commons is perhaps more appropriate for patterns that are offered for free than those offered for sale. Off the record, an attorney commented that Creative Commons "allows people to be stupid," because it doesn't protect the individual creators' rights in the way they think it does, so please be aware you may not automatically be protected in the way you want to be. With that in mind, however, the licenses created by Creative Commons include:

☆   **Attribution by**

You let others copy, distribute, display, and perform your copyrighted work – and derivative works based upon it – but only if they give credit as you request.

☆   **Share Alike**

You allow others to distribute derivative works only under a license identical to the one that governs your work.

☆   **Non-Commercial**

You let others copy, distribute, display, and perform your work but for non-commercial purposes.

☆   **No Derivative Works**

You let others copy, distribute, display, and perform only verbatim copies of your work, not derivative works based upon it.

For commercial (read: for sale) patterns, you are probably better off sticking with a "regular" copyright notice, since most designers don't allow reproducing their for-sale patterns under any of the conditions detailed above.

8   http://creativecommons.org/about/licenses

What to do if your copyright has been infringed

First of all, keep everything in writing, as much as you possibly can. You should ideally already have a lawyer to whom you can turn in these instances (if you can't afford one, law schools often hold clinics where you can ask questions, or look for a local branch of Lawyers for the Arts).

In most one-on-one cases, where a single person is copying your patterns and you know who they are, and how to contact them, a letter or email explaining that you hold copyright to the material he or she is distributing, as well as what you expect, such as ceasing distribution of the pattern, may do the trick. Often non-designers do not fully understand the implications of what they are doing when they infringe on your copyright, although music-sharing and other high-profile lawsuits have certainly made it less difficult to make this argument.

One tidbit I learned during my time working at the law office: never *threaten* a lawsuit. You either file one or you don't. Start with the letter or email that outlines what you expect to see happen, and give a timeframe/deadline for response. Your next step is to seek legal advice and begin work on a case, or to file a small claims lawsuit, which, although much cheaper to pursue, may not be right for every situation. One problem with small claims cases is that even though you may win and be awarded monetary damages, they cannot issue any sort of ruling that will keep the copyright in-fringer from continuing to infringe, and you cannot pursue a copyright case in small claims court.

If you receive a C&D (cease and desist) letter, don't ignore it! Ask for the basis of their claim, don't admit or deny anything, and be professional. Call your lawyer or Lawyers for the Arts for advice on how to proceed.

Trademarks vs. copyrights

Short version: if you want to put Mickey Mouse / your favorite sports team's symbol / college logo / any other graphic that is not something you made up yourself: **DON'T**. Not unless you are spe-cifically working for Disney, the Boston Bruins or Harvard University, to use some examples, and have been given their guidelines for logo usage. Almost every large company, university or other organization has logo usage guidelines in place specifying how, where and when their logos can and cannot be used, right down to specifications for what colors are allowable, and how words can be abbreviated.

What's the difference between copyright, trademarks and patents? Here's one explanation[9]. But if you stick to the above advice and don't use images or logos that belong to someone else, you should be fine. One very frequently asked question: stitch patterns themselves are not copyrightable, but a person's presentation of them is. You can use a stitch pattern from, say, the Barbara Walker stitch treasuries, but you *can't* photocopy her chart and stick it in your pattern.

9 http://www.lawmart.com/forms/difference.htm

For additional articles on copyright and its relationship to patterns and intellectual property, see arts and crafts lawyer Tammy Browning-Smith's website http://www.artsandcraftslaw.com, more specifically, this page[10] and the article "Copyright Myths Uncovered."

Contracts

I may have worked in a law office once upon a time, and I do look awfully good in a suit, but I am not a lawyer and I am not your lawyer and there are no lawyers within 100 yards of me right now and let's just all agree that lawyering is not happening here, OK? What I am going to tell you about contracts is mostly: common sense, designed to give you a basis for understanding what contracts are meant to do, and a means of supplying resources to help you find further information.

A good starting place on writing your own contracts can be found at:

http://24ways.org/2008/contract-killer

"But I don't want to write a contract! I just want to understand what this one says" you exclaim. Patience, grasshopper. In order to understand a pre-existing contract, it's good to have a solid foundation in what a contract *is*, and what goes into a good one, then proceed accordingly. The above article will help you immensely. To paraphrase it very briefly, contracts should cover:

- Who is getting hired for what, how much they will be paid, and how/when
- What both parties agree to do
- What is, and more importantly, is *not* included
- What happens when people change their minds

A knit-specific example:

You [designer name] are being hired to design Your Fantastic Sweater for the fall issue of KnitMagazine, to be delivered no later than [3 months from now], complete with fully-written pattern, using KnitMagazine's stylesheet. You will be paid $400 when the issue arrives on newsstands.

We, KnitMagazine, will provide technical editing and schematics. If you choose to provide charts or other schematics in our preferred format, Program X, we will pay an additional $20 per chart or schematic.

In the event we do not publish Your Fantastic Sweater, you will be paid a kill fee of no more than $100.

[Signed — you, KnitMagazine's representatives, etc]

10 http://www.artsandcraftslaw.com/id7.html

This is not a real contract, but it is enough of a sample to provide everyone (you and Knit Magazine's representatives both) with all the information needed from our checklist.

You know which design is being commissioned, and for how much, as well as how much you will receive if they decide not to publish it (the "kill fee"), or if you choose to supply the charts. They have acknowledged that if you don't, they'll supply the charts along with the technical editing. You know when you're going to be paid, and that you need to use the stylesheet they supply when formatting your pattern. Make sure they specify who will do the photography and provide yarn, too.

Where to nitpick? Were I offered this contract, one of my first points of contention would be getting paid "when issue arrives on newsstands." What if the design gets moved forward? I would ask for additional clarification there, such as "You will be paid $400 when the issue arrives on newsstands, or no later than 15 October 2010." Also, do I want to bother making the charts if they might not accept them? I'd ask for an example of an acceptable chart file to save time for everyone, even if that isn't written into the contract itself. I'd expect them to send one with the stylesheet, in fact.

You should also be aware there are many online resources at your disposal, among them LexPublica[11] and Nolo.com[12], so click over to read more sample documents until you're comfortable with the terminology, or at least comfortable enough to know what to ask your actual lawyer as needed. You can also use the checklist above to flip the text in your head. What is this clause specifying that I need to do, or that the other party will do? Exactly which rights to my work are they buying from me?

Which rights? OK, sorry to make your head explode, but there is more than one different set of rights you can sell to any work, be it a pattern, article or book. An excellent, albeit decade-old explanation is available online at the site referenced in this footnote[13]. Summarized:

☆ **First serial rights:**

The right to publish the pattern or article for the first time in any periodical. All other rights remain with the author. First serial rights can be limited by geography unless sold to an online publication, because the internet is accessible worldwide.

☆ **One-time rights:**

Also known as simultaneous rights – this grants the licensee the right to publish the work one time on a non-exclusive basis.

11 http://lexpubli.ca
12 http://www.nolo.com
13 http://www.writerswrite.com/journal/dec97/cew3.htm

☆   **Second serial (or reprint) rights:**

Publication may publish the article or design after the piece has already been published elsewhere. These rights are also non-exclusive. Book excerpts in a magazine typically fall under this category.

☆   **All rights:**

Just what it says. Designer/author is giving up all rights in the work and the publisher may publish the work in any format (including print, electronic and who knows what else in the future) without providing additional payment to the author. **AVOID WHENEVER POSSIBLE.**

☆   **Subsidiary rights plus dramatic, television and film rights:**

These rights are not usually an issue with knit-related patterns, articles or books, but you never know when Yarn Harlot: The Motion Picture might make it to a theatre near you someday. (The tagline on that movie poster, of course, would be: "She warned you you'd need more chairs!" And the trailer would feature exhausted bookstore employees, plus a lot of knitters holding socks).

☆   **Work for hire:**

If you are actually employed as a full or part-time employee by KnitMagazine, i.e. not a free-lancer, and create something for them in the course of your daily job duties, unless otherwise specified, they typically own that work you created, copyright included. In a knitting context, work for hire agreements are usually long-term pattern licenses, or multi-contributor books edited by a single author who gives up their rights to the editing and text contributed to the book.

AVOID IF AT ALL POSSIBLE UNLESS THE DEAL PAYS ENOUGH TO MAKE IT WORTHWHILE TO YOU.

☆   **Electronic rights:**

Changing *every* single day. The most important thing to remember is to lock down the specifics when you sign a contract. A few years ago, major book publishers' contracts often specified that electronic rights gave them the right to produce a CD, or a DVD or your work. Many of them have not updated those contracts in ages – and really, when's the last time you bought a physical CD of anything?

The phrase "including but not limited to" is your friend here. Cross out an overly-broad or general phrase such as "Publisher reserves the rights to produce an electronic edition of the work." and make it even more specific: "Publisher reserves the rights to produce electronic versions of the work, including but not limited to e-books, videos, and DVDs. Publisher may not produce single pattern downloads without prior permission from author." Or whatever floats your boat…

Personally, I would be overly cautious with signing over any electronic rights at all. As publishers see how successful Ravelry and other online pattern sales venues have become, many are (not unreasonably) trying to make a quick buck chopping up any knit pattern book in which they own all rights in order to sell single patterns, too. Watch your back. You can read a literary agent's take on the quickly-changing world of digital rights in Chapter 7.

One more site that can help you clarify what good contracts look like (and bad ones, too!) is:

http://keepyourcopyrights.org/contracts/clauses

The material on Keep Your Copyrights was written by academics at Columbia Law School with the intention of educating authors about their rights, and encouraging them not to give away more of their rights than necessary.

CHAPTER 5

Writing patterns

We've examined how to spread the word about your work, possible venues where you may want to sell, even other ways to make money while you're doing it – but what about the actual mechanics of pattern-writing? As much an art as it is a science, pattern-writing is a solid mark of your skills as a designer. There are plenty of knitters out there who can knit beautifully without a pattern, yet they would be lost if they tried to write it all down. Don't let this happen to you.

☆ Establishing a format

One of the most important things to do when you first begin to write patterns is to establish a stylesheet for yourself. In fact, it's one of the criteria on which you are judged when applying for membership in the Association of Knitwear Designers! What is a stylesheet? At the most basic level, a stylesheet establishes your patterns' written identity – which abbreviations do you use? Which measuring system? (Metric, English or both?) What elements do you consistently include in every pattern? For me, there's always a Notes section that discusses things the knitter may want to know which don't neatly fit into the pattern directions, as well as information on recommended blocking techniques, a thank-you section with the names of my technical editor and models, and the copyright information I referenced above in both the final section and in the footer of each page.

Stylesheets also establish the look and feel of your patterns – my pattern name is always in the same font, followed by "a [*pattern type*] by Shannon Okey for knitgrrl.com," and the main pattern photo. The body text is always the same font and size. The subheaders ("Front," "Back," "Sleeves") are consistently bolded. Any large charts are placed at the very end so they won't disrupt the overall flow of the pattern, and also because knitters are more likely to pull out those pages and use them alone during the course of knitting the pattern.

This improves my workflow in several ways: when I sit down to write a new pattern, I first open and copy an older pattern that is similar, if I have one. I start by replacing the yarn information. Since I have a tendency to use several of the same yarns quite a lot, starting from an old pattern means I don't have to retype the yardage and other information over again, and I remain consistent in the way I list that information. For example:

2 skeins Malabrigo Merino Worsted (100% Merino wool, 210 yds/192 m per 100 gm skein; color Glazed Carrot).

when copied over and changed for color and amount will become:

4 skeins Malabrigo Merino Worsted (100% Merino wool, 210 yds/192 m per 100 gm skein; color Lettuce).

and not accidentally end up:

4 skeins Malabrigo Merino Worsted (100% Merino, 210yds/192m per 100 gm skein, color Lettuce)

Take a closer look there. See the differences? The 'accidents' in the retyped version include no 'wool' after Merino, no space between 210 and yds (as well as 192 and m), a comma instead of a semicolon after 'skein,' and no period after the closing parenthesis. Consistency is important. A missed period here or there may seem like nothing now, but wait until you're managing a large library of your design work.

Reusing old patterns to draft new ones also helps remind me to put in information I may have otherwise forgotten. When I delete the old information and replace it with the new, I'm reminded that I've forgotten to measure the row gauge, or count the number of buttons needed for the placket, and can take action accordingly.

What if you don't have any patterns written yet? Knitty.com's style guide is a great starting point and will illustrate many of the items typically needed in a pattern. You can find it from here:

http://www.knitty.com/subguide.php

Study other designers' patterns you enjoy, too. Don't copy their layout! Instead, get a sense of what information they include that you find particularly helpful. (Linking to appropriate tutorial videos on YouTube to help the reader with a tricky concept? including a piece of knitter's graph paper so the knitter can chart his or her own initial for a mitten back? what stands out?)

Creating your own stylesheet and formatting will also help you when it comes time to submit to another publication. Typically, magazines have their own formatting stylesheet, and will expect you to use theirs. Yarn Forward, the magazine I edited, specified that the designer should include a choice of three alternate yarns in three price ranges that could be used in the pattern instead of the yarn pictured, as well as wraps per inch (a yarn weight measurement used by handspinners) to make substituting handspun yarn a snap. If you are commissioned to do a design for a magazine, be sure to follow their style guide or stylesheet directions exactly – no one likes to re-write a pattern that hasn't been done in the appropriate way. If they don't automatically send you a copy of the stylesheet – *ask*.

☆   **The importance of charts and schematics**

These aren't for you, pattern architect. They're for the benefit of the skilled carpenters out there who will actually implement your design in their neighborhoods, using their own hammers and yarn.

Hammers and yarn. Talk about mixed metaphors – but you get my point! Presumably once you knit a sample of your pattern, you won't be knitting another one immediately. However, knitters using your pattern are going to refer back to the schematic not only as they knit, but also to help them decide which size to knit – or whether the shape is appropriate for their body type at all! Accordingly, you should include as much information as is relevant and necessary to help along the way. A typical schematic looks like this, except there will be measurements in the locations where I've made notes for you:

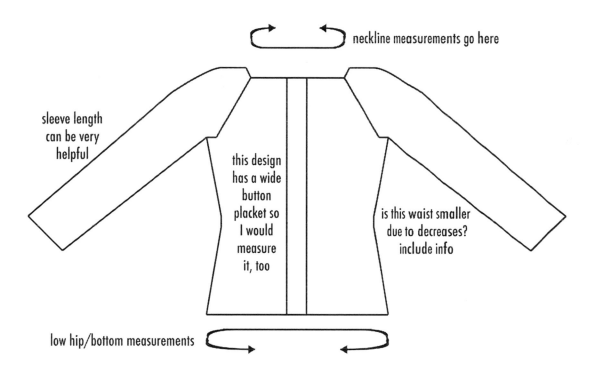

neckline measurements go here

sleeve length can be very helpful

this design has a wide button placket so I would measure it, too

is this waist smaller due to decreases? include info

low hip/bottom measurements

Similarly, for colorwork and particularly for cables, many knitters prefer charts to line by line directions. It's your job as the designer to include whichever format gets the information across in the clearest, most concise way. Often I find myself debating "how many lines is too many lines for a pattern repeat?" In most cases, unless the lines are very similar and easy to memorize, anything over 5 lines long gets charted.

Charting has its own conventions to which you need to adhere no matter which software or method you use to display your charts. For example, most lace charts do not chart the plain (all purl) alternating rows, only charting the lace rows themselves. Some books have attempted to make things "easier" on the knitter by charting all stitches as they would appear from the public-facing side of the fabric, but that is not the usual way to do it. When in doubt about how to chart something, or if you cannot find an existing pattern with a similar chart, provide a written explanation of how YOU intend the chart to be worked in your pattern directions.

Don't forget the chart legend/key! There is no one single set of chart symbols (most publishers create their own libraries in Adobe Illustrator or the like if they don't use an off-the-shelf product such as Knit Visualizer), and your customers will want to know that *your* circle-in-a-square is a purl and not, say, a bobble.

Design software

Some will argue that most knitting software programs are nothing but a "glorified calculator." That may be true when the software simply plugs gauge/stitch count into an existing sweater shape template, but there are also a large number of extremely useful programs that serve knitters and designers of all skill levels and working techniques. The major programs used by designers include:

- Knit Visualizer (http://knitfoundry.com)
- Intwined Pattern Studio (http://intwinedstudio.com)
- Cochenille (http://www.cochenille.com)
- Intwined Pattern Studio (http://www.intwinedstudio.com)
- Adobe Creative Suite
- Microsoft Excel/Microsoft Word
- Sweater Wizard/Sock Wizard/etc (http://www.knittingsoftware.com)
- DesignaKnit (http://www.knitcraft.com/knitcraft/products/dak/dak7.php)
- Knitware (http://www.greatknitdesigns.com/desc.htm)

Some programs seem to be more useful for machine knitters, but all claim to serve handknitting designers as well. Most will allow you to download a demo version for trial, and many are available for PCs and Macintosh alike.

Knit Visualizer is primarily used for charting. It's my most-used single knitting-specific software, because it is very easy to create great-looking cable and colorwork charts that can then be inserted into any pattern document file. Users fill in a grid with symbols chosen from a menu at the side of the screen.

Knit Visualizer also automatically generates a legend/chart key which will include every stitch you've used. Used in conjunction with Adobe Creative Suite (I use PhotoShop or Illustrator if I want to tweak the legend or assemble multiple chart pieces into one – sometimes Knit Visualizer breaks up a particularly wide or large chart into multiple pages), you can make great charts in a flash. On the Macintosh, I tend to use the print command, choose "Save as PDF," and edit the resulting PDF files from there.

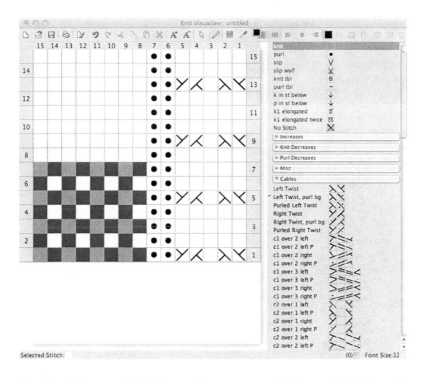

Intwined Pattern Studio is another program similar to Knit Visualizer that can be used for charting. Here's what it looks like in use:

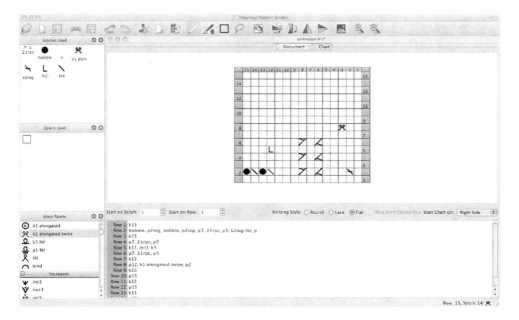

I like that it gives you the opportunity to chart for in the round, flat or lace knitting, and that you can switch back and forth between the document you're creating and your chart.

☆ Excel and Illustrator tutorials

If you don't want to invest the money for Knit Visualizer, you can use your copy of Microsoft Excel to generate charts as well as pattern information! As long as your charts are clear and easy to understand, it doesn't matter what you use to make them (unless a magazine specifies otherwise). Designer Marnie MacLean has done some of the most comprehensive online tutorials on using Excel for knit design:

http://www.marniemaclean.com/words/tutorial/excel

She also created some amazing tutorials for developing schematics in Adobe Illustrator. You can refer to them here:

http://www.marniemaclean.com/words/tutorial/illustrator

Even if you're not quite ready for the information presented in all her tutorials yet, you will likely find a use for them someday. And if you don't want to make your own symbols, you can use the knitter's font found at

http://home.earthlink.net/~ardesign/knitfont.htm

☆ Crochet symbols

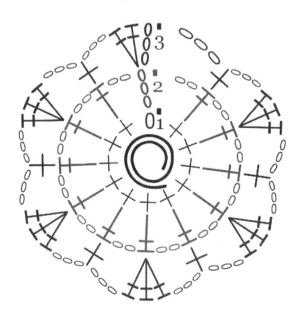

For crocheters, there is SymblCro (http://www.nhswinc.com), designed for drafting circular crochet motifs. In addition, I highly recommend the books *Blueprint Crochet* by Robyn Chachula and *Crochet Me: Designs to Fuel the Crochet Revolution* by Kim Werker (Interweave Press), both of which address crochet symbols in a clear and easy to understand way. Designer Amy O'Neill Houck says: "I would note that most crochet symbol charts are actually drawn by hand in a graphics program. There is a crochet font called

SBFillet.ttf[14]. It was designed for filet crochet and linear charts, but I find it easier to draw my own." Longtime crochet tech editor Julie Holetz notes: "I use Adobe Illustrator to draw my charts. There's also the Stitchin Crochet font.[15]"

Stitchin Crochet font creator Adriana Hernandez of adriprints press provided the sample motif above, which was created using Adobe Illustrator and her font, typing on a circular path.

☆ User accessibility

One other thing to remember about all charts, knit or crochet, is that they cross linguistic boundaries a written pattern can't – many American and European knitters love and can follow Japanese or German patterns without speaking a word of the language because the charts are clear and easy to understand. By making charts available for your patterns where possible, you enable many more potential customers to follow your pattern, even if English isn't their first language.

If you would like to print knitter's graph paper (individual cells are wider than they are tall, just like most knitting stitches), you can create any size you need at: http://www.tata-tatao.to/knit/matrix/e-index.html

☆ Technical illustrations

Although technical illustrations aren't always a must (and I would argue that a good clear photo or two does wonders to explain anything you can name), if you'd like to read a good writeup of one way to do them in Illustrator, check out:

http://curiousknitter.blogspot.com/2010/02/knitting-with-adobe-illustrator.html or http://techknitting.blogspot.com (her 'Subject Index' will help you find things quickly)

For more on artistic illustrations and photography, see Chapter 7.

Sizing

Sizing is a challenge for all designers and publications, but for very different reasons. Often less experienced knit designers don't know how to grade (multi-size) their patterns – a good technical editor is worth their weight in gold if you find yourself in this position and need help. Moreover, unless you are writing to a particular publication's specifications, you must decide how broad a range to include in your pattern. This is another situation where you cannot please everyone, but should try your best to be inclusive. Although several publications (including Knitty.com and Yarn Forward/Inside Crochet) have made efforts to include larger sizes – YF's bust size range on all patterns goes from 30-50" – this isn't always the case.

---

14 http://www.sbcrochet.com/crochetsoftware.shtml
15 http://new.myfonts.com/fonts/adriprints/stitchin

When Knitty.com began requiring larger sizes on all submissions several years ago (their current guidelines require all adult garments to go from XS to 3X in women's sizes, and S to 2X if the garment is for men, adhering to the Craft Yarn Council guidelines throughout), there was a small uproar from some quarters, and massive cheers from the majority of knitters. Depending on whose statistics you believe, the average American woman is now a size 14. Her British, Canadian, Australian and other counterparts are similarly sized, and one third of all American women are a size 16 or larger. You are missing out on a very important potential demographic if you ignore the plus size side of the spectrum.

Ample Knitters, an online mailing list which ran from 1998-2006 and its successor lists (as well as the website http://www.ample-knitters.com, which has a wonderful resources section, not to mention the Ample Knitters Ravelry group at http://www.ravelry.com/groups/ample-knitters), is one place to learn about the issues larger knitters face in regards to shaping, style and a number of other considerations. Two of the best books currently in print on the subject are *Big Girl Knits* and *Big Girl Knits 2*, both by Amy Singer and Jillian Moreno. Classic Elite Yarns hired Moreno to produce the first of several Curvy Knits pattern booklets as well. Even Vogue Knitting recently addressed the issue of pattern sizing on its editorial pages!

Joan McGowan-Michael of White Lies Designs (http://www.whiteliesdesigns.com) is another designer beloved by larger knitters, because her designs are feminine and flattering, yet include sizing and shaping that work for bust sizes from 30" to 60". Check out her interview in Chapter 12.

Ysolda Teague has created a hybrid of the Craft Yarn Council (CYC, also sometimes referred to by their old domain name, yarnstandards.com, or as CYCA) and British Industry Standard sizing charts, which you can find here:

http://ysolda.com/support/sizing

For other sizes (men, children, baby), as well as information on proper measuring, check out the CYC website at:

http://www.craftyarncouncil.com/sizing.html

They have also provided symbols for their standard yarn weight system and difficulty levels that you can include in your patterns with proper attribution. This is an example of a CYC skill level marker:

INTERMEDIATE

This is an example of the CYC yarn label for a worsted/aran weight yarn (16-20 sts per inch):

 As more and more yarn producers adopt these symbols for use on their labels, it makes sense to include them in your pattern if appropriate. 'Worsted,' 'Aran' and other word-based yarn classifications often mean very different things in different countries. For example, in the UK, what an American calls 'fingering weight' is referred to as '3-ply,' and although more and more users are finding patterns via the internet / learning additional terms for various weights, why not simplify where possible?

Various countries' yarn terminology is posted online at Ravelry.com, along with WPI (wraps per inch), a measurement frequently used by handspinners:

http://www.ravelry.com/help/yarn/weights?highlight=12

Getting help: test and sample knitters

Test knitters are another tool in your arsenal when you want to give patterns a trial run before release. You can find them online (http://www.ravelry.com/groups/search?query=test+knitters), on mailing lists, or even by posting a call for knitters on your blog. Test knitters can be compensated in a variety of ways, from cold, hard cash to free patterns and yarn.

When paid in cash, test knitters are generally paid per yard or meter of yarn knitted – rates vary by region, but 15-25 cents per yard is typical, making a 1000-yd sweater anywhere from $150-250. Keep in mind that good test knitters and sample knitters are often jealously hoarded by other designers. You can ask who knits their samples, but you may not find out!

Another alternative is to turn to a sample knitting service such as Fair Trade Knitters (http://www.fairtradeknitters.com), a production handknitting service that creates jobs and provides training to a womens' knitting cooperative in a remote area of Ecuador. Turnaround time is quick and if you can provide the schematics and swatches they ask for, you'll receive a professionally knitted sample at a reasonable price. I've used their services in the past when time was an issue for a book deadline, and have been very pleased with the results.

Tech editing, layout and more

Tech editors are similarly hard to come by – I have three that I used on a rotating basis, depending on who's available at the time. I asked the one with whom I most frequently work, Alexandra Virgiel, for some insight into what she does and how it relates to you, the designer.

What should designers know when hiring/working with a tech editor?

The tech editor can do a lot for your pattern, but garbage in is still garbage out. Make the pattern as good as you can before it goes to editing. If the tech editor has to interpret notes on a napkin, there is a greater possibility for error. Also, make certain that you write down what you actually knit, not what you meant to knit and then changed along the way. If for some reason the pattern doesn't reflect the knitted garment, explain why (i.e. sample is a little tight in the armhole, added an extra 0.5" to depth in pattern).

Most tech editors are happy to give advice on sizing, wording, etc. while you're writing it up. It's easier on everyone if you ask questions first, write second. Do agree on a deadline, and be available for questions.

What tools do you find most useful for your job?

I run a cheap and mostly open-source office. All text and schematics get done in OpenOffice. Charts in Knit Visualizer. Chart cleanup (sometimes) in GIMP and/or IrfanView, a nifty freeware image viewer and super-basic editor.

Should designers expect to pay extra for priority service, grading, etc.?

This varies by tech editor. I charge a flat rate per pattern that includes a schematic and any charts needed. That costs X. Grading as well as editing costs approximately $X * 2.5$, Generally you can have as many sizes as you want, within the limits of the design.

If your tech editor charges by the hour you can save money by doing your own charts and schematics and just having them checked over.

Tell me a horror story from the world of tech editing...

The worst project I ever worked on: fifteen patterns with no gauge, no sizing, wrong yarn info, and little resemblance between the patterns and the garments, which looked unwearable (photography later bore that out). Worse, the designer/author saw nothing wrong with that – they were "improvisational," and anyway it would all be magically fixed in editing, right? Don't be that guy. Your customers can tell when you've half-assed it, and if you don't give the tech editor anything to work with, God only knows what kind of patterns you're going to get back.

☆   **Where to look for tech editors**

The Indy Pattern Designers' Resources group on Ravelry is one place to look for tech editors if one isn't directly recommended to you by another satisfied customer (http://www.ravelry.com/

groups/indy-pattern-designers-resources) – you can also find graphic designers, copy editors and other help there. The Association of Knitwear Designers (http://www.knitwear-designers.org) can also connect you to a list of accredited technical editors who have been juried according to their standards.

One technical editor who has worked with an exceptionally large number of designers and publications in her career preferred to remain anonymous in sharing the following tidbit with you:

> *I **have** told publishers that certain designers' patterns aren't worth the paper they're written on (or the bytes, since they're mostly digital, but yes, I have received pencil-written patterns –oh, the pain!) and that the publisher has probably paid me more to edit a pattern than they paid the designer in the first place. Those designers are few and far between (thank God!). I'm usually very patient and try to help a designer hone her design and pattern writing skills, but when a designer clearly doesn't know what she's doing and resists help or refuses to answer questions or emails, I feel compelled to let the publisher know.*

A good tech editor is invaluable, and when a magazine, publisher or designer finds one they like and can trust, chances are very good they will prioritize their relationship with the tech editor over their relationship with you unless you are a Big Name that compels them to act otherwise. I don't want to panic you! Rather, I want to encourage you to develop a good relationship with your technical editor(s) and know that, like a good ad sales rep, they're not there to harass you, but to help you.

For even more about the world of tech editing, read the interview with Charlotte Quiggle in Chapter 12.

☆   ## Recent innovations in tech editing and pattern testing

Patterndraft (http://patterndraft.com), an online collaborative program that can be used simultaneously by designers, tech editors and pattern testers, entered beta testing in late spring 2010. Operating on a subscription model, the software streamlines communications among the people who are working on a pattern, allowing for immediate updates and changes, revision tracking, shared calendars and a single location to find all information relating to a pattern during its testing and tech editing stage. It's encrypted, too! Check the website for current prices and information.

CHAPTER 6

Making sales

Before you can start creating patterns to sell, you need to know about your potential market(s) and other factors that will influence how you produce your pattern line. If you choose to sell only digital patterns instead of print, for example, you can afford to be a little wordier in your explanations, because you're not paying extra for each printed page.

In addition, if you take the time to learn more about how sales generally work in the handknitting industry (some options include: direct to consumer, wholesale direct to yarn store, wholesale through a distributor, direct through sales reps), you'll have a better handle on not only the potential market, but also ideas on who to contact when it's time to expand. Preparation is key. You might want to produce beautifully packaged patterns on CD-Rs that include lots of photos and PDFs and a video demonstrating how to do the special stitches you've developed, but if yarn stores don't want to stock them, you may need to reconsider your plans. So let's take a look at the ways you can produce and sell patterns, and what the implications are for you, the designer, both from a rights perspective and, importantly, profitability-wise.

Selling wholesale

Designers can make a good living selling patterns wholesale if they are willing to put a lot of time into sourcing reasonably-priced printing solutions, not to mention work with many different yarn stores and other wholesale customers along the way.

(Yarn companies often commission or buy patterns that have been designed specifically for their yarns, for example).

Pattern wholesaling generally works like this:

> • Designer produces a line sheet with all of his or her designs, and ordering information. Line sheets are like order forms, but often have images of the products for sale. Most designers also make something similar to host on their website, but it's good to have a printed version for offline events such as trade shows.
> • Orders for patterns are taken either directly by the designer at a trade show or in person at a LYS. Orders can also be taken by a sales rep (see below).
> • Patterns are typically priced at one half their retail cost (this is called keystone pricing, or keystoning), and therefore marked up 100% by the shop selling them.
> • Patterns are purchased with a minimum order amount (either per pattern or per order).

The advantage to wholesaling is that it keeps down the amount of administrative hassle by prioritizing fewer larger orders over many smaller ones. Automated online systems make it easy to handle dozens of online orders with no need for input from you, but printed pattern orders still have to be packed up and shipped off.[16]

Most designers set a per-pattern or per order minimum. The pattern sales cooperative I founded, Stitch Cooperative, currently sets a 3-pattern minimum for each print pattern ordered rather than a specific total number of patterns or dollar amount, based on the principle of "if you're printing and shipping one, you might as well print three copies while you're at it." This also helps ensure that the yarn stores have sufficient stock on hand – once one patron purchases a pattern, typically their friends at the store will want one, too.

The major challenges of wholesaling are printing patterns at a reasonable cost, and keeping down overall postage/shipping costs. The color laser printer I am currently using costs anywhere from 12-15 cents per color page (*any* page with color on it), which doesn't sound like much until you're doing the math on a complex 7-page pattern. Let's take a look at the numbers:

- Pattern is **$5** (retail price)
- Shops purchase it from you at **$2.50**
- Pattern costs **95 cents** to print and another **2 cents** for the plastic binder sleeves shops expect.
- You are earning **$1.53** per pattern sold, not counting paper cost. This is also assuming the sale didn't come from a sales rep, who would also take a cut.

If you need to visit the post office to send that pattern out, you've just killed 10 minutes of your time, too – better to set a minimum number of patterns so you have a chance to recoup your non-monetary time investments as well.

You can also turn print pattern wholesaling over to a third party such as Bryson Distributing,[17] which creates altogether new issues to consider.

Is it any wonder designers are turning to direct online PDF sales these days?

Kim Dolce of Dolce Handknits, who currently works with Bryson, says this about what having a distributor has meant for her business:

"For the discount my distributor receives, I'm provided with access to a distribution channel I would not otherwise have had at my disposal or at the very least would have taken me years to put together. While I'm ultimately responsible for my own marketing, the 12 sales reps working for the distributor in essence become my sale reps and my pattern line is shown in hundreds of shops across the country. I'm also freed from much of the business of doing business. Instead of invoicing,

16 (Hey, it's 2010 already. I want my jet pack and my transporter beam, OK? No fair!)
17 http://www.brysonknits.com

packing and shipping 3, 6 or 12 patterns at a time, I ship a carton of hundreds of patterns to the distributor who in turn handles the fulfillment of those smaller shop orders. Nor do I have to worry about being paid or following-up with delinquent accounts. I only have to concern myself with one check arriving in the mail 30 days after an order ships. Which means the distributor is taking on much of the risk of doing business that would otherwise be mine.

I knew I wanted to do hard copy patterns and keep my business wholesale. I considered my options – representing myself, finding sales reps, going the distributor route or starting up a cooperative type of distributorship with other designers. When I looked at everything that was important to me, the things I didn't want to deal with and those I wanted control over, I knew a distributor was the best option for me. About 6 months before I was ready to launch the line I attended another TNNA show with a list of distributors I wanted to meet and another list of sales reps to talk to as a fallback.

To be honest, while I had the names of other distributors on my list I had one name at the top. I knew Bryson Distributing handled Fiber Trends patterns and I couldn't think of a more recognizable and successful independent pattern line than that. It turned out some distributors didn't handle leaflet patterns and had no interest in doing so. One was interested in taking over the printing and other aspects of the business that I wanted control over. Bryson's model was more traditional, it's a sizable company and what I wasn't aware of at the time, Jim Bryson really values what we as designers do. I was pretty much flying by the seat of my pants, but as luck would have it, Jim Bryson was interested in my line and was looking to pick up something new about 6 months from when we first talked, so the timing was perfect."

New technological possibilities for print

There are several new technology-based solutions that may help alleviate the print pricing problem somewhat, among them Magcloud[18]. Magcloud was designed to print magazine-style booklets of at least 4, but no more than 100 standard US letter size pages. It currently costs approximately 20 cents per page, not taking into account their frequent sales and other discounts. If you're already paying close to that for your printing anyway, you might as well upload your pattern PDFs and let them take care of the printing and shipping for you.

Magcloud uses paper that is FSC-certified (from managed forests and verified recycled sources), and is 50% recycled (10% post-consumer, 40% pre-consumer). Short issues (16 pages or under; most patterns will fall into this category) are printed on 100# paper.

(The # symbol is shorthand for "pound," and refers to the paper's weight. 100# is heavy stock. Typical copy paper is usually around 20#).

Similar 100# paper stock costs approximately $7.50 for 500 pieces at office supply stores, or .015

18 http://www.magcloud.com

per page. Pennies and fractions of pennies DO add up, so you need to take them into consideration over the long term. Generic brand standard sheet protectors (the current default for most yarn stores purchasing single patterns) are $19.99 for 200, or a little more than .09 apiece

Using an example 8-page pattern:

Printer ink **13 cents** (using the average of high/low costs on my current color laser) per page, or **$1.04** total
Paper costs **12 cents** (assuming non-double sided printing)
Sheet protector **2 cents**
It will cost me **$1.18** at a bare minimum to print that pattern myself. Magcloud will charge $1.60 to produce the same thing or slightly better, *and* they will ship it out, too. (They'll even "ship to group," using a mailing list you establish, which makes pattern clubs or autoship pattern programs for your existing clients not only feasible, but simple!)

Ask yourself: is your time worth 42 cents?

If someone told you they'd pay you 42 cents to stand in line at the post office, would you? Even with my DYMO postage meter and printer[19], I often find myself needing to go to the post office, and it *always* takes longer than I expect.

The Magcloud model works like this: you set a markup of your choice on each item sold, over and above your print costs. If I'm selling that pattern at retail for $6 (yarn stores buy it from me for $3), I will earn $1.40 per pattern sold when I sell it to a yarn store, or $4.40 selling direct to consumer at the full $6 price.

It's not perfect, but it's the best competition I've seen for printing it yourself.

Other printing options include short run offset and digital printing. One printer I like, JakPrints[20], happens to be located in Northeast Ohio near me, but they do jobs nationwide, and can compete nicely on price thanks to the slightly lower cost of living here. An 8-page catalog-style layout similar to our sample pattern above costs $710 for 250 copies, or $735 for 500, so using the second number (because paying an extra $25 for twice as many copies seems like a no-brainer), our 8-page pattern costs $1.47 each.

Yay, we just saved 13 cents each compared to Magcloud!

Until someone finds a really bad pattern error and you are stuck pasting corrections over the remaining 400 copies piled up in your garage next to 7 other boxes of patterns…

---

19 I have an upgraded DYMO LabelWriter 400 that can print postage through Endicia for Mac. More on this when we talk about postage and shipping.
20 http://www.jakprints.com

See where I'm going with this? Stick to shorter print runs and print on demand when you can. You never know when someone might find an error, or you might decide you want to change something, or any number of other things. Unless, of course, someone just ordered 500 copies of your pattern. (*Wake up! You're dreaming.* This advice applies to single patterns more so than, say, books, where it definitely makes sense to do larger print runs to drive down costs wherever you can).

In addition, the more patterns you have to offer, the more space you will have to find in your home or studio for them, storage-wise. And fulfillment services aren't cheap! Shipwire[21] is one fulfillment service that will take those boxes out of your garage and ship items out as they're ordered, but it's designed more for physical objects than something like patterns.

If you choose to go with a distributor-based model, as Kim Dolce did, you may very well find yourself in the position of needing to print 500 copies of each pattern! There are many reasonably-priced printing services available online these days, and you can often get a better price somewhere that's not local to you. Check out 48hourprint.com and some of the other options listed in the Resources guide at the back. Another added benefit of using such a printing service is that you could have the patterns shipped directly to your distributor, a space-saver if you live in a small apartment or don't have storage space to spare. Order sample prints from the various services and compare before you commit to one – paper and print quality **does** matter.

Postage and shipping

If you plan to ship your own products, be they patterns or the cool new stitch markers you're selling on the side to bring in additional income, you'll eventually have to deal with postage, shipping and our friends in the big delivery trucks.

☆   **Lesson one:**

Avoid the post office as much as possible. Don't get me wrong, I love my friends at the post office. Before I had a dedicated studio space, I spent a lot of time there checking my PO box. But unless you live in some mystical fairyland, chances are good that a post office run is going to kill at least a half hour of your day that would be better spent knitting or finding new customers.

As mentioned above, I have a DYMO LabelWriter that can print postage. Today, however, I would recommend the slightly newer DYMO LabelWriter 450 Twin Turbo model, which can print both postage and packing labels at the same time. On mine, you need to swap between the roll of digital postage stamps and the roll of labels. The LabelWriter 450 works on both Mac and PC, and there is no ink/toner because it's a thermal printer. Labels aren't dirt cheap but they are reasonable compared to writing everything out by hand, securing PayPal shipping forms onto envelopes with tape, or other alternatives. In addition, it looks more professional, and that's what we're aiming for here.

21 http://www.shipwire.com

You can, if you receive payments for orders in PayPal, print a shipping label and pay for USPS or UPS shipping directly inside PayPal, but again, it takes time to tape the resulting label to the package unless you use their Click-n-Ship[22] labels. (At $9 for 25 labels, they're not cheap!) Other countries' postal systems may have similar labels available to their customers, if you don't live in the US. Check with Canada Post, the Royal Mail, Deutsche Post or whoever your national carrier happens to be.

A special note on shipping, border issues and more from Canadian designer Kate Atherley concerns key shipments from the US to Canada and vice versa, from a designer's perspective: "Shipping across the border (to/from the US) is expensive, takes too damn long and is risky. We have to consider customs – improperly labeled, a package might get stuck at customs for inspection, and then there's always the risk of having to pay import duties and tax. If you label something as a sample or having a low value, chances are it won't be held and you won't have to pay anything, but I feel like it's a crapshoot. There is no simple overnight or 2-day option that's affordable – I've had packages that have cost me almost my entire design fee to ship. This means that the deadlines are often compressed. If you ship out yarn to me from the US, it can take a week or more to arrive, and then I have to allow another week or so at the back end for it to arrive – that's 2 weeks out of my knitting time."

☆   **Lesson two:**

Set up accounts with the major shipping companies (UPS, FedEx, etc). If you are an Etsy.com seller (it's currently free to join, even if you never sell a thing), look in "your Etsy" at the "shipping options" section on the left sidebar[23]. You'll find a link that says *Save on shipping with Etsy and FedEx*, and a passcode. Copy the passcode and click the link. As of this writing (January 2010), Etsy accountholders qualify for the following discounts:

Up to 21% off select FedEx Express® U.S. shipping
Up to 18% off select FedEx Express international
Up to 20% off select FedEx Ground® shipping
Up to 20% off select FedEx Office[SM] services

That adds up!

Check with your local chamber of commerce and any other professional groups to which you belong, such as TNNA, they may have also negotiated savings on shipping that you can use. Long experience has taught me one can only fit so many patterns in plastic sleeves inside a flat rate Priority Mail envelope, so sometimes using UPS or FedEx works out better, both price-wise and cost-of-shipping-supplies-wise. FedEx and UPS will deliver their shipping supplies to your door.

22 http://tinyurl.com/y9ht85h
23 https://www.etsy.com/shipping_profile_edit.php

☆   **Lesson three:**

It is always wise to use mailing/shipping services with tracking numbers, but particularly for larger orders. You never know when you might have a negative encounter with a customer who claims they never received what you sent.

Both UPS and FedEx have a $100 liability on all packages unless otherwise declared, and additional fees paid[24]. Here is yet another good reason to keep excellent records (from clause 49.2, Liability Limits, in the UPS Tariff/Terms and Conditions of Service

> *UPS's liability for loss or damage to a package containing* **documents** (emphasis mine, and next section snipped for brevity)...*is limited to the replacement cost of the media on which the content is recorded.*[25]

In other words, good luck getting them to pay you $5 per pattern on that box of 100 patterns you just sent out, or even whatever it cost to print and produce them unless you can prove it. Record-keeping is key! It's an imperfect world, and there are no perfect solutions, only good ones. Don't let the perfect be the enemy of the good when choosing what's right for you. UPS, FedEx and other trackable shipping services have both advantages and disadvantages. Losing one shipment may not make or break you, but if you get to the point where you have dozens of packages going out per day, it adds up.

Sales reps

Sales representatives are the public face of a knitting brand – people who travel from one yarn store to the next bringing new skeins of happiness plus the latest patterns and gadgets. A great sales rep should have excellent relationships with the shops in his or her territory (if not, you may suffer blowback from stores who don't like dealing with that rep and therefore won't end up stocking your patterns). It can be difficult to find an established rep who is willing to take on just patterns – the best ones have their hands full already! – but ask around. The winter and summer TNNA trade shows feature bulletin boards with reps who are looking for new lines – it can be worth your time to go to the show just for this alone.

Doing the digital math

Selling digital patterns is simple, cheap, easy and allows you to reach buyers anywhere there's an internet connection. What's the catch? Well, there are a few, actually. This is a topic dear to my heart (we all have our biases), because I think that the rising interest in knitting has been nurtured and sustained with growing internet participation over the past 5+ years. It's easier now than ever to find someone who shares your passion for knitting online, even if you live in the tiniest, most

---

24 http://www.fedex.com/us/services/terms/popup_tc_groundtariff_body.html#declared
25 http://www.ups.com/content/us/en/resources/ship/terms/service.html – you'll need to download the text saved as a PDF in order to read these, look for "Liability Limits"

remote outpost. Previously, knitting's popularity seemed to run in 10-year cycles (some observers say 20-year). Up in the early 80s, down in the early 90s, up in the 00s with no signs of stopping yet!

Bringing the internet and knitting together has maintained not only a high level of interest in the craft itself but also a steady demand for quality patterns and instruction. Here, at the start of 2010, online-only classes are starting to become not only viable but popular, for example, and the same with e-books. They may not supplant printed directions entirely, but they're giving them a run for the money. You may even be reading a digital version of this book right now!

The cost of producing pattern PDFs is miniscule compared to printing them, even when you include the costs of being online (having an internet connection, a computer, appropriate software, etc). It's important to evaluate not only how digital products have an impact on your bottom line, but why. No hypotheticals here – if no one is paying what you are asking for your product, you're making zero. I won't tell you what to charge for your pattern or product – determining the right price for *you* is your job – but I can give you an idea of how your prices affect your earnings and how to consider choosing online sales venues. Let's look at a recent example in the knit design world.

In November 2009, Knit Picks, the popular online-only yarn company, started their Independent Designers Program (IDP) in a small, pre-release test. It went live, with full promotion to their mailing list and website, in January 2010. The program allows independent designers to sell patterns that use Knit Picks yarn and retain 100% of the proceeds. The catch? All patterns retail for $1.99, when patterns sold online or in yarn stores typically cost $5 or $6 each.

The largest and most recent amount of publicly-available data (March 2010) is that 293,000 patterns, representing $1,500,000 in sales have been sold on Ravelry.com. This is an average per-pattern price of $5.12, and of that amount, 98.8% of the money earned went directly to the designers.

Full disclosure: at the time of this writing, I am preparing a handful of patterns to sell in the Knit Picks IDP. I've also been following discussions about the program online and in mailing lists targeted to knit designers. Hopefully you've already read the section above about the more tangible costs inherent in print patterns, which will make this next explanation all the more clear.

☆   ## Using a pattern with a retail cost of $5 as our example:

- I can sell it myself on my website and net **$4.55** after PayPal fees.
- I can sell it on Ravelry and net $4.55 and their (small) tiered commission after the month's sales are totaled…using the 98.7% figure above, probably more like **$4.49**
- I can sell it on Stitch Cooperative's new digital affiliate system through a yarn store and net **$3.64** (the post-PayPal $4.55, with an additional commission to the LYS that sold it, too)
- I can sell it on Patternfish.com and net approximately **$3.00** (60% of $5).
- I can sell it wholesale, printed, to a yarn store and get $2.50 (but probably more like **$2.00** by

the time you take printing into consideration, etc).
- I can sell it with Knit Picks in their new program and get **$1.99**.

Of course the most rational way to sell that pattern is the first, but it relies upon both getting people to visit your website *and* getting them to buy. This shouldn't be a problem if you follow the best practices for social media we discussed earlier, but as I mentioned, social media is more for building long term relationships than it is for driving direct sales. Ravelry is a clear winner on that front.

The digital affiliate system my pattern sales cooperative developed is good, but it relies on yarn store owners to not only sign up for the program but also actively promote it. The current economic crisis also means that many yarn stores are not buying as many print patterns as they once were (although this may change going forward), so that makes the fifth option unattractive for now.

(Not to mention all that printing/shipping takes up time I could be using for more productive work, such as creating new designs. Never forget to account for all the time you put into your business!)

Other online venues such as Patternfish.com take varying percentages of the sales price (in Patternfish's case, as much as 40%).

To me, selling with Knit Picks' program made sense because they offer a huge built-in audience, they'll promote the patterns, and I don't have to do anything I wouldn't already have been doing (knitting, photographing, making charts). In addition, Knit Picks is not taking rights to the design, as most magazines (or major publisher book deals) would, and I believe that the economies of scale will work in my favor here, i.e. selling 100 $1.99 patterns instead of 20 $5 ones.

Why? For one thing, that's 100 potential new fans who will seek out my other work if they like the pattern they just bought. I can also justify it as a form of subsidized advertising – I get to share in Knit Picks' 700,000 unique site visitors per month in exchange for taking a little less than I *might* have made elsewhere. ("Might" being the keyword there...the only thing certain in knitwear design is death, taxes, and an income that swings up and down). And it may even revive interest in older patterns that have slowed down sales-wise over time.

☆   **Are you hurting other designers by taking less for your work?**

A popular designer allowed me to include her side of a lengthy conversation we had about the Knit Picks Independent Designer's Program here on the condition of anonymity. I think this is worth including because it not only shows you a counterpoint and different reasoning behind why another designer chose not to experiment with the program, but it also makes it all the more clear that you need to carefully consider the implications of any business decision as it concerns *you*: your values, your beliefs and what you find important in life. She says:

"I think that the people who get in early get extra publicity and less competition, and so it may be a very good program for them, but as long as they intend to scale with no limits, there is simply no way that future contributors can expect the same type of response.

To me, this makes the point of an up front advance somewhat moot. If you used your advance to pay a tech editor (or if your advance doesn't cover much more than you spent on a tech editor) and your patterns aren't earning you enough to even reclaim your pattern, then there is no spreading the wealth around. It's largely risk free for the company sponsoring it. At worst, they are out a few balls of yarn and a nominal fee that is well below the going rates for patterns. At best, they get back everything they paid in the advance and sell oodles of yarn in the process. In addition, I just hate seeing individual PDF downloads offered at such a low price. I think, in the end, this hurts all self publishers.

I agree with you on building up a large library of patterns so that I might sell a few of each a month and get enough from them to make it worth my time. [author's note: see *The Long Tail: Why the Future of Business is Selling Less of More*, a book by Chris Anderson] There *is* a cost, however, to making patterns available for sale that's more unique to pattern design than to other types of digital media: we do *constant* support for our patterns. As long as a pattern remains online, no matter how well vetted, tested, tech edited and error-free it is, there will always be support questions and if a pattern is more popular there are simply more opportunities for people to misinterpret instructions and need help.

So when you look at a pattern in 10 sizes, with complicated instructions and many possible areas for confusion, fitting problems, poor yarn choices and so on, the more that pattern sells, the more support will be required. I recently had to pay to have a tech edited pattern re-tech-edited because it had become clear that the first tech editor did a horrible job. Before I made that call, I was spending a heck of a lot of time doing support for the pattern and decided that money spent re-tech-editing was a better value than hours spent trying to figure out all the problems and creating updates.

All this is to say that the retail price for the pattern has to cover not just the time I sunk into creating the pattern but also the ongoing maintenance. We can be all too quick to forget the value of our time, and $1.99 per pattern means that we have to sell at least 4 patterns for every hour of support we are doing just to reach minimum wage (ish) and frankly, I think the work I do is worth far more than minimum wage!

And while I agree that business models tend to be self regulating, I find most fledgling designers (yours truly was one of them) far too willing to undervalue themselves for a chance to publish. So, just like many of us who have been around the block a few times have given up on submitting to print publications, we'll probably also forego a program like this one if it doesn't serve us well. However, there is always a glut of willing designers in the wings who are happy to take our place. In time, when all patterns come down in price because consumers won't agree to higher prices anymore, your $1.99 will no longer be competitive for price alone, and new patterns will either have to be exceptional, or you will need to push your prices even lower. There'll be a point where it simply won't be worth people's time to design, unless money is not a factor for them.

But you know, I'm sincere when I say that I really don't begrudge anyone their business choices. Each indie designer has to make tough business choices and there is *always* a trade off, so while I'm adamant in my stance on these programs for me, I totally get why people choose to participate for the same reasons that I understand why individuals want or need to shop at discount and big box stores versus mom and pop shops. I think everyone should weigh the pros and cons but ultimately only *they* can decide what the right choice is. I also feel this way about yarn substitutions and picking which size to knit when one is between sizes!"

☆   So what's the solution?

There is no one solution, there are only the solutions that are right for you!

Using myself as an example, I sell in all of the above venues plus an Etsy shop (http://knitgrrl.etsy. com), as well as my own online and brick and mortar shops (http://www.knitgrrlstudio.com/ shop)…and I'll likely add others as they appear and make sense to me. You never know where you will pick up new fans. It's the same as the social media number crunch above – some people are only on Facebook and Ravelry, some are on Ravelry and Twitter, some are on all of the above – so if you want to reach them, you should be, too.

As long as there are no contractual difficulties (such as an exclusive contract to sell on only one site), you should choose as many different sales outlets as makes sense for you. Different websites have different audiences and you may be surprised where you sell best! One tip: keep a running list, spreadsheet or database of where all your patterns are currently being legitimately sold. Post it on your website, too! If someone has copied your pattern or is otherwise distributing it without your permission, it's not rare for an internet Good Samaritan to let you know so you can take appropriate action. In addition, when you release a new pattern, you'll have a checklist of everywhere it needs to be sent or uploaded.

☆   Don't despair...

I know as a reader seeking expert advice that it can be really frustrating to hear *you* need to decide what options are right for your business, especially if you haven't yet had to choose *any* at all. However, as I've mentioned previously, this career does not have a standardized path to follow. As various factors continue to change the industry on a daily basis, you will be better off if you educate yourself on the history of how things have been done previously (as well remaining open to new sales methods, software, and social media) than you will be if you choose only one method of selling your work and stick with it forever. Don't be afraid to change gears. Audiences change. Software changes. You can, too.

Money, money, money

Selling patterns isn't like your childhood lemonade stand, though for all I know, these days kids accept credit cards for those, too. You've got a product, now you want to get paid. What are your options, particularly online?

☆   **(All roads lead to...) PayPal**

PayPal is, like it or leave it, the 800-lb gorilla of online sales facilitation. Just about every online sales service, be it Ravelry, Patternfish, Etsy or others yet to be developed, not to mention every e-commerce software (ZenCart, osCommerce, Shopify, etc) ties into PayPal. Why? More people have PayPal accounts as buyers or sellers than almost any other service, and you don't even need an account in order to buy using PayPal. (As a buyer, you can manually input your credit or debit card information instead).

Canadian designer Kate Atherley, on currency and other considerations:

> *I like to think that PayPal makes this all fairly transparent/irrelevant, and I don't know any Canadians who are worried about this sort of thing – we all know that credit card companies just do the conversion and take care of the math. We are forced to shop in USD all the time. But I also recognize that this attitude comes from being the smaller country with the smaller currency. It shouldn't be relevant, but it is. And I don't honestly know how to fix this, other than user education. I've got patterns priced $5 on Ravelry and $5 on Patternfish but they are different $5. I like to sell in Canadian dollars to Canadians, and Ravelry doesn't (seem to) let me. And then there's the niggling sense that I'm violating tax laws somehow...*

By making these cross-border transactions simple, PayPal was the first online payment service to nearly erase national borders and open the world's bank accounts to even the smallest business.

☆   **Google Checkout**

For customers who dislike PayPal (there is a large and vocal anti-PayPal contingent out there), Google Checkout is a viable replacement, and if at all possible, you should offer both payment options in order to maximize the number of customers who will feel comfortable shopping with you on your website. E-junkie, my primary digital download sales vehicle outside of Ravelry.com, and Payloadz (an older service which some designers still use) allow you to offer both PayPal and Google Checkout as payment options when you sell patterns or other items through them.

☆   **WorldPay, Amazon Payments and other options**

These aren't widely used or supported when it comes to making payments for patterns, although that may change as time goes forward. WorldPay is a UK online payment service (for a list of past and current payment solutions, see this page at Wikipedia: http://en.wikipedia.org/wiki/List_of_ on-line_payment_service_providers, keeping in mind that most of them are no longer around!)

☆ Checks and other things made of paper

Although it's normal to be paid via check when you're dealing with distributors, it's up to you whether you will accept checks, money orders and other forms of payment from individual customers. One word of advice? Wait for the check to clear *before* you ship the order!

☆ Accepting credit cards

Merchant accounts are easier to set up now than ever before. I've used the same company (Merchant Warehouse – see the Resources Guide for more information) in two of my businesses now, and it takes all of about ten minutes to do the application and get things set up. Depending on whether you're selling online, or online *and* in person, there are many different options for you to consider.

Another merchant account service, ProPay, which is frequently used by the craft show crowd, would be a good option if you are doing a lot of trade or craft shows. There is a tendency to overspend at in-person events, and if you're able to offer payment via credit card on the spot, chances are you will make sales you wouldn't normally have made, which balances out any monthly or annual fees. In addition, if you're using a PC (Mac users need to run it through a virtual terminal), ProPay's MicroSecure Card Reader is tiny enough to carry anywhere compared to a larger terminal with printing capabilities (such as my Nurit 3010 machine). One less thing to make space for in your trade show packing!

☆ The future...

Square (https://squareup.com) is a new way of accepting credit cards using your smartphone or other digital devices which doesn't require a full merchant account setup. One advantage Square may have for the independent designer is the ability to accept credit cards for orders somewhere like TNNA or Stitches a few times a year without maintaining a full merchant account at all times.

CHAPTER 7

Proposals and Publishing

Or, how to say "I do" to writing for magazines and books. Writing and designing for magazines and books is often first among the major goals of an aspiring designer. Get your work out in the right place at the right time and you can parlay it into wider notoriety with what is essentially free advertising.

> *To this day I still kick myself for being lazy and not getting my submission together on time for the first Stitch 'n Bitch book by Debbie Stoller. (Sorry, Debbie. It was my loss...congrats on selling over a quarter of a million copies!)*

So what does it take to get published? I'll walk you through the steps so you can create your own success story. First of all, I'd like to address a question that comes up again and again, namely...

Do you need an agent?

Short answer: *not necessarily*, though it can definitely help. Unlike the fiction market, the knit-writing sphere is a lot smaller and more open to newcomers. You aren't always going to end up in a junior sub-editor's slush pile...in fact, you might end up speaking directly to your future editor at a trade show or other event long before you write your first proposal. But if you have a difficult time with proposals, or find yourself so busy you can't keep up, having a great agent on your side is an invaluable asset.

☆ **Working with an agent**

Agents are an amalgam of many good things when it comes to book publishing contracts. They're like having a lawyer who knows not only all the ins and outs of a book deal's contract, but also all the editors at all the publishing houses (three of whom they just had lunch with last week), and what they're buying or not buying...in short, your agent can be your best friend when it's you versus Giant Publishing Company X.

Heretical though it may seem, you don't always need an agent to get a book deal. I love my agent, and though I'd had success landing book deals without her, she does more watching my back contractually than deal-finding. She's also an invaluable sounding board with a vast amount of expertise, well worth the standard 15% she earns when something gets signed. I will admit I resisted for a long time, but after a long talk with Jennifer Hansen of Stitch Diva Studios in which she pointed out all the time I was spending dealing with [problems X, Y and Z at Publisher ABC] was time I could be designing, I realized I would be better off with one than without!

☆   **Tips for finding and working with an agent**
    (from a top New York City-based literary agent)

- Craft titles are a world unto themselves; research agents who handle titles in the field and target them first
- If you have colleagues/friends who are repped by these agents, ask them for an introduction: an agent will always pay more attention to a referral from a client than a query that comes in cold
- Unlike your editor, your agent is going to want whatever you want, so once they're on board, be up front with them about your priorities and goals – are you anal about photography and want to be involved in all shoots?; are you terrible with tech editing and want them to hire someone to do it?; do you need to be able to retain the right to sell certain patterns individually on your own? – so that they can do their best for you before the deal is in contracts, when it's often too late to secure those kinds of concessions.

Here's another anonymous tip from an author who has written several major publisher books:

> *"If you do get an agent for book publishing make sure that she's not friends with acquisitions editors. We got royally screwed with* [name redacted] *and* [name redacted] *on that, and didn't figure it out until it was too late."*

I asked one literary agent about the problems she encounters with her client-authors. Expectations too high? unable to be flexible? won't listen to the advice she gives...? She responded:

"My authors are all angels [big grin] But seriously, it's important to be realistic – publishing is in tough shape right now, and craft publishing has been consolidating at a rapid pace. Publishers are more and more focused on platform and unwilling to take a risk on someone 'unknown,' so advances are lower and it's harder to secure contracts. Understanding the marketplace and working with your agent to create as compelling a proposal as possible is key. Also, the publisher may ask you to jump through some hoops before signing you up. Even if you've sold scores of designs to magazines etc, they may still ask you to send them some actual garments, and/or some of the patterns. If you really want the book deal, you should do it."

☆   **What's a platform?**

"Platform" is a word you'll hear a lot when speaking with agents and publishers. It basically means "fanbase" coupled with "what do you have to offer *us?*" In other words, if Martha Stewart designs a paint line for a home improvement store, it's not because she's hurting for cash. It's because both brands have something to offer each other – Stewart has hordes of loyal fans who like to do home improvement and crafts projects, and the store can handle sales and marketing for what will likely be a smashing success, periodically sending her a Publisher's Clearing House-sized check.

You may have a platform already but don't know it. Does your blog get 100,000 unique viewers a month? Do you have 10,000 rabid Twitter followers? Are each of your patterns on Ravelry being knit by 1000 people? You can make a case for what you have to offer based on something like this – publishers love numbers and statistics!

☆   Where are publishers heading on the digital rights issue?

And how can we, as independent designers and authors, be ready for it? Our anonymous agent friend fills us in...

"Publishers these days are making land grabs for rights. Everyone is scrambling to secure as many rights as they can so as not to be left out in the cold when new formats take over. Scary, right? But, your publisher is your partner, not your adversary (I hope), so you want to work with them to exploit rights as effectively as possible. Since we don't yet really know how much many of those rights are actually worth, I'd encourage everyone to set terms of license on as many speculative type rights as possible (or on the entire agreement) – perhaps grant the right, but for 3 years, or 5 years, and then there has to be a renegotiation and you're free to revert at that time if you want. Or if the right isn't exploited within a few years, ask for a reversion so you can do something with it yourself. Make sure you earn some share of revenues on every little thing – from microtransactions and advertising they may attached to your work in some digital context, to reprints etc."

Smart advice! (*See, I told you to really read and think through your contracts, didn't I?*)

So with all that buzzing in your brain, let's talk about the three major types of publishing and how you go about doing them: magazines, books and the expanding world of independent or self-publishing.

☆   Proposing to a magazine

Putting together a magazine proposal is fairly simple if you read and follow the instructions! But if you are not sure where you'll be submitting your work, you can create a basic proposal and then tweak it with the elements requested by Magazine X. I have taught entire workshops based on assembling the elements of a successful proposal, but it all comes down to this:

- Did you follow the publisher's directions?
- Did you make an effort to put together a compelling submission?
- Is your work creative? Does it stand out, quality-wise?
- Did you make a good first impression with your email or other contact?

If so, you are well on your way to landing in the pages of a magazine. Now sit back and be prepared to wait for a while: one of the hardest parts of magazine submission is not knowing how long it will take before you hear back from the editors. This is one variable that can swing from mere hours to months. I'll admit that during my tenure at Yarn Forward, I made more than one 'yes, I will take it!' decision immediately. (Then again, we were a monthly, which meant a very quick turnaround per issue).

Estimated time from receipt of submission to acceptance or rejection ranges from a week to six months. The editors I spoke with all emphasized that they do not hold things up any longer than they absolutely have to (they want to clear their inboxes as much as you want to hear back from them!), but the profession being what it is, sometimes changes to the magazine lineup (*remember the 'follow through when you commit' designer example at the beginning of the book?*) necessitate taking a little more time to confirm whether they will be able to use your work.

And although I don't recommend sending an endless stream of follow-up emails (again, they're trying to clear out their inbox in order to get to you), it's not excessive to send a status query after 6 weeks or so, especially if the submission is seasonal and could be sent to another publication in time. Things do get lost in the mail, after all. Be polite, and more importantly, brief!

On the flip side, if an editor contacts you for information about your submission, be sure to reply as soon as you can with all of the information he or she has requested.

☆   Proposing to a book publisher

Book publishers are like magazines with a longer lead time. Typically, you'll submit something similar to a larger magazine pattern proposal, with a table of contents, samples and more information included. Please see Appendix B. I've reproduced the book proposal template I first created for my Knitgrrl book series at Watson-Guptill, and have adapted for all my proposals since. No matter where you are submitting work, creativity, professionalism and patience will all help you along the way.

☆   Self-publishing

Are you an ultra-organized control freak who enjoys spending all of your free time working? Then self-publishing may be right for you.

Wait!
Come back.

I didn't mean to scare you...sorry. However, self-publishing is not something one just wakes up and decides to do for a lark. There is definitely a learning curve, a sizeable number of variables to manage, and the options are changing every single day. The pros of self-publishing are many (increased income, better control over end product and marketing, speed) but don't kid yourself, there are also many cons. In order to put out a quality product, you'll either have to learn a lot about design software, or you'll need to pay someone with the requisite skills (and by the way, freelance graphic designers earn a *lot* more money per hour than fiber arts designers do). Most self publishers throw in the towel, buy a lot of books on Adobe InDesign, and make the best of it. See the Resources guide at the back of the book for some useful starting points. Are you also prepared to hire (or barter services with) technical editors and other knit-related professionals?

At a bare minimum, text-wise, do you have someone with excellent proofreading and editing skills who can look over the work before you publish it?

Yes, you are very good at reading over your own writing, I know.

*No, you shouldn't be the **only** one reading it before it gets published.*

Look, I've written 12+ books and countless magazine articles at this point, and I readily admit to needing an outside editor, if only to tell me when to shut up.

In the interviews section (Chapter 12), quite a few of the featured designers have chosen to go the self-publishing route, and explained why. You can join their ranks if you are willing to go the extra mile to put out a quality product, and there's no excuse not to these days! With quality POD (print on demand) services at your disposal, you don't even need to print thousands of copies up front that might end up sitting in your garage for five years.

One word of warning: beware the value-added services offered by some POD services, such as editorial and marketing. Even if they have the best of intentions (they certainly don't have reasonable price tags), the chances any editor working for a general-interest printing service knows anything at all about knitting/crochet/etc is slim to none. You're better off finding a volunteer editor or reader group via your website, Ravelry, etc. Think of them as test knitters for your writing.

Photos and illustrations

No matter where or with whom you are publishing, the right visual images can make or break your chances for success, whether you're doing a magazine proposal or releasing your pattern for sale online. People are very visually-oriented: if you can catch their attention successfully, you have a better than average chance of closing the sale (or getting the magazine commission, or whatever you are doing). You don't have to have an art degree to do great photos and sketches, either – there are a wide variety of tools at your disposal, including "cheats" that'll make it look as if you've been doing fashion illustration since you were five.

Melissa Wehrle (read her interview in on page 172) kicked off a series on knit-related sketching here: http://www.neoknits.com/2010/03/sketching-101-flat-sketching – if that's too daunting at first, try starting with a Fashionary or Hokey Croquis sketchbook (fashionary.org, hokeycroquis.com). You can download some figures to try on both Fashionary and Hokey Croquis's websites, too.

Franklin Habit, an expert in appealing visuals (http://the-panopticon.blogspot.com), creator of this book's cover image, and knitter extraordinaire shared some of his opinions on the power of images:

Can you comment on the power of visuals for a knitter?

I think it's a given that when it comes to selling a pattern, visuals are of paramount importance And I don't just mean clear schematics and excellent photographs; I also mean handsome layout and good typography. Especially in our brave new world of self-publishing, a professional overall appearance will help to give the impression that the designer is reliable and the pattern will be well-written and error-free.

As both a photographer and an illustrator, you come to visual images from two very different directions – do you think that knitters relate to visual learning more so than most disciplines?

I think that as a person becomes an experienced knitter, s/he can't help but become a more visually-oriented person. To knit well, you have to learn to notice small details that most folks might ignore – the direction of a cable twist, the method used for an increase or decrease, and so forth. Knitters grow accustomed to looking closely at their knitting, and I'd be surprised if that tendency didn't carry over into looking closely at other things.

Any tips for photographing knitwear?

My number one tip is to get to know your camera. It's not expensive equipment that makes a good photograph – it's knowing what to do with the equipment you have. Study the manual and play with your camera. Keep it with you, test the features and photograph *everything* until using it begins to feel instinctive. Trying to improve your photography skills when you only pull out the camera to snap a finished object is like trying to learn to knit by working three stitches a day.

Is a bad visual image worse than no image at all when it comes to getting information across in a knitting pattern?

It can be, if the image is misleading. A schematic or photograph that doesn't honestly represent the reality of the pattern is going to cause a mess of trouble for your customers, and lots of luck trying to get them to trust you again! If a designer's illustration or photography skills aren't solid, better in the long run to hire someone else than to try to fudge it.

☆   **Effective photographs**

If you want a crash course in effective knit-photography, reading designer Jared Flood's website (http://brooklyntweed.blogspot.com) and carefully observing how he highlights specific aspects of whatever he is capturing is one way to do it! Knitting photography is a special breed unto itself: you need to consider *what* you are trying to show in the image before you actually do it. Do you need to emphasize a special stitch pattern? Is the collar or buttonband joined in a special way that would make more sense to the knitter if viewed close up? It helps, especially if you have more than one item to photograph and limited time, to make a shot list in advance that catalogs all the images you need to capture. This not only saves time, but ensures you'll get all the shots you need – when working with a model or with a limited amount of time to complete the shots, you won't need to struggle to remember everything (and inevitably, miss something)!

Photographer and knit designer Lee Meredith (http://www.leethal.net) answered a few more questions for me about the delicate relationship between knitting and photography:

How does your photography training influence your knitting, and vice versa?

This is tough, because they surely influence each other, but I don't know exactly how; I had been studying photography for years when I started knitting, so I'm sure that way of thinking has always been a part of my knitting since the beginning. I'm definitely all about the finished work in my knitting projects, not the process, and I'm always visualizing a piece – the shape, colors, construction – before I start and as I knit. My background in all visual arts (I also studied studio arts quite a bit) heavily influences my knit design choices; I think much less about fashion and trends when I design knitwear, with my focus on visually interesting lines, color combinations, and details. As for my knitting influencing my photography – for the last few years, I've hardly done any photography outside of my work, which is mainly knitting and other forms of crafting, and just shooting for fun. I am definitely into shooting knit fabric and yarn, because it's beautiful to capture, and I probably take my knitting photography experience into other subjects, without being conscious of the connection.

When you're paging through patterns online or elsewhere, what sticks out like a sore thumb to you as a photographer visually? What are your pet peeves, and how can designers fix them to make their photos better?

I hate it when a photograph of a knit item is treating the model as the subject instead of the knit-wear – either the knit object is at an angle where you can't see the design well, or is out of focus. It's great to have a styled photograph of the finished object on a model, but designers (or stylists) need to be sure the photo functions as a visual reference for knitters.

Unedited digital photographs bother me – the photos that digital cameras (especially nicer, more professional ones) produce are meant to be edited, for color, contrast (levels and curves), sharpness, etc. The photos straight out of the camera are kind of a blank slate, usually dull, often a bit dark, which is on purpose so that the photographer can mess with them and make them exactly as they want, so when designers use digital photos with no editing, they are usually dull and could be so easily fixed. (All cameras should come with some basic software that will do the simple jobs needed to make a dull photo pop).

And, bad photographs in general – it's so easy to take decent photos now, compared to the old film days. If you're a designer trying to sell your pattern (or just get it noticed), it's important to make it look its best. Simple steps: no flash, use natural light. If it's night, wait till tomorrow to photograph the piece, go outside or beside a big window – if it's super sunny, shade or indoors is best, not direct sunlight, and if it's overcast, then outdoors is excellent. Make sure the shot is in focus, and there's no motion blur – with most point-and-shoot cameras, there's no need to worry about this as long as you have good light, but if you're indoors using light through a window, you may need to use a tripod, or just use a table or wall to keep the camera steady. Take many shots! Digital cameras make this no problem, and any professional will tell you that this is their secret! Take twenty or thirty photos instead of two or three, and you'll be much more likely to have a few fabulous ones in the mix. Take the same shot a few times, because maybe one will have slight motion blur or the model's face won't be perfect, problems you might not see on the LCD screen, but when editing through them later you'll find that the fourth shot was much better than the first three. And, again, edit the shots before sticking them into your pattern – levels and curves (or brightness and contrast), cropping, and sharpness should all be considered. If you need guidance, look at knit pattern photos that look great, and try to copy the look of those, or find tutorials or guides online to help out.

CHAPTER 8

Advertising

Why is social media at the very front of this book and advertising at the back? The vast majority of designers do not have a supersized budget to spend on advertising. In fact, even larger companies are shifting their ad spending to online sources such as Ravelry.com, as Jonelle Beck of South West Trading Company explained earlier in the book. That's not to say print advertising is never effective, or that it's a bad idea – it's simply one of many options, and it's a good idea to educate yourself about all of them.

☆ **Online advertising**

There are many different options for online advertising. Among the favorite locations for designers to advertise are Ravelry.com and Knitty.com, although there are certainly many more to choose from, including Google Adwords, Facebook, etc. As with all advertising, you need to consider who will be most likely to see your ad: if you make sock blockers or sock yarn, you'd be better off advertising on a sock knitting website, for example. Online advertising has a singular advantage in that it is cheap compared to print advertising, which makes it easier to test out if you're just getting started, and often you can change up your photos or text mid-campaign (which is impossible with print – once it's printed, it's printed).

☆ **Cooperative advertising**

In addition to her design work, Jennifer Hansen of Stitch Diva (http://www.stitchdiva.com) manages Fiber Buzz, an advertising cooperative service that creates editorial-style "Top 10 Picks" ads for placement in major knit-related publications such as Interweave Knits, Yarn Market News, Knitter's, knit.1, Vogue Knitting and Knitscene. Each ad's cost is divided up ten ways, making it more reasonably priced for each participant, and the clear style and 'voice' of the ads are memorable and effective (see past ads at http://fiberbuzz.com/top_10_picks.html).

Etsy.com offers another form of cooperative advertising (full details and upcoming calls for participants are here: http://www.etsy.com/storque/search/tags/cooperative-advertising). Here's how their program works:

- Etsy purchases ad space in magazines (targeted to the craft- and handmade-friendly audience), covers half of the cost, and designs the ad.
- Etsy sellers are able to purchase spots in the ad at the discounted rate.
- Ad includes your shop name, a single item image, price, and category.

Ads are limited to one spot per seller, per advertisement, as with most cooperative ads. It's important to have VERY clear photography that sends a message even at a very small size – for example, I used a bright red version of my hat pattern Reboux in a co-op ad that went into BUST magazine, and got a ton of phonecalls from friends all over the country when the issue hit newsstands. That color just *jumped* off the page visually. BUST, ReadyMade, Venus Zine and several other non-knitting magazines with a sizeable craft-friendly reader base often offer discounted ad space (BUST's Product Showcase, for example).

☆   **Print advertising**

There's no way around this fact: print ads are expensive. Sizeable print ads in the "premium" magazines will set you back thousands You can help yourself by learning more before you start blindly charging full page spreads to your credit card! I spoke with advertising managers from the top two knitting magazine companies, and you can learn a lot from their years of experience.

Leanne Pressly, a former ad manager for Interweave Knits, launched The Wool Wide Web[26] in 2010, a marketing consulting firm for the yarn and knitting industry. Her invaluable advice will save you time and money.

Look for the 'advertising' page on your favorite magazines' website. Leanne says that a lot of magazines are very proprietary about rates and information and don't post them online, but you can look in the magazine or online masthead for the ad rep in your area and call or email for a media kit.

For magazines that do print information about their subscribers, circulation or readers, you can learn quite a bit. For example, Venus Zine announces on their advertising page that 92% of their readership is female, and 49% of their readers sew, knit or crochet. Pretty good odds, no? Consider taking out ads in non-knitting magazines because your product will already stand out from the other advertisers, but remember that ads are more effective the more often you place then in a single publication. It's well-documented that frequency helps sell your product better, plus most publications offer a frequency discount so your per-ad price will decrease with more insertions.

Leanne pointed to one study showing a 25% increase in readership when an ad was placed in 12 monthly issues versus just six. Another study in Business Week also found that advertising in twice as many issues increased readership by at least 25%. You can read about it here: http://www.riger.com/know_base/media/ad_frequency.html

Circulation figures are another factor to consider. ReadyMade has more than 3 times as many subscribers than the major knitting magazines. Which one is going to be seen by more people? And ReadyMade's subscriber base is 81% female, not too much lower than Interweave Knits or Vogue Knitting, so you're reaching a similar group of subscribers.

26 http://www.thewoolwideweb.com

Leanne notes that you need to look at several demographic factors (age, gender and income) when evaluating whether a magazine is right for your target market. "For example, Knits and Knitscene are both 90% female, but Knitscene appeals to a much lower income and age demographic," one that would be better suited to a less expensive product. "The bottom line is to have a clear understanding of *your* market, and match that to the demographic of the readership."

"Also, beware of tricky language and know which number your sales rep is quoting. Readership or distribution is *not* the same as circulation," says Leanne. "Be sure you're comparing apples to apples when evaluating the magazines. Circulation is the best number to use and reflects the number of subscribers and copies sent to the newsstand. Look for the strongest numbers on the subscriber side. Those are the most loyal readers. You can print and send all the mags you want to a newsstand, but if the sell-through is low then nobody sees your ad anyway."

Keep your eyes peeled for the "statement of ownership" that appears once per year in most magazines in order to qualify for discounted postal rates. It will tell you a lot about the circulation and subscriber numbers.

When asked what else can designers do to maximize their print ad dollar, Leanne offered the following "age old" advice, or so she called it:

- White space (in other words, uncluttered design)
- Clear incentive
- Call to action
- Time sensitive (set expiration date on any offers).

"I always advised my yarn folks to *show* the yarn. This is a very visually stimulating craft niche. Showing a logo of a sheep instead of a beautiful skein of hand-dyed yarn is a mistake. Use the space to show your products."

- Color is better than black and white – go smaller if that means affording color.
- Make a position request – sometimes the media kit says there's a charge, but 90% of the time, the rep will just do it and not charge for it. You won't get best position *every* issue, but maybe your first one. Top right hand facing is best.
- Ask your rep for feedback on what's in the issue and match your ad content. If there is a 4-page feature on eco yarns, then promote your eco yarns. Cables, sell aran yarns; Lace, laceweight yarns (you get the idea). Sometimes you can even get yarn requirements and promote a kit for a certain pattern that will be featured.
- Change your ad! Keep same colors, fonts and logo for branding consistency– but readers get bored by the same "we sell yarn" ad in every issue.
- Use a tracking code for results – "mention KnitsApril" for free shipping so you get a sense of how effective a campaign is, but *don't* rely on this as the only indicator of whether your ad is working! Print ads are a tool for strengthening your brand, not

necessarily instant sales. Integrated approaches work best (print and online) so you're getting the branding benefit, but also a return on investment for the online ad (which elicits an instant click and purchase).

Myths and truths about advertising, according to Leanne:

- A bigger ad *does* convey bigger company, better service, more professional and trust-worthy. If you can afford to run with the big boys, do it.
- Get to know your ad rep! They're not there to just sell you stuff, they do have a *lot* more influence on what gets into the magazine than you think. "I can think of 10-20 instances where knowing what my advertiser was doing (new product, pattern, etc), then discussing it with Lisa or Eunny (the editors of Knitscene and Interweave Knits) landed that item elsewhere in the pages of the magazine."

SoHo Publications (Vogue Knitting, Knit Simple, etc) advertising manager Rose Ann Pollani shared some of her tips and tricks with me as well:

Advertising is about delivering a consistent message. You are better off running a smaller ad in every issue than a big, splashy ad once per year. Frequency always gets a discount. On the other hand, if you want a big splashy fall issue presence, be prepared to back it up with smaller ads throughout the year.

Know your product and know your target audience, then find the publication that reaches it the best. Vogue Knitting readers tend to have a high income – 75% have an annual family income of over $50,000, whereas for Knit Simple it is around 22%. If you have a very expensive product, then Vogue Knitting would be your target audience. KnitSimple skews slightly younger than VK, and these readers are more likely to have children at home. Most knitting magazines are around 90% female...it's the nature of the beast, so gender selection is not really an issue in our industry.

Keep your ad to ONE topic. If it's a needle ad, then don't add yarn to it. Have the best needle ad you can, then do a separate ad for your yarn. Be sure to include a website and phone number (you'd be surprised how many people forget); a physical address is no longer needed. Ads can also be image ads without a call to action – it's really more important to think about consistency.

If you want to see how good your ad looks, then cut out the ads that you like from regular magazines. Lay them on the floor with your ad and see how well it fits in. Do the same with other knitting mag ads.

Color vs. black and white? Color and b/w are the same price for us today. Black and white is fine if you are trying to make a graphic statement, just don't let it look cheap.

Premium positions and position requests? We charge more for premium positions, like the back cover. In terms of positions inside the covers, we will lock them in for advertisers who sign an annual contract.

Do you tell clients what's coming up editorially so they can create their ads to suit?

We always email our regular advertisers and let them know what is coming up in the next issue. If we are doing something special then we will target people who might not be able to be a regular advertiser, but it might make sense for them to invest in promotion in a particular issue. For example, in VK Fall we have a big needle section for advertisers, so we will be especially targeting companies who make/wholesale needles and we will be really promoting that section to our readers. Of course, it makes it more valuable for our regular advertisers to be in an issue that is getting special attention too.

How often do you recommend your clients change up their ads? Do readers skip right over an ad they've seen a dozen times before?

That depends entirely on the company. If you have a great needle ad, then it can run for a year, or even several years. Yarn needs updating more often. Some stores have a signature ad that they run many times too. While it might seem readers skim over an ad they have seen before, there is always the subliminal message, and the recognition factor. Sometimes repetitiveness helps this.

What are your top tips in terms of doing well in print advertising?

- Add web ads to your print budget – they are less expensive, but add to the repetitiveness of your message and your brand building.
- Know your target demographic.
- Team up with others to create "group" ads.
- Have your ad professionally designed – don't do it yourself unless you have a graphic design background.
- Remember your brand and keep the look and message consistent.
- If you are social networking, add the buttons to your ad.
- If you are advertising in a publication, then push the publication to everyone you can – you need to help get your message out there too!
- Most magazines have product pages – send products, patterns etc for review. This way you can gauge response and then find the magazine that best fits your product.

CHAPTER 9

Further education

Knitting- and textile education differs all over the world. It's fair to say that the UK has an advantage over the US and Canada, in that its university-level education for handknitting is much more comprehensive. American schools tend to include handknitting as an afterthought in textile or fiber arts degree programs rather than treat it as a specialty or field all its own. Finding a knitting-specific degree course can seem close to impossible, so most students choose fashion design or a related path and fill in the blanks.

Australia, as *the* major high-end wool exporter (producing 50% of the world's Merino), is a special case – a quick glance at any fashion or industry-related website such as:

* Council of Textile & Fashion Industries of Australia, Ltd: http://www.tfia.com.au
* Australian Fashion Council: http://www.australianfashioncouncil.com
* Australasian Textiles & Fashion Magazine: http://www.atfmag.com

will often feature a focus on wool and its end products you almost never see in a similar US publication. Accordingly, there is an emphasis on textiles education, and research – the Commonwealth Scientific Industrial Research Organisation (CSIRO) has a fascinating RSS feed, if you're interested in staying on top of the latest high-tech advances related to wool:

http://www.csiro.au/science/Wool-Textiles/whats-new.xml

CSIRO has also worked with The Australian Wool Textile Training Centre (http://www.awttc.com.au), which was developed in 2006 in response to the need for more wool textile training and skills development.

Next door in New Zealand, which is second only to Australia in wool exports, the The Textile & Design Laboratory of the Auckland University of Technology (http://www.tdl.aut.ac.nz) offers training on high end Shima Seiki knitting machines and more, both as a part of their textile and fashion design curriculum and as a service to non-students alike. According to their website, "Virtually anyone can access the Textile & Design Laboratory's (T+DL) facilities for the purposes of research, training, product development, sampling and even small scale production." The lab can even help you break into the knitwear market, as they want to support emerging (as well as established designers). Though their focus is, naturally, more based on machine knitting, should you happen to be in Auckland, it never hurts to network!

Back in North America, The Knitting Guild of America (TKGA) offers its Master Knitter program, and the Canadian Guild of Knitters a similar accreditation. While not specifically design-oriented (they're more skills-based), if you'd like to ensure your knitting skills are up to par with other industry professionals, this is one way to check.

If you're interested in teaching, The Fashion Institute of Technology (FIT) in New York City offers the Craft Yarn Council's Certified Instructor Program (http://www3.fitnyc.edu/continuinged/CPS/CraftYarnCouncil.htm) as well as continuing education, online education, certificate programs and of course, undergraduate and graduate programs. From time to time, other knitting classes appear in their curriculum, too. The Pratt Institute (http://www.pratt.edu) periodically offers knit-related classes and has several faculty members with interest and experience in the field. Rounding out the New York-based offerings, Parsons The New School for Design (familiar to most as the setting for television favorite Project Runway!) offers both handknitting and machine knitting classes.

Designer Melissa Wehrle, a graduate of FIT, remarked:

"I took the full knitwear design program at FIT, it is definitely geared more towards the industrial side of the industry, i.e. working with overseas factories, etc. From my previous experience, not too much handknitting will be discussed, there's an emphasis on machine knitting. I was in the 4-year program and received very little instruction on handknitting and designing your own hand knit garments. However, the teachers were very knowledgeable in handknitting and were more than willing to answer questions, help solve problems, and give suggestions on hand knit garments included in your collection."

She also wrote a related 5-part series on her blog – Melissa's experience at FIT is parts 1-2B, and there's also information on her first fashion job out of college, as well as 'A day in the life of a sweater designer.' You can read it at http://www.neoknits.com/category/fashion-experience

The Academy of Art University in San Francisco offers a BFA and MFA in Knitwear Design. Knitwear students from the school have gone on to internships with Alexander McQueen and Azzedine Alaia, and while it's almost exclusively machine knitting, the MFA students learn handknitting, and the knitwear 1 online class is entirely handknitting. The Academy's online courses – such as FSH 124.OL: Knitwear Design – offer valuable knowledge for the self-taught designer, such as building a comprehensive collection. They even offer an entire fashion degree online (http://online.academyart.edu/fashiondesign.html).

The Fashion Institute of Design and Merchandising, with campuses in California, also has a knitwear design program (http://fidm.edu/academics/majors/fashion-knitwear). About her time at FIDM, designer Cassie Miller says: "What I learned there has definitely helped my knitting design ability. I learned a lot about fitting the human form in patternmaking and draping, and drawing schematics on the computer and by hand. I took a grading class, too, and wish I had paid more attention because I still get headaches when I grade my knitting patterns. There isn't really any emphasis on knitting in the fashion design program, but there are classes on machine knitting in the textiles program. The tuition for FIDM is rather expensive in my opinion, but I recently noticed at my local community college there is a pattern alteration and sewing class, so there are definitely always other options."

If you're interested in high-end machine knitting and a more art-focused approach, the Rhode Island School of Design (http://www.risd.edu) often offers continuing education classes in knitwear design and handknitting. Liz Collins, a well-known fiber artist with considerable machine knitting expertise, is now on the faculty there.

Philadelphia University (formerly the College of Textiles, http://www.philau.edu) was founded in 1884 as the first textile-specific college in the US, but has since expanded its curriculum. It includes majors in textile engineering and fashion design. There are frequent knitting class offerings with an emphasis on machine knitting.

Finally, the Art Institute in Miami (http://www.artinstitutes.edu/miami) teaches knitwear courses periodically. Check with your local fashion schools and colleges. Not every school may teach a full knitwear design program but they often have one class here or there if there are faculty members with interest in the subject. Moore College of Art and Design in Philadelphia teaches machine knitting, for example.

☆   Programs in the UK

Central St. Martins College of Art and Design in London offers not only a range of degree programs but also numerous knit-related 'short courses,' and Knit-1 in Brighton (UK) offers ultra-intensive and lengthy design courses (http://www.knitdesigncourses.com). I have a visit to Knit-1 on my "must do" life list, to be honest! Nottingham Trent University offers a full degree course, complete with paid internships at top design studios, including Prada, Gucci and Alexander McQueen. About the course:

> *Our award-winning BA (Hons) Fashion Knitwear Design and Knitted Textiles is an exciting fusion of fashion and fabric design, allowing you to develop a creative balance of both disciplines. The only course of its kind in the UK, it has a universally established reputation for design innovation in knitted and woven clothing at every market level.*
>
> *During the course you'll learn to control the whole creative process, from fabric design and creation to garment design and manufacture. You'll gain a full understanding of modern day design and production practices and graduate equipped for a career in innovation and development.*

You can read more about their course at http://tinyurl.com/knitdesignBA

DeMontfort University in Leicester sponsors an annual industry event called FAME (Fashion, Arts, Media Eastmidlands) which features exhibits from fashion and related companies to give students and visitors alike advice on how to "get in and get on" in the industry. Designer Fiona Ellis attended DeMontfort, and found it extremely useful for her future career in design because of the presentation skills taught alongside the actual art of design. (See the Yarn Forward articles referenced below for more on her experience there).

Gloria Currie did a National Certificate Clothing Technology course at Cardonald College in Scotland, as she had her own machine knitwear business and wanted to learn how to design. She says: "It was great for learning how to pattern draft, but didn't include the steps of taking a pattern block." ['pattern block' refers to both a sloper and the final full scale pattern draft – using the measurements from the full scale pattern draft, one translates those measurements into a written-out pattern] She later did a 3-year part time machine knitting course which covered all aspects of knitwear design, such as how to use a machine, draft patterns, use a formula to work out shaping and so on, and has since moved on to designing her own handpainted yarn.

When choosing a program you should also look at what other resources are available to you – for example, the University of Southampton's Winchester School of Art's library (UK) recently acquired the Montse Stanley and Richard Rutt collections, and has over 5000 knit patterns in its Jane Waller Knitting Pattern Collection (among, if not *the* most comprehensive collection in the world). The Library also sponsored the In the Loop: Knitting Past, Present, and Future conference in 2008, and has materials related to the conference in its archives.

Designer Claire Montgomerie's articles on knit education in the UK appeared in Yarn Forward magazine issues 13 and 14 (there's also more on the In the Loop conference in issue 13). Both back issues are available online via Yudu at: http://www.yudu.com/library/20144/KAL-Media-Ltd

Two other interesting blog posts on this topic are available online at:

http://andreatung.blogspot.com/2008/07/so-you-want-to-study-knitwear-part-1.html
http://andreatung.blogspot.com/2008/07/so-you-want-to-study-knitwear-part-2.html

Knitting machines

If you're alarmed by the frequency of machine knitting in the course catalogs above, don't be. In an academic/design program setting, speed is paramount, and many students are planning to work with mass produced knits rather than the handknit market. While it's fair to say that handknitting dominates the pattern-sales market, there are plenty of conferences and events dedicated to machine knitters, too. Sue Jalowiec of BT Yarns (she was the first person to show me how to use one of my knitting machines!) sponsors several per year. See her site for more information:

http://www.btyarns.com/servlet/the-INSPIRATION-Conferences/Categories

There are also a few designers who are talented in both hand- and machine knitting. Triple threat

Lily Chin (add crochet to the preceding categories) uses her machine collection to develop concepts quickly. Lily once told me never to sell a knitting machine – they are hard to find in good working order, and compared to twenty years ago, only a handful of manufacturers sell them new.

The most common knitting machines you'll find new today are the Bond Ultimate Sweater Machine (often abbreviated USM) and the Silver Reed models – the mid-gauge LK-150 is typically the most useful for handknitters looking to switch over or add to their repertoire.

Angelika's Yarn Store (http://www.yarn-store.com/knitting-machines.html) has a number of articles you may find interesting, including "What Every Hand Knitter Should Know Before Buying a Knitting Machine, or Is Machine Knitting Cheating?" Is machine knitting "cheating"? Some interesting perspectives are available in this Ravelry thread:

http://www.ravelry.com/discuss/designers/94988/1-25

What's most important to remember, though, is that machine knitting is not just an easier form of handknitting. You can't just throw some yarn at the machine and walk away. So is it cheating? Well, it depends. If you're passing it off to a retail customer as handknit, sure. If you're using it as a design development tool? No.

However, if you're machine knitting samples for pattern development, you should always strive to have the sample reknit by a test hand knitter before publishing the pattern. Not because the gauge is different – as you surely know, all knitters knit differently, and "not getting gauge because the sample was *obviously* machine knit" is just a high-level excuse for being too lazy to switch needle sizes – but because there are many more ways to manipulate stitches by hand than there are for machine, and you should take that into account if you can make it easier on the hand knitters purchasing your patterns.

☆ Designer Marnie MacLean's machine knitting notes:

- With the more affordable/accessible machine models ribbing, garter, and other mixes of knit and purl stitches on a single side are far more time consuming to work than basic stockinette and simple lace patterns.
- Machines do an amazing job with colorwork because the tension remains consistent.
- You have to be pretty creative to make the sorts of seamless garments that are preferred by most knitters these days. It's generally only possible if you have a machine that can do tubular or ribbed knitting, and it won't be easy.
- A machine will allow you to plow through some of that stash you've been acquiring and will never be able to knit in your foreseeable lifespan. (But let's be honest, it's not as if you won't decide you should buy more yarn regardless).
- Accurately determining gauge is paramount on a machine. This involves not just

working a swatch but washing it and letting it rest. Since machine knitting is worked under tension, there's no way to check things as you go, you must have a plan in mind.

- Machines are louder and less portable than handknitting and thus this become a factor in when and where you can use them. If you do most of your knitting while watching TV with friends or family, or on the subway, your machine is going to languish. (That said, banging out a sweater in a weekend is a beautiful thing).

- Machines like the Silver Reed LK-150 can do some things that can't be (easily) done by hand knitters, such as tuck stitches and a sort of two toned knitting where the purl side of the fabric looks like one color and the knit side looks like another color.

- I love combining the large swaths of stockinette worked on a machine with delicate hand worked trim in knit or crochet.

CHAPTER 10
Professional organizations and associations

There are several organizations you may want to join that will help you as a professional designer. All have different membership requirements and perspectives, but one of the best ways to establish yourself, make contacts and network is to get involved.

The National Needle Arts Association – TNNA

1100-H Brandywine Blvd,
Zanesville OH 43701
Phone: 1-800-889-8662
Email: TNNA.info@Offinger.com
http://www.tnna.org

TNNA, established in 1975, is probably the most widely-recognized needle arts industry association in the US and even overseas. It is an international trade organization representing retailers, manufacturers, distributors, designers, manufacturers' representatives, publishers, teachers and wholesalers of products and supplies for the specialty needlearts market. In their own words, TNNA "offers its members opportunities to discuss and exchange ideas, learn new techniques, obtain valuable business education, address industry issues and, most importantly, 'do business.'"

TNNA sponsors two major tradeshows and two smaller ones each year. The winter tradeshow, held in January, is typically located on the west coast in California (usually San Diego, sometimes Long Beach), and the June summer show – the more critical one to attend, if you had to pick – is held in Columbus, Ohio.

The summer show is where fall and winter trends are presented. These trends represent a disproportional segment of the industry given that most casual knitters tend to knit more during the colder months, and so companies and designers save their biggest, splashiest launches for that show.

Outside the January and June shows, The Needlecraft Market in September and the Nashville Show in February are "cash and carry" shows allowing retailers to purchase immediate stock as well as place orders. In January and June, yarn store owners can only place orders with companies and designers, they cannot actually walk out the door holding a box of your latest pattern! All show attendees must show proof of business ownership, which limits the audience you reach only to qualified buyers.

TNNA also offers a wide variety of member sections and groups. Sections are based on your membership category (retailers automatically become members of the retail section, while affiliate members may choose the section that works best for them). If you're reading this book, chances are you would want to join the designer/teacher group.

Among many TNNA benefits are discounts from a wide variety of service providers (shipping companies, car rental, etc). They also provides professional development, such as classes and special presentations at the shows, how-to books (their business advisory series includes *Marketing Needlearts*, *Trade Show Tips* and *Working with Manufacturers' Representatives*), and from time to time, they also issue survey results about the industry that can help your business.

TNNA sponsors Stitch 'N' Pitch events and the Pathways into Professional Needlearts (PiPN) program or college students. I've had several PiPN interns over the years – it's a great way to not only provide mentoring to a college student, but to get some help for your business during the summer months. You might even learn something from them, too (I know I have)!

TNNA, as a trade association, is open only to verifiable businesses providing services and/or products for the needlearts industry. There are three types of membership[27]. The likeliest category for those of you reading this book is Affiliate Member.

Business identification requirements for affiliate members are not as steep as they are for some other membership categories. As an example (see the TNNA website for more, especially if you are applying for a retail membership as an online or brick and mortar store):

Designers must provide:

- Three letters of introduction from current TNNA Wholesale Members representing their product segment
- Published work (i.e., printed pattern published within the last 2 years, full copy) OR published article (published within the last 2 years, full copy) OR a letter from a current TNNA Wholesale Member stating that you are actively designing for them

Teachers must provide:

- Resume or biography
- Published work (i.e. magazine, show or conference)
- Outline of class projects they have taught
- A letter of introduction from a current TNNA Wholesale or Retail Member

Chances are good your local yarn store is a retail member, so there's one possible letter of introduction. If you've designed for a specific yarn company, talk to your contact there about a wholesale member letter of introduction.

---

27 http://tnna.org/MemberBenefits/MembershipRequirements/tabid/118/Default.aspx

Association of Knitwear Designers – AKD

http://www.knitwear-designers.org

The Association of Knitwear Designers (AKD) is an independent organization dedicated to promoting the art and business of knitting. AKD provides professional accreditation, networking, education and assistance to knitwear designers worldwide. With two levels of membership, Professional and Associate, AKD strives to meet the needs of designers at all levels.

Professional level membership is juried, and applicants must provide an original, self-knit garment, a resume, and one's past history of professional endeavor. There are several categories of professional membership, and members can be accredited in one or more areas:

- Author Designer
- Teacher
- Technical Editor
- Editor/Publisher
- Gallery Knitter
- Retailer
- Yarn Manufacturer

AKD actively promotes its members to yarn companies, conference organizers and publishers via its member showcase and accreditations listing.

Associate level membership is open to newer designers who want to increase their skills and professional contacts. New members have a period of two years to prepare for entry into the Professional level, during which they may request mentoring by a professional member.

Design Lines, the AKD newsletter, is published six times annually and mailed free to all members. AKD also offers a tearsheet service, which allows members to receive multiple copies of their published designs at no charge (no more sending your mom out to Borders to buy out every copy of a knitting magazine).

In collaboration with TNNA, AKD members are able to work with the newest unreleased yarns, and spotlight their efforts in the Great Wall of Yarn display area at the TNNA trade shows.

Kim Dolce of Dolce Handknits says: "I was willing and able to make the investment in attending a show, and I think that goes a long way to assuring yarn companies, distributors and shop owners that you're a professional and you're in it for the long haul. Membership fees for both AKD and TNNA are both very reasonable and in my opinion well worth the cost. I can't begin to place a value on what I've gained over the years from those two associations, particularly my regular attendance at TNNA shows."

Crochet Guild of America

Crochet Guild of America
1100-H Brandywine Blvd
Zanesville OH 43701
Phone: 740-452-4541
Email: CGOA@Offinger.com
http://www.crochet.org

The Crochet Guild of America is a professional development organization for crocheters managed by the same company as TNNA. Each year CGOA hosts the Chain Link conference, and serves as a starting point for those looking to join a local guild, much like its sister organization TKGA (see below). CGOA publishes Crochet! magazine and administers the CGOA Masters program, for testing advanced skills.

Robyn Chachula, the current CGOA professional development chair, says: "CGOA has professional and associate members. Regular CGOA members are welcome to apply to be either a professional or associate member for free. Professional members have been earning an income from the crochet industry for 2 years. Associates are member who want to start a crochet career. Members include designers, contract crocheters, conservationists, yarn shop owners, tech editors, magazine editors, etc, and associates can request a mentor with whom to work one on one. All professional and associate members are enrolled in our email group, where they can ask general questions, such as "do you know who to contact for yarn at…?" or "would you write this like *this* or *this*?" On the list we try to keep members up to date on any happenings in the industry and let it be a safe place to discuss questions with other professionals. Once a year we hold a conference day, where we bring in speakers on anything that supports being a professional in the industry. Magazine editors, publishers, contract lawyers, designers all have spoken at the conference day."

The Knitting Guild Association

The Knitting Guild Association
1100-H Brandywine Blvd
Zanesville, OH 43701-7303
Phone: 740-452-4541
Email: TKGA@TKGA.com
http://www.tkga.com
TKGA publishes Cast On magazine, administers the Master Knitter program, and hosts an annual conference for its members. It is a non-profit organization of approximately 11,000 individual members and 280 affiliated local member clubs/guilds.

☆   **The Knit and Crochet Show**

The Knit and Crochet Show (http://www.knitandcrochetshow.com) is held at the same time as the annual CGOA and TKGA conferences, and features classes, shopping and more. This is another potential venue for you to teach outside of Stitches and other consumer shows.

CHAPTER 11

Standing out

I've had this conversation more times than I can count – in a world where designers often have a difficult time feeling as if they are valued creators, how can we distinguish ourselves and stand out? How can we not only make a difference in the perception of professional designers, but also make ourselves and our customers happy?

If you do this for a living, you will have at least one sleepless night over this topic, I guarantee it. A "dark night of the soul" where you're about to throw down your needles and hooks for good. You are not alone. Let's talk about the ways you can distinguish yourself, and hopefully dispel some of the worry that you're not doing the right things so you can get down to business and be successful. This chapter does discuss marketing and branding, but that's not the only thing you can do.

☆ Specialization

Don't be afraid to specialize! If you have a signature technique or project type, it's a great way to get recognition and become a "name" in that specialty. For example, designer Sivia Harding is well-known for her complex knitting designs that incorporate beads. Miriam Felton of Mimknits is known for lace shawls. They both do other types of projects, but when I put on my editor hat and think "OK, who could I call for a project that involves beads?", Sivia comes to mind first. Ditto for shawls and Miriam. In addition, it's a great way to build your market quickly.

Imagine you are a shawl knitter who has purchased a Mimknits pattern at your LYS. You love it, you had a great experience knitting it, you can't wait to knit another, so you visit Miriam's website and see she's designed several other complex shawls that are right up your alley – whose shawl pattern are you most likely to purchase next?

☆ Amazing customer service

It's one thing to provide a product, it's another thing to provide appropriate customer service. This isn't just about pattern support, or your public image in social media (as someone who seems approachable and doesn't scare off customers). It's about providing the kind of service you would want to experience, and making your customers not only happy, but willing to recommend you to their friends.

You can learn a lot from other industries in this regard. Zappos.com (online shoe sales and more) has amazing customer service – read http://mashable.com/2009/04/26/zappos for just a taste of what they do. John DiJulius, author of *Secret Service: Hidden Systems That Deliver Unforgettable Customer*

Service grew his salon business from one employee to a total of five salons and spas, 150 employees and 750 to 1,000 new clients per month. Amazingly, his salons retain 70% of their new clients, double the industry average. And although his tactics may seem focused on larger organizations, you can put his principles to work for you. The DiJulius Group, his consulting firm, says that it helps companies "Make Price Irrelevant." When you're worrying that your price is too high or that free patterns are going to cut into your sales (and so you give up, or cut your prices), his philosophy can help change your mind. Take a look at http://www.thedijuliusgroup.com for more information, read his book, or read this article:

http://www.sbnonline.com/Local/Article/3219/82/0/The_loyal_treatment.aspx

particularly the part at the end on the power of referral business.

DiJulius points out that everyone likes to feel appreciated, and that you can improve your customer's perception of you, not to mention the likelihood that they'll recommend you to others, by following up. It could be as simple as using the "recommend these other patterns" screen in E-junkie (the pattern download service allows you to select some or all of the other patterns you have for sale with them to be recommended to pattern purchasers on checkout), or sending a thank you email a month after purchase...whatever you do, stay in the customer's mind as not only someone who wrote *one* pattern they liked, but as a potential source of *other* patterns they might like. Invite them to join your special email list, where sales are first announced and discounts offered – get creative!

☆   Pattern support

Few designers can utter the words 'pattern support' without groaning at least once. Operating on the "you'd never say that to her face!" principle, pattern purchasers can be pushy, rude and plain obnoxious via email. These are the horror stories that come to light when designers get together in a large group, usually punctuated with "No, she did NOT say that to you!" and "Oh, you think that's bad, well..."

Stop and remember for a moment that however pushy, obnoxious and raised-in-a-barn the customer seem to be, it is your responsibility to not only anticipate potential problems, alleviate them where you can, but also to respond to the truly irritating customers in a way that will keep them coming back for more.

Frontline defense: set up an "errata" page on your website and post any errors found in your published patterns (along with the fix, or "information coming soon" as soon as it is reported to you and confirmed). You may also want to start a group for your patterns on Ravelry if you haven't already – often users will walk each other through any tricky spots without need for serious

intervention on your part. If you can find a volunteer moderator to help with the group, you can free up more time for designing, too.

Responsiveness: when you receive an errata report, even if you can't check out its accuracy right away, promptly respond to the person who let you know with a "Thanks for this, I'll look into it and get back to you as soon as I can"-mail. Customers hate to feel ignored, and like to believe that something is being done right away. You should also periodically check your spam folder – you never know what might end up there.

Extra credit: set up a Google Alert with your name in it (and/or your company name). If someone posts that he or she is having a problem with your pattern on a blog, etc. but doesn't bother to reach out to you, you'll get a notification and be able to click over and respond. How's that for proactive? Go to http://www.google.com/alerts to set yours up. It's like having an especially nosy neighbor keeping her eye on the internet for you.

☆   Effective Partnerships

Identifying and forming effective partnerships that help both parties shine are also a great way to stand out. I asked dyer/designer Anniken Allis (http://www.yarnaddict.co.uk) what advice she'd give to designers who want to work with independent yarn dyers like herself, and she said: "Ask! Most indie dyers, even those of us who design ourselves, love seeing designs that use our yarns."

☆   Marketing and branding

When you are a one-person business (as most designers are), you need to put a special emphasis on making sure your marketing and branding messages are consistent and allow you to build both a visual and 'company' identity. Do you have a logo? A specific font you always use? Take time out to consider the overall visual "personality" and public face you are showing to the world.

☆   Develop something new

Designer Stefanie Japel pioneered the use of online networking application Ning.com to offer online classes. Her willingness to teach other teachers quickly spread the concept, and the ability to teach groups of students no matter where they live enabled her to expand her offerings. I spoke with her about teaching online.

How did you develop your online teaching concept and initial classes?

First, I familiarized myself with the kinds of classes that other online teachers were offering. How long they are, how much they cost, the end goal of the class (making a doll, a quilt, a painting, etc.) and then tried to scale my classes to that, with a knit object or specific skill being the end goal. Then, I tried to choose two projects that seemed like they could easily be interpreted and taught using a combination of video, PDF handouts, and live chat.

One of my classes details the process of recycling t-shirts into yarn, and then how to dye the yarn, and finally walking through 4 patterns. The second class just walks the knitter through a lace shawl pattern, but at the same time teaches students how to read lace charts, how to 'read' their knitting, and how to fix mistakes. So, while each of the initial two classes is very simple in premise, there's a lot of technical information rolled into them.

After I ran these classes a few times, I made them into "self-guided" classes because I had created enough material that a student could work through it without my help and still come up with the finished result. This has been a great way to offer the classes at a slightly discounted rate so that a student could try a class and then maybe sign up for a more involved class at a later time.

My next step was to create classes for a more adventurous knitter, like "Design Your Own Shawl" in which students choose their own shawl shapes, choose their stitch patterns, and I teach them how to create their own publishable knitting patterns. So they work through how to chart out their lace, how to choose stitch patterns that work together, how to format a pattern and do the photography. Several students have already published their patterns and are teaching classes on their own patterns. This is one of my favorite classes to teach.

Did you think they'd take off as quickly as they did? What about them works for you, and the students?

The success of this idea came as a complete surprise to me. I have taught over 300 students to date (April 2010), and have a total of about 850 people registered on my classroom network. I was very concerned that the information would translate to video, and that I would be able to engage the students and make everyone feel as though they're getting the same amount of attention that they would in an in-person class. So far, I've received a lot of very positive feedback and many students have taken every single class that I've offered.

I think that even though on first thought the idea of video recording myself teaching seems like it would be somewhat removed, or seem less 'real', the student perceives the video as being in real time. Or at least has the impression that I've created this video with them in mind. I'm still presenting lots and lots of "face time" in each class through these videos and addressing individual questions.

The live chats and the forum really give us all a chance to get to know each other, and I do feel like I'm making real connections with my students. (And those students who are naturally shy or who don't *want* a connection aren't obligated to participate or comment, they can just passively take the class.) So it seems to work well for every type of student.

The way that the classes are designed is to have all of the material posted to the site, so that students can really work though everything at their own pace. They don't have to rush to keep up with everyone, or to wait for the slower students.

☆   **Standing out isn't a chore, it's a challenge. What can you do to provide a memorable, worth-every-penny experience for your customers?**

(You can take notes here if you like. Unless you're reading this digitally, in which case that might be difficult).

CHAPTER 12

The interviews

I think the two best ways to learn are by doing, and by learning directly from someone who is already successful. This chapter will take you behind the scenes with many top designers and other industry professionals who are active and successful in the field right now. Designers, magazine and book editors, technical editors, self publishers – they all have something to teach you. Consider this a multi-year internship condensed into a number of printed pages.

What's more important is that while many of them agree on a few basic facts (the internet has changed the industry, or that self-marketing is important), not all of them are in lockstep with one another, so no matter what your personal opinions, you will find something to challenge your current ideas and hopefully give you new ones.

YSOLDA TEAGUE

Website: http://www.ysolda.com
Twitter: @ysolda

Right place, right time, right designer. Ysolda Teague is a stellar example of what the right kind of social media networking can do for your business, and she is definitely a product of talent, hard work and the access of the internet. Ysolda has embraced many of the concepts we've already discussed, and I think it is easily argued that Ravelry has played an exceptionally large role in her success.

Did you actively plan to be a knit designer or did it just happen? How?

It happened pretty accidentally, when I first started knitting I don't think I even thought about how there were real people behind the patterns. I remember when I first encountered publications like Knitty and Stitch 'n Bitch that had those little designer profiles, I was surprised to find them because I'd never thought about the designers before. My surprise was quickly followed by: "these people don't sound all that different to me, maybe I could do this." I'd already been improvising my own projects, I was hopelessly bad at following patterns and was fascinated by the structure and logic of stitch patterns. Reading those profiles introduced the idea of turning my improvised projects into patterns and then I started posting photos of my completed knits on craftster.org and realised that people actually wanted to make them.

My first pattern was published in Knitty, and I honestly had no idea what a big deal it was, I doubt I'd have submitted if I had. I'd only discovered the magazine fairly recently, and didn't know how many readers they had. They made it all seem rather accessible, I read the submissions guidelines, I worked everything out on graph paper and I scanned in my film photos. This was only 5 years ago, but it's easy to forget how much this world has changed in this time. So I was going through the submission notes and checking I'd done everything when I got to the section for my profile, I'd certainly read enough of those to have no trouble writing it, but it suggested that I could include a link to my website.

I didn't have a website, but I didn't want to seem too amateur, so I thought I'd better set one up. No one really read it until a few months later when my Knitty pattern showed up on the cover, I got several thousand hits, and realised both that Knitty actually had a few readers and that if I wanted to keep some of my newfound fans I'd better keep doing this. And so I have.

What role has the internet played in your success? (from blogs to social media to Knitty and Ravelry) And why? What makes it such a game-changer for the modern designer?

If it weren't for the internet I doubt I'd be doing this at all, let alone successfully. The internet is full of ways that make being a designer easier, but the most fundamental thing is that it makes it seem accessible. Although I'm sure it seems insanely overwhelming to new designers, there's a lot of information out there about being a designer. Ravelry and other forums provide a place to meet and converse with other designers of all experience levels, and many designers are highly visible online. I still meet people who, when I explain what I do, react as I once did with "I'd never thought about there being real people behind knitting patterns," but at least now they aren't knitters.

I think that level of accessibility is important, without it I'd certainly never have thought designing could become my own career. Of course, lots of people did make successful careers designing before the internet, and there are still designers who don't find the internet is crucial to their businesses. For me, however, the internet has made it possible to work successfully in a way that suits my personality and interests. I enjoy having such a direct relationship with my customers, writing the blog, taking photos, and generally doing all of the work that goes into self publishing and promotion. Not only do I enjoy those things, but I find it hard to give up control over them, working in a model of submitting a sample and pattern to be styled, photographed, re-written and promoted by someone else doesn't suit me at all. Although I'm now finding myself delegating more and more, and I've found that the internet has made it easier to make the necessary connections for that, I still like being the one in control of my final product.

You don't do a lot of designs in print magazines. Why?

Well partly it's because many of the print magazines don't offer terms that work for me, but mainly it's just that I prefer to focus on my self publishing business, and that doesn't leave a lot of free time! There's a lot that I like about magazines, but if I'm considering publishing a design with someone else I try and weigh up the pros and cons compared to self publishing. Frankly, self publishing usually offers more.

Tell me more about Whimsical Little Knits 1 & 2 – *why did you decide to do both digital and print editions? Is one more popular than the other?*

Whimsical Little Knits 1 & 2 are collections of patterns for small things, loosely centered around the idea of designs that would make good gifts, for others or yourself. I'd like to tell you about how I put a lot of thought into planning their format, but it wouldn't be true. I was already selling individual patterns digitally and when I decided to do a collection it seemed like it would be fun to release the patterns one at a time. More than anything, I just hated the idea of working on a project for months without anyone seeing it. So I started with the idea of a digital pattern collection released in a installments, that knitters could sort of subscribe to. I really love books as physical objects and had some ideas I thought would be fun for that, so I decided to also offer a printed version, and since the subscription element would be digital, and I thought the PDF would be helpful as a backup, I bundled them together. It was really all a bit spur of the moment, I tend to decide to do something and figure out exactly how to do it later. Not sure it's an approach I'd recommend, but it seems to be working out ok.

What are your dealbreakers in a contract – what won't you agree to under any circumstances?

Most importantly I won't give up my full rights to the design or agree to indefinite exclusivity, which really amounts to the same thing as long as the publisher stays in business. It's also important to me that I'm able to review and if necessary make changes to the final pattern before it goes to print, since any problems reflect negatively on me. The crucial things are that I'll have some control over how my pattern appears and that at some point I'll be able to add it to my self published line.

At what point did you realize you needed to bring in additional help?

I realized I needed additional help several months before I actually did anything about it. I'd been talking about hiring an assistant for a while, but I was daunted by the task of finding the right person. Then I happened to have my friend Sarah help out at an event and realized that there was no way that I wanted to do that sort of thing by myself again. Luckily she had lots of skills that were perfect for the job and had no desire to become a designer herself, important since I knew I'd never be happy assisting another designer! Things have become a lot more organized, but the thing that's relieved the most stress is that she handles all of the customer support. I love that my customers feel able to ask questions, but actually responding to them all in a timely manner was really wearing me down and taking a lot of time away from actually designing. As my business have grown, I've also hired more people to other things, like graphic design and sample knitting, so that I can really focus on the aspects that interest me and best use my time.

TRISHA MALCOLM

Website: http://www.vogueknitting.com

As Vice President/Editorial Director of SoHo Publishing Company, and editor-in-chief of Vogue Knitting, Trisha Malcolm has had an impressive career in the business and offers some great information below...

How did you get into the industry?

I learned to knit at 4, crochet at 7, and spent hours watching my mother draft sewing patterns and make most of our clothes. Then, as a high school teacher in Australia I taught Home Ec. and assorted craft classes, while knitting and sewing in my spare time. After leaving to travel the world (like most Aussies and Kiwis!) I ended up in New York for a week, and an offer to share an apartment came up. An ad in the New York Times for an assistant craft editor at a magazine caught my eye, and with my teaching and crafting background I got the job. There's no formal training for being an editor at a knitting or craft magazine – you learn it all on the job.

Where do you see the industry heading?

I've been in or on the periphery of this industry for a long time now and it's changed a lot over the years. The two biggest changes that have taken place were the huge growth of knitting in the mid 00s, and the way knitting and the internet have really connected to form a brave new knitting world. Since knitting is so much about the yarn and needles, they will always evolve, but basically stay the same. In my crystal ball, I see that the real (r)evolution will be in patterns and in community.

Patterns will become more internet based and will be sold more in singular (granular) form than in published collections – we are already seeing a decline in the sale of books that are just pure pattern anthologies. Books need to be more based in technique and innovation to really grab attention any more. Patterns will not be free; sure, there will always be some free patterns, but too much money is spent on patterns to give them away and I think we will see a movement back towards more paid patterns. Free patterns cheapen the value of a pattern and cheapen the work and talent of designers.

This doesn't mean that magazines will go away. Our sales are as strong as ever. Magazines bring news and an editorial point of view that you cannot find in another arena, and readers trust magazines. Internet magazines have not evolved yet to take away print versions, and may never do. You cannot take your iPad into the bathtub with your glass of wine!

With community, we will see Ravelry evolve, and other groups will pop up as well. Knitters like to connect with each other and talk about their work and their passion so there will be other forums for that too.

Facebook will evolve too – it's already the 5th largest nation on earth, and last year passed email as the way more people communicate with each other on the Internet. Every brand and designer is able to create it's own mini community. We will be able to create more virtual events though Facebook as well.

New types of real world events will add to the notion of community too. VK•LIVE, Sock Summit, the recent Men's Knitting Event are examples of new events which are targeted to specific groups within the knitting whole rather than just knitters in general.

In society we are seeing a shift back to hand-made, home cooking, urban gardens and being more sustainable ourselves. Local is the new global. Knitting fits right into this trend and will continue to be very popular because it is, and will become more so, a part of our new ethos.

What do you wish someone had told you when you first got started? And/or what kinds of mistakes do you see designers making all the time (especially newer ones)? How can they stand out from the crowd, professionalism-wise?

I wish someone had told me that there was very little money to be made in this industry!!! For all the work I have put in over the years I could have made a small fortune in a well-paid industry... LOL. Seriously, I wish someone had told me how much time everything takes. My ideas are too fast and frequent for my hands to keep up with. I think that many other people share that problem as well.

In terms of mistakes from designers, more often than not, we see them in fit. A lot of people just don't know how to make something fit properly, and I would suggest to new designers that they take as many fit classes as they can (not that there are a lot out there) and use a few really good reference books to help you along.

As a designer, make sure you have your social networking act together. When your work goes to print, be sure to support the publications you are working for and blog/Facebook/tweet/email to promote yourself and your publisher. That is the BEST way to stand out – publishers promote your work and you promote your publishers. It's a win-win for all.

What kind of role does the Internet play in our industry, and where is that going? Do you see a special benefit in social media, for example? VK & the other Soho mags seemed to have expanded their internet offerings exponentially in the past year – was this calculated?

As I said before, the internet is very important to us in terms of patterns and community. For a magazine that is only printed every few months, it also has the benefit of immediacy and of talking to our readers to remind them we are not asleep between mailing dates.

For many years, magazine publishers had been watching what is going on online and had been hesitant in making a commitment. Remember that we are professionally publishers as well as being part of the knitting world. We spent a long time formulating what we should do with our Internet presence – we attended many industry conferences on the subject before making our decisions.

In terms of our pattern store, this is something we have been debating in our company since 2004. We even wrote an RFP that year! Our idea was to make patterns available for individual sale, since we have a huge amount of content. Not everyone in our management was convinced it would work so it was shelved for quite some time. Eventually, it was put into place and now it's growing and getting more profitable all the time.

What do you like to see in submissions? (pattern and/or editorial) Do people generally follow the submission guidelines – or again, if they don't, what are the big pet peeves and what you wish people would/would not do?

Think of your professional work as a collaboration, and be in touch, ask questions if you have them, send a photo of your work so far. If you think you need to change something, send off an email and let someone know. Another mistake: If someone sends you yarn for a project and it's not working out, then contact whoever has hired you. Too many people are too afraid to speak up and when the project is finished, everyone is disappointed. Also be wise enough to know when too much contact becomes annoying.

In terms of your professional identity, it starts with the presentation of your design submission. We no longer expect it to be mailed in–though that is great if you want to! If you are emailing, be sure to get it together so that your sketch is not the size of a postage stamp, or too big to print on a page – and the same with your swatch. Swatch in a color that when scanned, it can be read when it's printed out. We don't choose from the screen, so be sure everything prints properly and is clear and understandable.

Another tip about publishing: It's like Rome – it takes TIME. If you submit an idea, leave it be. Publishing works in cycles. Book ideas are generally assessed by an editorial committee only 3 or 4 times a year, magazines not many more times than that. Hold off on the emails and calls – they are not a good way to stand out. And don't send the same sketches to more than one place. If you get them back, then send them off elsewhere.

The best designers send their garment, pattern, contract and invoice together. You quickly get a bad name if we get the garment but have to bug you for the next month for a pattern.

We are often asked if a designer can post their pattern in other places. When someone buys your design, they own it. Give it up and move on to your next design. If you have more designs than you can get published, you now have the opportunity to create your idea and self publish on several websites. The two should co-exist. If someone likes your work in a magazine or book, they are more likely to search you out elsewhere and buy your patterns.

What do you see as the most influential traits/activities when it comes to being a successful designer? What do great designers have in common, or have that sets them apart from lesser ones?

Great designers are truly professional in their presentations, they have exacting standards, and they usually have a signature look/sense/style that sets them apart. They build a body of work that holds together. Most of them teach. They appear at stores. They work tirelessly to promote their point of view and their work, and they love to teach others. They have web sites, blogs, Facebook pages, they participate in the industry – they attend trade shows at least once a year and use it as a time to teach or to network with others.

For me, more importantly, almost every designer I have had the pleasure of meeting has been a really wonderful and very nice person. I have enjoyed their company tremendously and many have become personal friends. People in this industry are generally respectful of each other's work. They don't bitch about each other, they aren't jealous, they get on, and they celebrate each other's successes. Part of that is that they have their own niche they have developed, and they are confident in their work and love what they do. And they are not emotionally needy. If you personally can't rise above extreme bitchiness, then look for work elsewhere. Most people here are really nice, and that's something you don't find everywhere – if you aren't one of them then no one will want to work with you.

Do you think the "up/down" knitting cycle is shortening up a bit? (Various people say knitting gets popular in 10 or 20 year cycles... we've been on a sustained kick for a while – does the internet get credit for that?) What happens when all the superficial knitting fans get bored and drop off? Do you see a renewed popularity in more complex patterns/techniques/etc?

I'm not sure about the length of cycles, but what we have seen was this time when "everyone" tried to knit. It was "the" thing to do. Of course, many people moved on as they do with all fads. What we are left with then is a larger core group. Over the past few years we have seen many of these people evolve their knitting skills. Firstly, they couldn't get enough cables, right now it's lace, and there's another movement embracing color like it's a new religion! Complexity and challenging techniques are needed to stimulate a larger group of more experienced knitters.

Having said that, our readers of Knit Simple magazine (and we have almost as many as Vogue Knitting, told us in a recent survey that they only want easy projects as they are too busy for complex stuff. They mainly knit accessories, likes scarves and hats, and are very happy doing so!

I was really excited to see Vogue comment on model size ranges recently, and I know VK's also addressed this in the past – can you talk a little bit about catering to specific populations of knitters, whether it's by offering a magazine that's meant to have less complex patterns (Knit Simple) or geared at a younger audience (knit.1) or whether offering larger pattern size ranges has brought you kudos... how can you both stay true to your editorial vision and yet address specific needs?

This is a constant challenge for me. I appreciate that you liked me addressing size ranges, but so many readers missed the point and thought I was being condescending. It's really hard to get across to people that there are a lot of patterns that don't work when sized up for several reasons. They think it's our job to size everything up to as large as possible. I have accepted this is an argument I can never win! We have always tried to size patterns up and mark on the page those that are.

During the knitting rage there were more knitters and more money out there, so we were able to try ideas like Knit.1. However, now the economy is in a different place, we have pulled the title. The sales in the end did not warrant keeping it going. Sadly.

We have had much more success with Knit Simple. It evolved out of a publication with used to do with Family Circle called Easy Knitting. When it went away, it was at a time when there were many new knitters and we wanted to create a publication that helped them develop their skills and confidence. It now sells almost as well as Vogue Knitting, and there is very little cross over. In fact, 40% of these readers don't buy any other knitting magazines, so we have a unique market segment here.

Along the same lines, we did a VK publication a few years ago for MEN. It totally failed! We have found in our magazines that you need to be all things to all people and try to cater to the fringe groups from that base and in other mediums. Books, for instance, do better when targeted to a niche group.

What else? Got any specific soapbox-y issues we should talk about?

My biggest soapbox issue in the industry is always copyright. I get really upset when stores copy from magazines and books. It means that publishers and authors are being duped out of a sale. The more erosion of sales in publishing, the less material published. There are stores that will buy a single copy of a book and then photocopy any pattern the customer wants. I don't think that store owners get the extent of the damage they are doing. With any publication, they can make money from the sale, the publisher and designers get paid, and the customer goes home with more inspiration – which hopefully will send them back to the store for another project. If anyone has any ideas on how to break this vicious cycle then I would love to hear from you!

LILY CHIN

Website: http://www.lilychinsignaturecollection.com

Did you actively plan to be a designer or did it just happen? How? Where did you get your start?

It just happened. I've always done it, but always on the side until I realized that a liberal arts education means no great jobs and no definitive career path immediately. I started in magazines as well as ready-to-wear/manufacturing in the 80s.

What's the source of most of your income? Teaching, magazine work, books?

About half teaching and half designing. I don't do as much magazine work now but have been working on books instead.

Where do you see the design profession heading? Are there any differences between the knit and crochet side of things?

Due to the internet, lots of "dabblers" are now designing as opposed to dedicated, full-time designers such as myself. This is not a judgment of any kind, just an observation. Knit seems to still out-sell crochet even though there are more crocheters in the US. Knitters are more willing to pay for things.

What are your dealbreakers in a contract – what won't you agree to under any circumstances?

I don't have to do anything I don't want to. If a magazine wants all rights, I don't have to do work for them. I just won't offer designs that I want to keep is all. You don't have to take anything you don't want, and if you don't want to accept their terms, don't work for them.

What advice would you give a designer who's just starting out today?

Don't quit your day job. It's always been a low-paying field and always will be. Unless you're willing to put in more hours in a work week than most to earn a living wage, do it on the side.

If you could change 3 things about the design business, what would they be?

The low pay, the long hours and horrible deadlines.

How do you stay productive? What's your typical work week like?

I work *all* the time. Fear of not being able to pay my bills keeps me motivated. You have to really love this to death to put up with a lot of sh*t. If I didn't love it still, I wouldn't be doing it.

You've been in the business a long time, and maintained your popularity throughout – to what do you attribute your success?

Lots of hard work and originality. Don't put out stuff everyone's seen before. Try to be as different as possible. Play nice. Don't get the reputation of being "difficult." Meet all deadlines. Be accurate and write up instructions well. Dot your i's and cross your t's. Get the reputation of being reliable and willing to go the extra mile.

Is marketing yourself important? How and why? What do you do to stay at the top of everyone's head?

Marketing is *always* important. Why design if no one notices? That's why I said before – be as original as possible. Let your design speak for itself. Otherwise it's just all hype. This is not to say hype is all bad. I've been accused of being masterful at self-promotion. I don't think this is a bad thing. If my work didn't back me up, I would be all style and no substance. My über-outgoing personality is a big draw and I've always garnered attention because I'm not shy. I like it when people talk because that just means more recognition. I'm not afraid of controversy either. I'm of the "any publicity is good publicity" school. Just spell my name right.

ANNIE MODESITT

> **Website:** http://www.anniemodesitt.com
> **Blog:** http://www.modeknit.com
> **Twitter:** @modeknit

How did you become a designer? When did you begin designing full time? And what made you realize "that's it, I'm doing THIS full time"?

I started – as most designers do – as a knitter. I half-taught myself to knit at age 25 and after wrapping myself completely in my knitting mojo for a year, I began knitting for other designers, which led to my submission of designs to various knitting magazines. Most of them aren't around any more (Knitting with Simplicity, McCall's Needlework, Elle used to run a knit pattern every month) but I was fortunate to have designs in many of them.

What's the source of most of your income? teaching, magazine work, books. Where do you see this changing in the next few years?

When I first started my income was pretty much 80% design and 20% working at a yarn shop. After a few years of teaching, the percentages changed to 40% teaching and 60% designing. Once I'd written Confessions of a Knitting Heretic (and my seven other books) my income from writing changed to about 60%, teaching is about 30% and designing about 10% of my income.

I don't love that – I'd like to earn more from designing – but I think the way the industry is structured right now that's pretty much impossible for most folks.

Where do you see the design profession heading? Any differences between the knit and crochet sides of things?
I see crochet growing, and as long as the designs can remain fun and fresh and inventive that won't be a problem. There's a *huge* untapped pool of potential crocheters, and just about anything undiscovered can be a revelation to a new crafter of any stripe.

In knitting I see the basic categories of patterns remaining steady (easy and fast to knit, "expert" projects, gifts and small items) but I definitely sense a glacial move to embrace more challenging projects. This is wonderful, and I'm glad the movement is slow because – as a dieter – I know that gains won too quickly also fade very quickly!

The psychology of working toward more difficult knit goals is wonderful to watch. I've seen my own students move from, "Oh, I'm just a beginner..." to "I *must* get that Bohus design kit!" To my mind two things are responsible for this:

1. Sock knitters. They are the unsung heroines of the knitting world. By making useful, wonderful, hard to purchase and fun to create projects, they convince MANY knitters that knitting isn't worthless or silly – and that once you make a project on size 1 needles, a cardigan on size 7s is much less daunting!
2. The internet. Because many different techniques are available at a crafter's fingertips – through YouTube, various websites and online bookshops – folks who might be intimidated or hate to ask questions can be immediately gratified. Sites like Knitter's Review, Knitty, Twist Collective and Ravelry all engage the knitter to rethink the knitting community.

If a brick and mortar shop doesn't use these two motivating factors (socks and the internet) to persuade folks to visit their shop, they're losing out. I'm stunned when I still run across shop owners who eschew the web, I feel it's one of the best ways to allow brick and mortar shops to achieve a sustainable level of commerce.

And it's not going away.

What are your dealbreakers in a contract – what won't you agree to under any circumstances?

When I studied costume design we were taught, "Never tell a director, 'No.' Say, 'Yes!' and then tell the director what the cost will be. Let *them* say, 'No.'"

I feel that way about contracts. I try not to say NO, but I do say what the cost will be for a YES.

Having said that, I refuse to deal with organizations that I feel treat their employees or customers in an unfair way. That's a very subjective standard, and sometimes it's a hard line to walk, but it's the main problem I have with some large venue teaching shows or publishing conglomerates which work out sweetheart deals for some designers and teachers, but treat others as if they're not worthy of fair treatment.

As far as publishing contracts go, each time I fall into a contractual pit, I learn a new lesson. It's easier to say what I would try to avoid again rather than what the deal breakers would be.

Here are some things I've learned:

1. I won't work on a book unless the editor is a knitter. I'm tired of teaching my editors to knit.
2. A publisher *must* be committed to marketing any book I write.
3. A publisher *must* be committed to keeping my book on the shelves for longer than just a year or two.
4. I must be allowed to retain the rights to my patterns / book content to republish in future.

These are the main 4 things that stand out to my mind, and the main reason I'd rather self publish a book if it's at all possible, so I can control what happens after the initial interest begins to wane.

What advice would you give a designer who's just starting out today?

Don't expect to make a living on knit design, not right off the bat. By the same token, realize that if *you're* willing to accept a low fee, you're also relegating other designers to – in effect – accept that bad fee. Poor fees can be offset by reversion of rights or other nuggets the publisher/ magazine can offer. Ask for them.

If you could change 3 things about the design business, what would they be?

Union. Union. Union.

A Design Guild or Union which would support member designers could raise the living conditions *and* the standards of the current yarn industry. A hand knit designer works harder for their dollar than almost any other professional I know (yes, I am biased...).

Graphic designers, actors, costumers, photographers, writers – these freelancers all have guilds or organizations that act on their behalf and have worked up scales of payment to which their industries adhere.

Hand knit and crochet designers don't have this. Fees for designs vary greatly, and there is currently no tool in place to provide professional, full time designers with the backup necessary to create a professional environment.

From my own observations of my fees for magazine design work, the current average fee for a hand knit project is just slightly more than the average fee in 1986, when I began designing. This is just wrong.

I would like to have a scale below which no guild designer would work. It would be on the low end, and designers with more experience or a proven track record could always negotiate above the scale. By setting this, a certain level of professionalism would be required of the designer, and the playing field would be leveled.

Sometimes *all* members of our yarn industry forget the following:

1. To the yarn manufacturers and yarn shops, the goal of a pattern is to sell yarn.
2. To the magazine, the goal of a pattern is to sell issues.
3. To a designer, the goal of a pattern is to sell themselves.

But – most important –

4. To the knitter who buys the pattern, the goal is to bring little bit of happiness.

Each facet of the above equation is dependent on the others, but the happiness factor must **NEVER** be overlooked.

How do you stay productive? What's your typical work week like?

Right now I'm not feeling very productive. I try to set some weekly or monthly goal and work toward that. My energy level and ability to dream up solutions to design problems varies from day to day, so I can't demand X amount of work on any given day.

I'm fortunate that I'm a pretty self-motivated person and can get a great deal of work done when I'm in the mood or physically able. I've learned from several painful sessions of 'beating myself up' that being down on myself doesn't make me work harder, but being *honest* with myself allows me to work smarter.

- I try to write a bit each day, either a pattern, article or on my blog.
- I try to knit a bit each day, some days more than others, to remind myself why I do this (love of knit and crochet!).
- I try to work on a class a bit each day, either by tweaking a handout, coming up with a new class or shooting some video for one of my online classes.
- And then I try to just keep on top of the financial stuff on a weekly basis – invoices not paid, taxes to report, ad budgets to figure and all the other really fun stuff.

You've been in the business for quite a while, and maintained your popularity throughout – to what do you attribute your success?

Healthy bribes.

Seriously, I have no idea. I have long tried to design things that I think are attractive, that I would either wear (or would *like* to wear if I had the figure for it...) and sometimes I even succeed.

I've been *very* lucky that some folks like my work, like my rather outspoken way of expressing myself, and enjoy my classes. I don't kid myself that I'm universally loved (nor should I be!)

I think the fact that I'm constantly energized, excited and – well – in *love* with the yarns I use keeps me interested. And, as my mother used to say, "Interested people are interesting!"

Is marketing yourself important?

Marketing is *very* important. I'm a member of several professional designer email lists, where folks who earn a good amount from their income from hand knit and crochet design work can privately speak about what demons they're currently facing. Several years ago there was a much greater negative reaction to any kind of "shameless self promotion" that a designer might engage in.

Whenever discussions came up where some folks admitted they found it a bit distasteful to market themselves, I made it clear that I was not ashamed of promoting myself at all. (I *would*, however, be ashamed of not paying the mortgage)

For a bit this may have made me somewhat of a pariah among some designers who saw marketing as something to descend to, something lesser than our chosen calling of designing. I believe the two go hand in hand. For a business to thrive, even if the business is just one person, marketing must be involved.

Unfortunately when a career path is viewed as "women's work," that our fees are little better than "butter and egg" money, marketing or promotion can be a difficult dance. On the one hand, a designer may want to be perceived as just some humble person sitting at home producing patterns for lovely knitted garments. On the other hand, that same designer would like to earn some money designing those patterns.

Marketing can be as simple as writing a blog so folks know who you are and having a web page, or as elaborate as mass mailings and ad campaigns in the major knitting magazines. I am not the marketer I know I could be, but I grab at every chance I get to keep myself (and my patterns) visible, because I do like paying that darned electric bill.

Why did you decide to self-publish Confessions of a Knitting Heretic*? What about that process was different compared to working with a large publisher?*

I self-published *Confessions…* because no one wanted to publish it. I offered it on CafePress.com, earned enough money to go to a printer, and each printing of the book led to more sales, which went right back into paying for more printing. I feel very strongly that if that book *had* been published by a larger house it may be out of print by now (as are some of my other books – very good books – but not big enough sellers to merit warehouse space).

It was only after I self-published that I realized how fortunate I was to have taken that route. I own the rights, I can republish the book in any way I want. I can keep in it print, no one can remainder it. I can recreate it in a more polished and complete format (which I hope to do in future) and I don't have to argue with anyone about what to keep in or take out.

And, most important, I earn a lot more money on a self-published book than I've earned on *any* of my publishing house books. It's a hassle to handle the printing, the storage of the books, and of course it's hard to pay $2,000 – $5,000 whenever I get a new shipment of books printed, but all of that is worth it in the long run.

Some of my books have sold better than others, but *all* of my books have earned a respectable amount and have definitely paid for themselves. I found Fern Reiss's series on self-publishing to be very helpful, especially in terms of setting a retail price for my books and marketing them.

You've moved into providing other knit-related products on top of your patterns (the flip books, audio books, online classes) – how have those raised your profile or brought you new customers?

New ways of reaching out to customers has *definitely* helped me to raise my profile. It's gratifying that by offering new ways to learn and think about knitting, more folks are feeling freer to experiment and not accept that there's only *one* dogmatic way to knit (or purl).

I'm currently enjoying a nice success with my initial offering of online classes on Combination knitting, and hope to be adding a few project oriented classes as well as technique classes like Knitting Lace and Working with Color.

TINA WHITMORE

Website: http://www.knitwhits.com

How did you start designing? When did you transition to doing it full time, and what factors went into that decision?

I've been designing since I was in high school – I started knitting when I was about 7 – but I was only designing sweaters for myself and occasionally on commission for private clients. I was working in graphic design and as a knitting teacher at my local community college all while training for and doing triathlons in my free time. I sustained a back injury skiing that put an end to the triathlons and left me fairly immobile for almost a year – at the same time my primary graphic design client moved a large part of their operations to Singapore. I was making a hat for a pregnant friend who ended up having an enormous baby – 3 hats later I finally made one that fit. I was encouraged by other non-knitting friends (with their own small businesses) to see if I could make a go of it as a business. I wrote up the hat patterns, bought some yarn from a local store, put together some kits and starting visiting local knitting stores and writing orders. I drove down to Los Angeles and sold more; only one store out of the first 20 I'd seen had said no. It seemed viable. I booked a booth at TNNA and then I had 50 stores buying from me. There was no conscious transition to full time, I just sort of created a monster and it took off very, very quickly and was lucky that it comfortably filled the gap left by the slowdown in the graphic design.

Tell me about Knitwhits – how do you differentiate yourself from other knit design businesses?

I'm not good at planning anything, so I can't say that I have a specific business model that I created or that I've followed. I think Knitwhits offers patterns that often have the appearance of being more challenging or maybe more funky and unusual, while still retaining very basic knitting techniques. I'm also driven a lot by color or a color palette. Without sounding too loopy, it's always the yarn that tells me what it wants to be, but it better be something interesting or I won't do it. I don't really study much what's going on in the knitting world, or what other designers are making. I do think that there are an awful lot of good very basic designs produced and I have no interest in reinventing the wheel. It's hard to improve on a Rowan cardigan!

How has your product line enhanced your design business (the mini skeins, the kits, etc)?

Well, that's sort of a which came first – the chicken or the egg. When I started, my thought was to offer kits with patterns being available but not the primary driving force (financially). As I learned the business of it all, patterns in and of themselves also have proven to be a big part of the business. I also got to a point where I was itching to make larger items, which led to the development of some unusually structured sweaters, cardigans and tops. Since these are not so "kit-able," I left them as stand-alone patterns – they have actually ended up being a large part of my business. I do offer some other items on my website that moved me for one reason or another. The mini-skeins seemed to fill a gap in the industry; interesting that there are other companies now doing the same thing, even some larger distributors are trying it out.

Tell me why you use Payloadz for your downloadable PDF sales instead of a newer option such as E-junkie.

Payloadz is fine, until it messes up which thankfully doesn't happen very often, but the customers let me know in no uncertain terms pretty quickly when the Payloadz site is down! I looked at switching to E-junkie for financial reasons but then Payloadz modified their fees downwards so I left it as is. To reprogram my site for E-junkie just seems at the moment more work than I want to get into – and I'm not convinced that it runs that much better than Payloadz. Maybe I've just had good luck with them, they don't seem at all bad to me. I think E-junkie has done well as the programming is basic if you have a simple enough website, and the price is right. It's also a bit of perception – Payloadz is the PC of downloads, E-junkie is the Apple!

How do you use social media to promote your business?

Ha! I don't – well...not so true. I recently started a Facebook page and I have sourced test knitters in the past on Ravelry. I do also have a Knitwhits Ravelry group, but with everything else as a one-woman shop it's hard to keep on top of it all. I like the Facebook page the best as I bring in odds and ends that I find online that relate to knitting, so it's not entirely a "new pattern – buy this" page that I see so much of. Snore pie with yawn sauce. I started a blog a few years back with the idea of it being about my dog and my work, but it's hard to find something interesting to say on a regular (or even not so regular) basis. And then when something does come up I sort of peter out before I get to blogging about it. I find blogging to be a bit self-indulgent honestly. Though some bloggers are very good and an interesting read for sure, I just don't think I am or ever will be one of them!

Talk to me about yarn support. I know you have had issues with a certain company in the past...

I'm pretty lousy at asking for yarn support. If I have an idea for something I tend to just buy the yarn, if I can I'll order at wholesale, if not, then I get it at retail. I'm not a "normal" designer though and I think many companies don't get that a pattern doesn't have to be in a book to generate income in yarn sales. Self publishers don't seem to rate with some companies and nothing but time and experience can change that. I think some distributors are familiar with Knitwhits but I don't have the name recognition of the designers who've gone the magazine and book route. I'm also lousy at self promotion... it's the English in me. I should add though that I do get approached a fair amount by yarn companies who want me to use their yarn, I do tend to shy away from it a bit due to my odd work style and the requirements of running Knitwhits on a daily basis don't really allow for me to set it aside to do a book or design for a magazine.

There is one particular brand of yarn that I've bought a lot of for my sweater patterns. I've done a lot of designs with this particular yarn company's yarns and they won't give me the time of day until I come to them with a book, and have told me as much. I've done the math and by extrapolating out what I've seen on Ravelry, in some 60% of my patterns sold using this company's yarn the knitter actually uses the suggested yarn. This also comes to some $250,000 in yarn sales for this company – nothing to sneeze at. Given that I've made them a pretty penny it seems cheap of them to not throw a bag of yarn my way if I ask. I tried to rise above it and continue with their yarn regardless, but I have a bit of a bad taste in my mouth. That being said, another company who I had never bought anything from gave me a skein of every color of their worsted yarn. I was floored. I eventually used the yarn in a few kits and now I buy a lot of yarn from them, so what was a small investment for them of 30 skeins has turned into a very happy symbiotic relationship. They are lovely people that offer very nice yarns in a beautiful color palette and I sing their praises wherever I can. I took some of their yarns and fibers on consignment to a few shows, this led to a new design in their linen yarn, and to my new found interest in spinning which has in turn led to Humanity Handspun... but that's another story! This company is such a pleasure to work with that I'm happy to promote them.

Talk to me about goal setting – I sympathize with what you wrote once on "had 10 goals, 2 got shot down"...

I'm as bad with goals as I am with plans. But I'm very good at lists. I have them all over my office! As a small business one can become a bit tunnel vision in one's ways. As long as things are humming along all seems well, but sometimes you need to shake it up a bit, if only for your sanity. Sitting down and clearing one's head of the every-day stuff can really open up some new channels. With the slowdown in the economy and in the knitting industry in general, to keep afloat you have to be open to new ideas, or create new ideas of your own. I don't know what I did with that list of goals I blogged about, it's somewhere under some other piles of lists on my desk but I do know that every time I've stumbled across it I've found that I can cross off another one or two items from that list.

Where do you see the industry heading?

I have no idea! I do tend to live in a bit of a bubble, but from what I see I expect continued consolidation for probably a couple more years. There are a lot of yarn companies and distributors hanging on by the skin of their teeth – though they would never admit to it in public. I've noticed cost cutting measures from my suppliers that have a trickle down effect primarily in their ability (or lack of) to supply my yarn when I need it, so I have learned to work around that. So far, since it's an industry issue, the retail stores have been understanding. I don't know that we will have the big knitting upswing of 2004-2005 anytime again soon. "They" say it's a seven year cycle, but I think it will be closer to a 10 – 12 year cycle this time before real sustained growth happens again. I'm not sure many people will be able to ride it out that long. Of course there are new people starting up stores, or new designers coming up every day but it won't be an easy climb.

What would you tell a new designer? or recommend to an established one?

A new designer? Don't believe that the internet is everything. I think the internet reaches but a small fraction of the market. That is of course changing, but there is a lot of hype over the web too. Also, I would say, take it seriously. Don't give away your work for free. Value what you do, and only offer a product of value. Be prepared to change your expectation of what a designer does. I spend far more time packing and shipping and slogging away at the computer on tedium than I ever do designing. Fortunately for me I happen to like that!

An established one? Yay!
To perk up a business? What moves you? What brought you to this business? What can you do to fall back in love with what you do (if you're not)? Are you designing for yourself or for what you perceive the market wants? If one is not working, try the other. Expand your knowledge and skills. Keep learning, it doesn't have to be in design, it could be something completely unrelated – I took up tribal style belly dancing last January and it's had a huge impact on how I design. You never know where or what can get your creative juices going, it may surprise you!

Tell me about your recent computer crash and why is it SO IMPORTANT TO MAKE BACKUPS.

If you ever hear that little voice in your head say: "hmm, I should probably back up my files," THEN DO IT!

I lost almost a year's worth of accounting which I had to recreate. Fortunately I was able to puzzle it all together, but I did lose a lot of day-to-day figures that I refer to (prior year figures) to see where things are going, so 2009 ended up being a bit of a vacuum. I only lost one pattern, but was able to dig up a PDF and redo that. I'm sure I lost countless other things, but I have no idea what. I had two major crashes in the space of about a year, it's not a lesson I need to learn a 3rd time. Then of course I spent many days trying to piece it back together, so it's not only the lost files, it's the lost time that is so frustrating and wasteful.

Knitwhits has a customer projects page – what do you gain by posting these projects? (does it show other customers they can do it too, get you free images you can use, what?)

The Knitwhits Flickr site is fairly quiet but Ravelry has filled that hole nicely. I think it's great for potential customers to be able to check out what other knitters have done with a design, colorwise, or to see how something knits up in another yarn or how it knits up at all! The photographs on a retail site are not always taken in a "real world" setting, so I think it helps the customer visualize a project and see if they like something or not. There is a community aspect to it as well. With permission I will use a customer or store's image in a newsletter or on the website, but again, it boils down to only having so many hours in the day. I also find it useful to see potential pitfalls, where a customer may have stumbled on my instructions. Lastly, I find it useful to see what the customers are actually knitting.

JOSI HANNON MADERA

> **Website:** http://iamintheloop.com
> **Website:** http://www.tensionmagazine.com

Where do you see the overall design industry (particularly crochet) heading?

I think things are looking up for crochet. There are more designers who understand clothing fit and construction than ever before, and that is changing the inaccurate perception that crochet is not meant for clothing. Another great trend is that yarn companies are once again focusing on their finer weights, instead of their thicker novelty type yarns – and that bodes well for crochet designers, too.

What do you wish someone had told you when you first started off as a designer? How did you get into the business?

I started designing at a very young age – my mom had a side business selling macramé, sewn housewares and clothing. Perhaps what my mom lacked as a mentor was a freewheeling spirit, but I think that gave my own willy-nilly natural self the discipline to care about form and function, as well as efficiency and precision.

I started designing for pay originally as a costume designer, and it eventually morphed into crochet. I chose crochet because of the lack of good stuff out there 10-15 years ago – so much different than the lovely pieces of my elders. My grandmother's crochet is way better than yours.

I'll bet money on it, because I'm still not half as good.

Do you earn most of your income from design work or do you do other things as well?

In addition to selling patterns, completed pieces, and designs (to others who reproduce them), I am a code monkey, photographer and tech editor. I handle all things technical for Croshay Design (website and publishing) and I am the editor-in-chief of Tension Magazine.

My code monkey skills also bring in an income, and I am always available for other crafty people who need a great website (custom shopping carts, anyone?). I want to bring yarn arts into the 21st century, as I believe digital publishing is the way to go. Not only does one not have the page count restrictions of print publishing, one can include video and interactive aspects to patterns and websites.

Note: Josi's website Art of Crochet includes many patterns with interactive sizing and video stitch guides – see http://www.iamintheloop.com/artofcrochet/patterns.php, and particularly Raspberry Fizz as an excellent example of how the online medium can push the limits of pattern publishing, particularly in terms of generating custom sized patterns.

What role does the internet play in knit design work these days compared to other more "traditional" information sources?

See above. The opportunities that digital publishing offers over print are not even all discovered yet. This is an exciting time to be involved in Self-publishing/independent publishing because people are now finally used to it. The average crafty person understands PayPal, downloading patterns, PDFs, etc. They are comfortable with getting their media through the internet, and in fact are showing signs that they prefer it.

What do you see as the most influential traits/activities when it comes to being a successful designer? What do great designers have in common, or have that sets them apart from lesser ones?

I feel great garment designers, first and foremost, have a love of, and respect for, the human body. They need their designs to be flattering, easy to put on and remove, durable, and stylish. No one aspect gets to be sacrificed for another.

"Design" is a sacred concept to me. It means something conceived with purpose, that the details are deliberate, and that the finished object functions as expected. I pray at that altar every day, and my penance for sinning = frogging.

What are your current career goals? How have they changed and why?

I am very excited and hopeful for Tension Magazine. I would like to set a new and higher standard for internet publication, crochet patterns, and compensation for participants.

What advice would you give a new designer? What advice would you give someone who's been around a while but needs a kickstart?

Write a business plan. It's not as boring as it sounds, because it is a way for you to focus your creative goals. If money isn't your goal, pick a goal and write a business plan around that. Maybe it is to get published in 5 different places in one year. Maybe it is to get a profitable teaching gig. Whatever it happens to be – take some time to write it out. The path will make itself apparent, and then it is up to you to walk it.

Why are you so pro-digital media/DIY?

I am under contractual obligation to not go into the details of why my experience with print book publishers was so horrible that I never recommend it. However, a digital contract is something I'd be willing to enter into because I am a control freak and I'd make certain I get to do the layout, etc.

MARNIE MACLEAN

Website: http://marniemaclean.com
Twitter: @MarnieMacLean

Where do you see the handknitting industry heading?

Crafts seem to be eternally cyclical in popularity yet the classics never seem to fully fade away. As long as there are fashionable sweaters in stores and people of various shapes and sizes, there will always be a group of people who want to make their own pieces, custom fit, in the yarn and color of their choosing. That said, the business side is changing and there are opposing forces at play.

On the one hand customers want instant access to patterns, at any time, they want lots of information and they want it presented clearly, accurately and attractively but they don't want to pay too much. Publishers need a way to make that model profitable and attractive to advertisers, while keeping prices low. And designers, more and more, are demanding fair wages, and greater control of their designs. As the customer gets more and more content and the publishers try to keep prices down, and with designers wanting better compensation, eventually, some concessions must be made.

The successful business model(s) will balance all of these factors and I don't yet know how that will play out.

What do you wish someone had told you when you first started off as a designer? How did you get into the business?

I wish I had been told...EVERYTHING. I knew nothing. I didn't know about gauge swatches, grading, tech editing, valuing my work, contracts, yarn support, submitting patterns, seeking out mentors. Nothing. I just knew I loved knitting and having been someone who had done a lot of sewing, I had some idea about basic garment shapes and proportions for my own size, but beyond that, it was all trial by fire. Luckily, these days, most of that information is available online and there are a multitude of forums in places like Ravelry, where aspiring and established designers come together to talk shop.

Do you earn most of your income from straight up design work or do you do other things as well?

I feel firmly (maybe too firmly) that designing is one business and teaching and lecturing and other related events are another business. Often, when people discuss the merits of one publishing venture over another, they mention that one might open doors for teaching events, but teaching pays what teaching pays and it pays you per hour for your work. Designing pays what it pays and that is usually a flat fee or royalties or an exclusivity period and then rights revert. So for me, I'm a designer, if I teach, I'm working as a teacher and I don't consider those overlapping in any way. I know that's sort of tangential to the topic, but it's something I feel pretty strongly about because I think people so undervalue their design work and this is often used as an excuse to accept paltry pay for one's hard work.

Now to actually answer your question, for all intents and purposes, 100% of my yarn related income is from designing. I am also open to doing teaching and events and articles, but right now, I've only committed to designing.

What role does the internet play in knit design work these days? Do you use social media in your business or find it beneficial overall?

I started online and have remained largely an online designer, both with my own self-published patterns and submitting to places like Twist Collective. I'm also active in social media and on Ravelry though I do those because I enjoy them, not as a intentional tool to drive up sales. I believe that some people probably have found my patterns through these social media tools but I also suspect that I've turned off a few prospective customers because I don't have a business-only persona there, so it may be a wash.

At the end of the day, you can't please everyone. I do see some people really using social media as a business tool and I think the problem is finding a balance. I'm likely to stop following someone on Twitter if I'm forever reading that they've posted another handknit Tabasco bottle dress over at Etsy. A little is fine but I am not looking to just get a stream of advertisements. I'm there because of the social aspects.

On the other hand, some designers, often those who are just trying to get their voice heard, lament that these social media tools really bore them and they get tired of reporting what they had for dinner. I think it's far worse for business to misuse a tool. If you are boring, even to yourself, imagine how others are responding. It's like having a rice cooker if you hate rice. A tool you don't like using is no use to you. Best to put your energies elsewhere.

What do you see as the most influential traits/activities when it comes to being a successful designer?

Most of the really popular designers, from what I can see, have found a balance between wearable and innovative designs and they always style their knits (or have their knits styled by a publication) in a way that's inviting and appealing. One really popular piece tends to snowball into more sales and if you can keep offering the sorts of designs your customers liked before, you'll have a steady stream of repeat customers.

Do you think where the design initially appears makes a difference?

I can't say that one type of publishing over another is more effective. There are certainly people who have done exceedingly well in print publishing only, but I do think having a strong online presence helps greatly. If someone sees another person wearing a great garment or reads a blog with a wonderful finished piece, they are more likely to buy the pattern if they can get it instantly.

What sets a great designer apart?

Very few of the really popular designers, that I know of have a substantial foundation and/or degree in actual apparel design so most designers start off knowing very little beyond what they've gleaned from patterns they've knit themselves. I suspect a good number of great designers never hit their stride because it can take so long to get up to speed on all the ins and outs of designing and working with tech editors and magazines and deadlines and picking yarns and then the pattern support and the unhappy customer and on and on. Some of what makes for a great designer is just trusting in yourself and forgiving yourself for not having it all figured out, and .

What are your current career goals? How have they changed and why?

For now, what keeps it fun for me is not making it my full time job. Firstly, I'm not terribly comfortable with having a lot of unpredictability in my income. One season may pay really well and the next may pay almost nothing. If I'm always worrying that I won't be earning enough then I'm not enjoying what I'm doing. But I also still consider knitting and crocheting my hobby, first and foremost, and if it starts becoming a chore to do it then I'm not going to be as creative with my work.

My goal is be sure that I respect my own work and my own time and try to produce patterns that people enjoy knitting and that produces great results. I don't think I'll ever stop learning how to write better patterns and that's exciting for me.

Tell me more about your tutorial series – why did you start writing them? They're mentioned in this book because they're incredibly useful, but how did you start? Were people asking you for specifics on how to use Illustrator and Excel, or...?

I don't think I made any conscious decision to do a tutorial series. Mostly, they came from reading blog posts or talking to friends who knit and discovering that they were hitting a wall with something. My feeling has always been that no one should opt not to design because they don't know how to execute something technically on a computer. Aspiring designers don't generally have a budget to hire a desktop publisher to build their charts in Illustrator but almost everyone has access to a spreadsheet application. Over time, my tutorials have just grown based on what I've found works and what people say they want to learn about. It's actually been really fun. In my various day jobs, over the years, I've been a desktop publisher and I've taught computer classes so it's a natural transition for me.

MYRA WOOD

Website: http://myrawood.com
Twitter: @myrawood

Where do you see the handknitting-and-crochet/design industry heading?

Independent designers are where the real growth is in our industry in terms of innovation and avant garde design. Unless the economy changes drastically, it's most likely larger book and magazine publishers will take even fewer chances than they already do and just publish generic titles with safe designs for the masses. High end, specialty books and better patterns will be self-published for both knitting and crochet.

Crochet is just starting to catch up to knitting in terms of contemporary fashion design and we're seeing more and more sophisticated crochet patterns available, which is changing the perception of crochet in a huge way. There are so many incredible crochet designers who make their designs available through higher end magazines, books and websites, and I see that trend continuing.

The surge in new crocheters and knitters will continue but I also think those that have a few years under their belts are looking to learn more involved techniques, which presents a great opportunity for teaching and self-publishing as well. We are seeing an explosion of self-published books and patterns since it's so easy to sell through the internet now and that will continue to thrive and grow.

In terms of yarn content, I think we'll continue to see a movement toward natural fibers and colors and away from the novelty yarns of a few years ago. People are experimenting with higher quality and hand-painted yarns and the designs will continue to reflect that, especially in the independent arena.

More involved stitch patterns and lace patterns are already topping the favorite pattern lists on Ravelry and other fiber-related sites, so I see lace becoming a mainstay for most knitters as they move from scarf and sock knitting into other interests.

Luckily, since the early 90s, knitting and crochet have resurfaced from the dark decades of uncoolness so the number of new needleworkers will continue to grow as tweens/teens and young adults spread the fiber love. Younger folks are also looking to hand work as the "new cool," since technology is now a given.

What do you wish someone had told you when you first started off as a designer? How did you get into the business?

I think it's crucial to find a good mentor to learn the ins and outs of the industry. There are so many incredible designers who have *been there, done that* and are willing to help newbie designers. I had an amazing mentor, Margaret Hubert, who told me what to expect so that I could be very realistic about my goals. She guided me through my initial contacts with publishers and patterns, making sure that I understood what and what not to expect.

Crochet Guild of America has an excellent, free mentoring program for any of their members interested in any professional aspect of the crochet industry. My best advice is find a good mentor and believe what they tell you. Many people have unrealistic expectations going into it and want to quit their day job immediately to make the big bucks. It doesn't work that way. Years and years of building your brand is necessary for any kind of income from the industry. It doesn't happen overnight.

Where do you earn most of your income?

The bulk of my fiber-related income comes from teaching at national venues, but that alone could never be enough to live on. I teach because I love to teach first and foremost. I also do graphic design work occasionally, produce independent books and patterns, and design patterns and write articles for publication. I've appeared on a number of fiber-related TV shows, so all of that together makes up my revenue source. It's important for me to wear lots of hats rather than concentrate on just one area to continue to grow creatively, be happy and earn an income at the same time.

What role does the internet play in your design work?

We've had a true paradigm shift in the needlearts world since the advent of Ravelry. There were many knit and crochet related blogs and networks before Ravelry, but the real change happened when Ravelry networked the entire community. The biggest change is that global opportunities now exist whereas previously most of the industry was primarily local; customers visiting their local yarn stores or big box stores for all of their knitting and crochet needs. Our customer base now spans the entire planet thanks to the web, and I do use my own website, Ravelry, Yahoo groups and Facebook to connect with existing and potential students/customers around the world on a daily basis. I update information about my classes and am able to promote my work to a much greater audience than I ever could without social networking. I find out about tons of new opportunities through the internet too!

What do you see as the most influential traits/activities when it comes to being a successful designer? What do great designers have in common, or have that sets them apart from lesser ones?

Well-written, properly tech-edited patterns and a great reputation sets the cream of the crop apart from wannabe pros. It's essential to treat everyone with respect, even if they are complete newbies, and provide quality customer service as well. Due to the internet, a bad reputation can spread like wild fire and sour a great designer's career if word gets around that they are surly or ignore their customers. Likeability is a great asset but there are a few "ghost" designers that stay out of the public eye.

If a designer interfaces with the public in any way through teaching, book signings, etc, they have to enjoy the social aspect or it's obvious to their potential fan base that they aren't really interested in them. Do what you love most and it will show. If you don't enjoy any single aspect of the business, stop doing it or it will negatively influence the rest of your career as well.

What are your current career goals? How have they changed and why?

My career goals are completely fluid. I've found, by following opportunities that arise and interest me, I've done a number of things I never dreamed of doing or even thought I'd like to do. I tend to be freeform about my design and my life and follow where the next step leads rather than rigidly adhering to any specific plan. That way I can experience different aspects and decide whether or for how long it suits me until the next opportunity presents itself.

That said, I do have constant dream goals. I'm always working on the next book or design in my mind but tend to leave my deadlines open so I can fulfill my creative desires as well as ensuring an income. The most important aspect of any career is to keep it fresh and continue to expand your own capabilities. I love learning new techniques that I can incorporate into my repertoire. Right now I'm obsessed with machine knitting, something I resisted but decided to try last year. I can see all kinds of new avenues for my designs that will affect my goals in years to come.

What advice would you give a new designer? What advice would you give someone who's been around a while but needs a kickstart?

Do what you **LOVE**! Don't second guess the market and try to figure out what will sell best. If you love what you design, others will too. Also, don't expect too much too soon. This is a long process that takes years to cultivate but with tender nurturing, love of what you do on a daily basis and the right attention it can happen!

If one trail turns cold, stop going in that direction. Nothing should be painful. If you hate the process, find another way that inspires you so that you love your days. It's entirely possible.
Tell me why you chose self-publishing versus working with a larger publishers.

Where do I begin? Self-publishing changed my life. After a horrendous experience as a new author with a rogue editor at a major publisher who took it upon herself to rewrite my book and redesign my patterns, I withdrew from my contract after 8 months of working together and literally started my first book over. After one year of restoring my content to its original vision, I finally produced the exact book I had in mind all along. I was elated and the reception from the buyers mirrored what I had suspected all along. There is a market for intelligent needlearts books that don't assume the reader knows nothing about their craft.

Large publishers need to dumb down their content to appeal to the largest number of consumers possible. They want to sell as many books as they can, plain and simple. As a self publisher, we have the luxury of producing special interest work for a niche market that the large companies won't and can't take a chance on. Self-publishing shouldn't be about trying to get rich by selling tons of books. It's done for the love of the process and the desire to impart exactly what you want to present exactly how you want to present it.

It helps that I have been working in graphic design my whole adult life but there are so many resources available through print on demand that allow anyone to write their own book these days! I'm currently working on my 5th self-published work, and although I have to wear every hat imaginable, I love the entire process. I can only recommend self-publishing to those who are interested in taking on at least a year long, all consuming project. Many people prefer to spend their time concentrating on designing alone so if that's the case, the other elements involved my not suit that type of designer. Also, no income occurs during the production of a book so that's another major consideration. I recommend going with a big publisher if none of that matters to you and all you want to concentrate on is the design aspect of your work. Self-publishing is a ton of work and a substantial investment, but the pay-off for me is well worth it.

JULIE TURJOMAN

Website: http://www.julieturjoman.com

Julie is the author of Brave New Knits, *and spent many months traveling all over the country to meet up with knit designers in their "natural habitats," their studios, houses, you name it. She's got a unique perspective to share on what's actually happening out there in the wider world of knit design. She writes:*

By now, most of the "knitting-is-the-new-yoga" trendsters have gone back to their yoga studios and left knitting to those of us who understand that it is unique unto itself – not a fad to pick up and then abandon when it starts to get challenging (because who ever got good at yoga if they didn't persevere?). And while that has not been a positive for the brick and mortar yarn shops that sprang up to take advantage of the trend, it has been good for those of us who know we will knit forever because the craft is an integral part of our lives, if not our livelihoods.

Yarn shops that continue to prosper do so because they have harnessed the internet, enabling them to reach a much wider audience than the knitters who physically walk in their door. They offer a range of yarns that encompasses both the stalwart traditionals and the new indie dyers. In addition, they offer a range of classes that allow every knitter to continue her knitting "education." By offering challenges for every level of experience, shop owners ensure that knitters don't get bored - and that helps keep them viable.

Knitting will not succumb to the cyclical nature of some other crafts for several reasons. Here are just a couple:

- One fact of today's technology is that many people have no opportunity to make something tangible; they sit at a computer all day and by the time they go home at night, they have nothing to show for themselves. Picking up a knitting project satisfies the craving many of us have to be productive, to make something intrinsically useful with our own hands;

- The yarn industry and independent spinners and dyers have caught up with the craft. While the classic yarns are still out there, who would have thought even a decade ago that knitters would have the infinite variety of fibers, range of colors, and pattern support that we enjoy today? It's mind-boggling!

I see a level of commitment and strategizing among twenty- and thirty-something designers that is extremely encouraging for the future of the handknitting industry. Many of the first generation of established designers really just "fell into" knitwear design as a career. They did not plan for it; rather, they recognized a natural ability and were able to combine it with (sometimes tenuous) personal industry connections to create what eventually became a viable career working for a major yarn manufacturer or print magazine. Timing and talent, rather than calculation, seemed to be their biggest drivers.

The difference I see now among professional designers who have established their reputations within the last three to five years is that they explore and educate themselves deeply in handknit design tradition and fashion. They set clear goals to establish themselves through various publishing and Self-publishing vehicles. Perhaps most important, they use the internet as a means to get the word out about their talents. They don't allow shyness or fear to prevent them from submitting their designs widely to knitting publications. While many of these designers deny having a specific

business plan, they nonetheless have focused goals for their career trajectories that were largely absent from the last generation of designers.

Blogging about our knitting has brought many of us an audience we could never have had even 8 years ago. Obviously, Ravelry has had an enormous impact on independent designers' ability to market themselves. Online magazines like Knitty.com and Twist Collective have had a similar influence on the exposure and name recognition they have achieved, successfully supplementing the reach of print magazines.

Great designers create thoughtful, unique patterns that have been tech edited and test knitted, minimizing the possibility of errors. They recognize that knitters come in all shapes and sizes, and routinely write their patterns to include a wide range of sizes. Whether they give a nod to current fashion trends or draw inspiration from the classics, each puts her or his own spin on them. An understanding of the characteristics of different fibers is evident in the choices they make to enhance their designs. Great designers create patterns that make the rest of us look at them in admiration and say, "Why didn't I think of that?"

While writing *Brave New Knits*, I was privileged to interview many established knitwear design stars as well as incredibly talented up-and-comers. We are fortunate that knitting is a "big tent" kind of world, and nowhere is that more evident than at conferences such as Stitches, TNNA, and Sock Summit. Our celebrities are generous with their time and talents, and willingly provide inspiration and advice to new designers. Although I hear from time to time about competitiveness within the industry, what I see more often are examples of mentoring and collegiality. To a degree, Ravelry and the ability to comment on blogs keeps us honest, but the right instincts are usually in play. Questions about patterns get answered quickly. Errata are corrected. Knitters rise to the occasion whenever a world crisis requires charity knitting or donations; i.e. the recent earthquake in Haiti and the OFA's Red Scarf Project.

What continues to trouble me is the pay scale for original patterns by the mainstream publications, although these issues are being addressed by some of them. Fair compensation for designers' work still has a long way to go within the more traditional bastions of the industry. New compensation structures that treat designers as business partners rather than as workers-for-hire are being developed, and that is encouraging. However, internet-based venues and Self-publishing put much more control into the hands of the knitters themselves, giving me confidence that it won't be too much longer before even the industry hold-outs step up to do what is right.

MIRIAM FELTON

Website: http://www.mimknits.com
Twitter: @mimknits

Where do you see the handknitting-and-crochet/design industry heading?

I see knitters learning to crochet, crocheters learning to knit and people becoming better educated and more independent. The trend toward everyone designing will eventually peter out with all the new people publishing patterns, and end with the new people realizing that they can make stuff for

How did you get into the business?

I designed a shawl and posted photos on my blog, and then people were asking for the pattern. It all snowballed from there when I realized that I actually wrote patterns very well.

Do you earn most of your income from design work?

Most of my income is from online pattern sales through Ravelry and my storefront. I normally do pretty well with wholesale pattern sales to yarn shops, but that has dipped since the economy went kabluey. I hope to be making more from teaching soon, and my book is coming out this year, which will be fun and hopefully add another revenue stream.

What role does the internet play in knit design work these days compared to other more "traditional" information sources? Do you see a special benefit in social media, for example? How do you use social media in your business?

I use social media right now to build excitement for projects I'm working on, to gather public opinion when I'm stuck on something, to update fans with progress, and to present my expertise on something when it is appropriate. I believe there are more ways I can use social media, but haven't had a lot of time to sit down and discuss them with some experts.

The internet is playing a huge role. Little old ladies have email accounts, and the next generation who *will* be little old ladies in the next 10 years already have email. Once knitters discover the wealth of knowledge and resources available online, it's only the die-hard techno-haters who refuse to avail themselves of it.

What do you see as the most influential traits/activities when it comes to being a successful designer?

Great designers are much different than great pattern writers. I know people who design amazing things, but their patterns are lacking, confusing, or downright BAD. Or vice versa, you can be a great pattern writer, including all the aspects of the pattern with perfect clarity and have an ugly, clunky or boring design that no one wants to knit. A great Self-publishing designer has a great creative idea, realizes it with fiber and then can either write the pattern themselves or knows when they need to outsource it to someone who can.

What are your current career goals? How have they changed and why?

I want to keep writing books and do more collections. I've done one-up patterns for so long that I want the challenge of designing things that go together but are not so similar that they are basically the same thing. I have a white whale of a book that I'm just beginning. It might take me 10 years, but I'll finish it someday. My goals really changed when I began designing full time. Before it was just a side gig, which made me money for fun and yarn, but when it became my career I had to start applying my business degree to it in ways I never had before. I had to think about marketing channels, and actually define a target market and demographic. I had to rethink how I ran the business, which has been good in some ways, and hard in others. It is easy to loose your creativity when you're rent payment depends on it. You begin to think about designing things that customers will love instead of designing things that you love. You have to get over that and keep designing things you love or else your work will suck.

What advice would you give a new designer?

Start getting involved in the community. If you came up with a really great bind off that's perfect for toe-up socks, then join the toe-up sock groups on Ravelry and when someone says "my bindoff isn't stretchy enough" jump right in and suggest yours. Make yourself available and be a helpful, contributing member of the knitting community. Name recognition is half the battle.

Also, don't ever forget that every contract is negotiable. And if the other party isn't willing to negotiate, you don't have to take what they're giving you. Remember that YOU are the one with something of value. They want your skill and your creative mind. If you're not getting what you want, then walk away. Don't sell yourself short just because this is a craft industry.

Tell me about your decision to self-publish.

The decision to self publish wasn't a hard one for me. I love learning and perfecting new skills, and I already had most of the skills needed to self-publish that I had cultivated over years of putting out single patterns. But if you are thinking about it, the important thing to remember is that you want to do it well. If you aren't very good at photography, then plan on hiring a photographer. If you aren't good with layout, get a book designer. The key is to be honest with yourself about what you can and can't do to meet the level of skill required to put out a good book. If you can't do a certain part, plan to farm it out to someone who can do it well.

ELIZABETH LOVICK

Website: http://www.northernlace.co.uk

A "p.s. at the start" from Elizabeth...

Re-reading what I have written I see I come back time and time again to money. The aim of a professional designer IS to make money. This is WORK, not a hobby. People are often amazed that I don't want to knit on planes etc. For me, such times are a delight – being able to sit and not HAVING to knit…. Anyone wanting to be a designer has to make that change in mind set.

Where do you see the handknitting-and-crochet/design industry heading?

If I knew *that* I would be rich!

I think the internet will continue to become more and more important both as a place to sell your wares and a place to buy (*not* the same thing!). It has the immediacy that folk want these days, and for the designer it has the added advantage of having a pretty quick turnaround time (no waiting for publishers and printers). And you don't have the same up-front expenses.

The biggest challenge to the industry is here too – any old fool can think they have a design and put it out there. And an awful lot of people are doing that (*awful* often being the operative word!). See later about professionalism – a pet soapbox of mine.

What do you wish someone had told you when you first started off as a designer? How did you get into the business?

Ill health (arthritis in the spine) stopped me teaching and I needed to earn money. So I did what my forebears would have done – turned to knitting. I then got fed up with knitting what others wanted me to knit (and for a pittance) and started my own label. That lead to selling my designs.

I had been working for myself for a while so knew what I was doing on the whole. I tell anyone who asks to start by looking exhaustively at the market before they do anything else, and get some training in the elements of business strategy and paperwork etc. That is far more important than a design course.

And another tip/essential. Grow a thick skin or give up now. Find your own way of coping with rejection from publishers and editors, and when people go on about what an awful design yours is in the current edition of Mag X. Same with teaching – you cannot please all the people all the time...

One story – I did a 3 hour Fair Isle class with 23 students I had never seen before. As any teacher knows, you reckon that, with the wind behind you, you can try to get one concept over per hour. So I did this class, and a couple of days later, a friend directed me to someone who had blogged about the class. How it was rubbish, how she couldn't see, how I had only taught 3 things, and they were try, tug and fudge. The friend expected me to be worried. I wasn't. Other people who didn't seen the demos the first time asked and I showed them again (*and again*) so that was her fault. And my aims for the morning was to get them to try, to pull stitches tight and to fudge....

Do you earn most of your income from design work or do you do other things as well?

Design, teaching, fiber tour operator, photographer. I also do all my own web design, publicity, tax stuff etc. My teacher's pension pays the mortgage, but if I want to eat, I have to design!!

Being able to take good pictures is vital to what I do – to be able to offer editors the combined package of words and pictures often makes the difference between getting a sale and not. I had taught photography, so knew what I was doing technically, but I did a freelancing course for photographers and the information in that was invaluable on the business side of things.

What role does the internet play in knit design work these days compared to other more "traditional" information sources? Do you see a special benefit in social media, for example? How do you use social media in your business?

Utterly and completely invaluable. For research (e.g. the fashion shows) and for selling. Couldn't do without it. For a long time I refused to blog – didn't see the point. Then over lunch with Jared Flood and Ruth Woolly Wormhead before UK Ravelry Day last June the topic came up. They both said I *must* have a blog. I took their word – and sales increased by about 30%! Ridiculous – it is only lightly veiled advertising with bits of tourist information, but it is read by hundreds.

What sets great designers apart from lesser ones?

For successful designers, quite frankly – marketing. I see beautiful designs which get overlooked and rubbish ones that are well marketed being successful. Get 'famous' and you can publish total rubbish. (No names!)

For great designers it is more difficult: a sense of line and what works, knowing when enough is enough!

What are your current career goals? How have they changed and why?

I am working towards a big book on Orkney knitting – huge area no one has looked at before. So much stuff it is difficult to get the time between other things, but I am gradually squirreling away designs for it!

What advice would you give a new designer? What advice would you give someone who's been around a while but needs a kickstart?

I answered this on the KnitDesign mailing list just the other day. My advice was simple: **Get a dog**. That will get you out walking, which is thinking time and design time in an environment (town or country) which should spark ideas. Also, go through the latest shows (on www.style.com) from all the fashion houses. They also help give you an idea of what is good and what is rubbish and why.

Professionalism is all. There are far too many people who don't do this and they give the industry a bad name. If you are a designer, knitting is *not* your hobby – it is **WORK**. I do think folk need to think things through – and be brutally honest with themselves.

Two tips – I know a knitter who is a competent knitter but not the brightest of souls. I write my patterns and articles with her in mind. If she can understand it, anyone can! Also – write out your pattern, then leave it for at least a week while you do another one. Then come back and proofread it. If you do it too soon, you will read what you *want* to be there, not what *is* there....

A story with a moral: I had been teaching on line (for free) and produced a pretty comprehensive set of notes on the subject. I put these online in the Yahoo group concerned, as PDFs done with a pretty primitive program.

A couple of weeks later, a friend in California went to a class on the same subject – at great expense. There were 10 or 15 people there. The teacher produced the first part of the hand outs – and Kathy recognized my notes intact, complete, with only the name changed. Being the lovely lady she is, she stood up, told the teacher and class that these notes were not written by the teacher but by me, and demanded her money back. The rest of the class followed suit.

In that case the person who stole my stuff got found out, and the shop owner made sure the woman didn't teach again in California, but it does show (a) how careful you need to be and (b) that you must be prepared for these things to happen.

Another point – if you become a name, even in a tiny pond, you cease to be you and become a Brand. These days, just as with sportsmen and authors, it is not enough to be a brilliant designer, you need to be good with the punters. Learn to keep that open friendly face, with the not-quite-fixed grin, and think of the money. Because, believe me, with some people, only the thought of the potential sales will keep you going. Most people are nice and most are reasonable, but there are others...

I think that with designing, like any other business, you need to periodically stand back and think, Where am I going? What is working well? What is bringing in money? What do I actually enjoy doing? Is there any other market I could/should be tapping? Even if the answers turn out to be steady as she goes, it is an essential exercise.

Work out what you are *good* at – the type of pattern etc – and what you are known for. Exploit this! But when you feel caged in by this, break out and do something different. Even if it doesn't make you any money, it will make you *feel* better! For example, I am now known for traditional patterns – lace, Fair Isle, ganseys – and for designs which will suit a large range of sizes. But I have just finished a knitted cotton skirt for teens. I will get the magazine money for it, but it won't have very much of a life outside that. Who cares? I have enjoyed it!

Since Elizabeth lives on Orkney, a very small island in the UK, I asked her if she would expound upon a few topics in particular, such as the role of the internet in building a business for herself.

Hurrah for the internet a thousand times over!! I can get people coming from thousands of miles away to do a class with me, but I can't get them to come from 15 miles away!

Things about the internet (in no particular order):

• Anyone can put a pattern out on the net and call themselves a designer. This is a great thing for people who are starting off in a small way, and who have the ability and drive to be professional (that word again) about it. But it does mean that the internet is overloaded with patterns, some excellent, some utter rubbish.

• Free patterns are the bane of every designer's life. I resisted for a long, long time before I put a couple up – ones that I give away with the yarn I sell locally. I don't give a direct link – only a link to my website, and they have to trawl down that before they get to the link. **Their price for the free pattern is having to look at what I have FOR SALE.**

• As I have said before on the KnitDesign mailing list, the problem with social networking sites for designers is twofold: (a) they are no fun, they are work – advertising work – every time I write a post on Ravelry, for example, it is Northern Lace who is writing – a subtle but important thing. (b) these sites, along with blogs etc, make the punters feel they know you – they are your 'friends.' And this means that they can take liberties with you – things which are fine between real friends but which go beyond what it reasonable. For example, I have been asked to resize patterns to their measurements (for free), to redesign using a different thickness of yarn (for free), to rewrite bits of my books for them (for free), to send them a few pages from a book (for free) 'because I don't want the rest so I don't want to pay for it'. If they see a pattern only available in a book, they don't see why I can't 'just' send them that one, etc. And the more outrageous the request, the ruder and more of a demand it becomes. Now, I hope I do my bit to help folk along, but it really isn't my job to teach them to knit (for free) or to spend an hour answering questions (for free) they could find the answer to with a couple of Google clicks. Help folk with patterns I have written – of course! But with every free pattern they have found on the net and which is written so badly even I can't work out what is meant – NO, NO, NO!

• Another beauty of the net is that folk need not know how small an outfit you are. They can't see the chaos/kids/dogs/dirty washing. They see your site and your patterns. And if they are professional in appearance you are, as they say over here, cooking with gas. (You would say 'good to go' I think!) But it puts and even bigger onus on the look of your patterns to do the marketing for you – you don't have a chance to talk to most of your customers – your online presence has to make the sale.

• And you can, of course, be anywhere in the world and can sell to the whole world. For example, there are only 20,000 people in my island group and less than 2,000 within a 10 mile radius of where I live. But I can sell through the internet to the whole world. I reckon that about 85% of my business is with North America, 5% Australasia, 5% Europe and 5% UK. You can go for niche marketing and reach almost everyone in that niche without leaving the house. Not to mention no postage costs, no delays in the post, no printing costs, no storage problems for you, no hiking to the post office in wind and rain…

- When you are talking via email, the punter doesn't hear your first reaction to their demand. I can say 'You stupid woman' to the screen, go away, have a coffee, come back and reply, calmly, that the answer to her question is on the front of the pattern. You do need to be aware of different cultures, though – I am getting to the stage of speaking fluent American, but I made some pretty big errors early on, such as saying, for a workshop, you needed a soft pencil with a rubber on the end. THAT is a perfectly respectable stationery item in the UK! And the time I sent a design for a skimpy vest to a US publication for consideration for the holiday issue...in the UK, the holiday issue is the one published in July for use on the beach!

- CDs. This is an example of how to get more money from what you have in the house – of using your skills to increase sales. One of my strengths is my photographic ability. I had thousands of pictures on my computer of places like Fair Isle and Unst, places people have heard all about, would love to visit, but probably never will. I also had PDFs of workbooks which need color but are not economic for me to print off singly. So I thought up the idea of putting the workbook plus a load of pictures on a CD-ROM and flogging that on the occasions where I meet folk face to face, and online too. As ever, it took quite a while to get together – sorting, editing and arranging photos takes a long time. I also spent quite a bit of time deciding on the look of the box and exactly what info to put on it – the usual marketing stuff. I wanted to make sure that (a) the design would last and (b) the basic template could be used for others in the same series (House Style again). There was quite a big outlay in money, too, but it has definitely been worth it. I have recently done a second run of three of the titles and am about to do the fourth.

MK CARROLL

Website: http://mkcarroll.com

Where do you see the handknitting-and-crochet/design industry heading?

Continuing to offer more PDF patterns, more internet presence and the ability to be responsive to what customers are looking for in a shorter time frame (with Ravelry, for example, designers and publications teams can quickly find out what a range of end users are choosing, modifying, subbing, etc., and take that into account for the upcoming seasons).

As for crochet: in the US, continuing (I hope, I really *really* hope) to integrate more into overall yarncraft and get to be more like *the rest of the world* (I am *so* annoyed with how in the US there's all this crochet-bashing, e.g. "hillbilly knitting," not meant as being any kind of compliment). I love that Knitscene and Vogue have both knit and crochet in their magazines, matter-of-factly and with no apologies. I have long considered the marginalization of crochet in the US to be very much a class issue – crochet is popular with communities that are not always held in high esteem or considered worthwhile markets by big companies (Lion Brand Yarn and Red Heart being exceptions, but in a way that I think still illustrates the class issue). I have also long been working to incorporate more Japanese-style informative instructions and have been working on generating pattern charts that break it out into step-by-step charts that look like the piece in progress (as much as that is possible). It is extra work for the pattern, and makes selling printed patterns cost-prohibitive, but PDF is great for that, and I have found that I now get hardly any questions from buyers for those patterns, because even if they don't know how to read a symbolcraft chart, the visual quality of the chart can show them very quickly and easily if they are on track. I've noticed more symbolcraft charts being used in publications, and am hoping that it's a continuing trend.

Yarn shops really need to step it up and offer more crochet support if they don't already. Hawai'i yarn shops are, if anything, more likely to have better crochet support than knit support – crochet has been big here for generations, and not being crochet-friendly would sink any shop here.

What do you wish someone had told you when you first started off as a designer? How did you get into the business?

Keep your copyright! Negotiate – don't just gratefully accept what is offered.

I submitted photos of pieces I had made to Debbie Stoller's call for submissions for *Stitch n' Bitch Nation* and bam! discovered that there was a demand for the things I made. I had already been selling/swapping finished items but I have never enjoyed doing production work – making the same thing over and over again bores me. Pattern writing seemed like a great way to respond to "oh I love that, can I buy it from you?"

Do you earn most of your income from design work or do you do other things as well?

At this point I am netting maybe $200 - $300 in a good month ($50 - $100 in bad months). I have not been spending much time actively promoting or publishing, though, and I have been taking a very long break from submitting to publications. My plan for 2010 is to have my website revamped this summer (and I'm going to pay someone to do it for me, although I intend to learn how to better use WordPress at some point), and then work on finishing up a batch of designs that have been in various phases of incompleteness for several months to *hrm, years* now, and every time I show my hand-dyed yarns off at the SnB, I get the nudges of "so when can I buy that on Etsy?" and think I might do some very limited runs and see if it's profitable.

In 2008 a couple of things happened: I started a new job that has been taking up a lot of my time and energy. I enjoy what I do as a CRM (Cultural Resources Management) archaeologist, but it feels very separate to me from yarncrafting. The second, and rather big thing, was that the nerve impingements in my neck, shoulders, and arms got to a point that I could not ignore (this blog post – http://mkcarroll.com/2008/07/the-devils-playthings – describes it in more detail). I'm also a licensed and practicing massage therapist, so I knew the signs, and I also knew that I had to rest my hands as much as possible. That meant cutting way back on knitting, crocheting, drawing, and using the computer, which meant putting my yarncrafting business on hold. I did try outsourcing more of the sample knitting and crocheting work but it got so hit-or-miss and stressful I chose to let go of trying that for now. I was fortunate enough to not need the income, and design work is currently the least profitable of my personal income streams, so I could let it go fallow.

And, actually, there was a third – one of the reasons I'd been doing more massage work was because the primary at the massage clinic, my dad, was out for a few months. He was very, very sick, and Mom and siblings and I were getting very stressed out about it. It took several months for him to recover, and today he's back to being the stubborn old coot we know and love. I could spend my one day off during the week sitting in front of my computer, or I could spend some of it with my family. Not a difficult choice these days, fortunately. When I started doing design work I was painfully broke and needed every dollar I could make.

The other things I could do I've tried a bit of. Teaching knit/crochet to kids at a couple of museum events, hosting a yarn-tasting at the state library. It's fun every once in a long while for me – I am an introvert and socializing, no matter how fun, is draining for me.

What role does the internet play in your design work these days?

It hasn't replaced walking around and checking out what people are wearing, reading books, flipping through old magazines, and troubleshooting what-I-want/need-in-my-wardrobe, but it can make it more readily accessible. My iPhone is my must-have when I leave the house.

Social media can help, but I've scaled back a bit on that too. For me, I find that I am most comfortable with keeping my personal life to myself, and using social media a bit to bounce around ideas, get recommendations, and see what other people are doing with knit and crochet. I recognize that it will likely mean being less popular as a "personality" but I look to what some other designers have managed to do without being a "personality" and that gives me hope.

What do you see as the most influential traits when it comes to being a successful designer?

A willingness to put in the necessary work. To buckle down and keep producing.

What are your current career goals? How have they changed and why?

As mentioned earlier, I've put the yarn business on the back burner. I have a lot going on with my other jobs and my personal life. A return to producing more patterns is in the works for me, updating my website to make it easier to shop from, and perhaps returning to designing for publications. My living situation is scheduled to change either this summer or early in 2011 and will hopefully mean having more time. Until then, I'm sharpening some of my skills (like taking your online classes!), continuing to scribble ideas down in my notebooks, and taking my time tweaking the designs I've been working on.

What advice would you give a new designer? What advice would you give someone who's been around a while?

New designers: don't invest more than you can afford to lose. Have a plan: what is it that you want to get out of this? Income? Popularity? Then focus on that.

Someone who needs a kickstart: take a break from yarncrafting and do something else, even if it's just a week or two. If it's been a while since you designed and made something for yourself – just yourself, with no thought to how marketable it could be, or which yarn companies might be interested, or how complex it would be to grade different sizes – go do that after you take your break.

What do you like about self-publishing versus working with a big publisher?

Self-publishing: I like being able to control what goes into the patterns, and holy sweet mother, does it take a lot of my time. When I write the pattern, make the sample(s), do all the photos, source the yarn(s), do the layout, do the publishing, do the marketing...it can take several months for me to get a pattern ready for sale.

One of the regrets I have right now is having signed over all copyright of a pattern to a book that turned out to be a best-seller – and not for the "I could have made more money" reason but because I trusted the copyeditor assigned to me and the pattern is full of errors. The editor has been unresponsive, the second printing still has errors, and it's *my name* on it.

KATE ATHERLEY

Website: http://wisehilda.blogspot.com
Twitter: @wisehilda

What do you wish someone had told you when you first started off as a designer? How did you get into the business?

I started out teaching, then selling my designs at the shop where I taught, and it broadened from there – LOVE Ravelry and Patternfish that I can now sell worldwide so very easily. Words cannot explain how amazing this is for me. I built my reputation in Toronto by word-of-mouth, and am using the internet to extend it past this fair city.

Do you earn most of your income from design work or do you do other things as well?

50% teaching, 25% tech editing/writing, 25% pattern sales. (I feel like this is off, should be getting way more from pattern sales. I have just given up the day job so I can focus on this fulltime.)

Has teaching knitting, etc helped you in your design work?

Oh yes. Being a teacher has improved my tech editing and writing enormously. I have an excellent sense of what is difficult to read/understand, and what sort of questions come up on a regular basis, and what needs to be well explained. And I'm significantly less tolerant of poorly written patterns for my own sake and for my students' sake. Being a teacher has also made me understand my own skill level and abilities. Just because I get something doesn't mean someone else will.

What role does the internet play in knit design work these days compared to other more "traditional" information sources? Do you see a special benefit in social media, for example?

It's great – I can get my stuff out there to the entire world. Other than the damn shipping issues, geography is irrelevant.
There's another dark side to such easy publishing, however. There are a lot of people out there publishing absolute rubbish. I had a student in a class recently pay $5 for a pattern on Etsy that didn't even give yarn or gauge info! I'll (grudgingly) forgive a freebie pattern if it's not complete or well written, but I was seriously offended by someone charging money for such crap.

And beyond the obvious stuff like that, there's so much self-published stuff that's not been through a tech editor or even a proofreader. The instructions might (hopefully) be right, but they can be incredibly poorly written. And it leads to such grief on the part of the knitter. We do lose knitters because they get discouraged by these patterns. Just because you got it online doesn't mean it's a good pattern. ARGH. This drives me insane.

And most people just don't know how to write a pattern. The poor quality of submissions I see even at Knitty [*as a technical editor*] is unbelievable. It's all fine in the context of a designer submitting to a publication that has an editor, but the thought of some of those making it out into the world in their original form makes my hair stand on end.

It's got to the point in my classes that I tell people to shy away from self-published freebies unless they come from a designer with a name and/or some experience. I point people to Knitty and Berroco and Lion Brand since I know they are all edited.

I *love* that I can publish corrections and update patterns quickly and easily online (mistakes do happen to everyone, after all), and that I can very quickly and easily look up a pattern to see if there's a new version or fixes or whatever.

As for the advantages of social media and blogs: I can build a following/readership. Cultivate a cult of personality, if you will. And I love being able to get feedback and engage with my customers. I make a point of providing technical support and answering questions. There's another local designer who sells way more than me, and has a bigger name, but I'm slowly catching up because I'm building a reputation for being accessible and helpful, and this other person has a reputation for being less helpful.

So people can know me and know my style, and hopefully come to trust my work.

What sets you apart as a designer? As a teacher? What do you see as important considerations in the design world?

I have a degree in mathematics and it's my key competitive difference. It makes me a good editor and a good pattern writer. First of all, I'm not afraid of the numbers, but also I've got a very solid training in logical thinking and instructional rigor. I know how to write good and complete instructions. It's also part of what makes me a good teacher.

Now, it's not required, but it means I'm a one-stop-shop. Some designers are amazing but suck at the tech side of things. There are designers out there who are more creative than me, but may not be able to write a pattern. I will never be Norah Gaughan for creativity and innovation, but there's a place for solid and accessible designs that are well-written.

I do believe strongly that great designers need to understand garment construction and fit. The February Lady sweater, for example, may be popular, and it may be well-written, but it's actually a terrible design. Have you knitted it? It's incredibly poochy and unflattering around the armholes and sleeves and looks like hell on many body types.

What are your current career goals? How have they changed and why?

I've only just started into this as my career – used to be a sideline. I gotta gets me a book deal. I have an idea – and now have time to write up a proposal. That's my objective at the moment. The book deal raises my name recognition so I can teach more. Love teaching – that will remain a focus for me. This is not about all my income coming from patterns – but I would like that number to grow. I also love tech editing.

What advice would you give a new designer? What advice would you give someone who's been around a while but needs a kickstart?

- **GET YOUR PATTERNS PROOFREAD!!!**
- Build a plan.
- Understand your competitive difference and focus on that and exploit it.
- Learn more about clothing fit, construction and design. Just because it looks good on/fits you doesn't mean it looks good on/fits everyone.

KAY GARDINER & ANN SHAYNE

Authors, *Mason-Dixon Knitting* and *Mason-Dixon Knitting Outside The Lines*

Website: http://www.masondixonknitting.com

How did you get into design, and how did the blog start? Which came first, chicken or egg?

The blog started back in the Early Blog Era (2003) as a grand experiment in public correspondence. We basically took our prolific daily emails to each other, and started putting them on the internet, with pictures. Kay had to buy a digital camera for the purpose of blogging. Big learning curve!
We never dreamed of designing a single thing until 2005, when we found ourselves with a book deal committing us to 30 fabulous patterns. By then we did have a lot of ideas. Not so much "designs" as things we wanted to knit but found very few patterns for in the world of handknitting at that time. We love collaborating with other designers – amateur and professional – who share our enthusiasm for Things Not Previously Knitted. (Or things that are under-knitted).

You've pretty much singlehandedly boosted both dishcloths and log cabin blankets into the stratosphere. What's it like to be known as someone with such specialization? How does it feel to be the Empresses of the Great Dishcloth Dynasty? Did that specialization help nab people's attention early on?

Well, it might be a little like Christopher Walken trying to get a role playing a character who's not creepy. He kind of owns that category. People are surprised to learn that we knit things that are not square, despite the fact that we knit things that are not square all the time! But we're thrilled that our instinct about blankets and other home items had such resonance with knitters. To us it felt like a gap in what was available for knitters. It felt like a big exciting world of color play and inventive, self-driven projects, that much of the designer world was not that interested in at that time. When we look at the thousands of blankets on Ravelry.com now, we feel pretty good about being the ones to put so many blankets out there, and to show that these kinds of items are worthy of being presented in beautiful book form. We think this kind of knitting has real staying power. People are always going to enjoy knitting blankets and other home items, and these are the kinds of projects that become family heirlooms, because they don't have to fit, they don't wear out, and they're so personal.

What have you brought to your design career from your previous/concurrent professional life?

Both Ann and I were drawn to write knitting books because we are so drawn to writing itself, and so passionate about the subject of knitting. We actually enjoy typing, no kidding. I fully expect that I will either knit a few rows or type a paragraph or two, after I am technically deceased. "And one more thing!" – will be my epitaph. Ann is the same way – the fingers move very quickly and the punctuation skills are a matter of religious fervor.

Ann worked in the publishing industry, editing BookPage, a magazine for bookstores and libraries, for many years. I had worked for years as a trial and appeals lawyer, which involves a lot of
writing. So we both have a solid grounding in describing, explaining, and finding something to say
about anything and everything. We didn't think enough had been said about knitting. We still
don't! Knitting is a deep, deep subject to us, full of both humor and human interest. Knitting is
often a metaphor for other aspects of life. So we wanted to write about knitting. Paradoxically,
though, we had noticed that books of writing about knitting did not hold our interest unless they
also had actual knitting – patterns and pictures – in them. A book about knitting makes you want
to knit (as a cookbook will make you hungry), and the reader could feel disappointed if there's no
knitting. So to write the kind of books we wanted to write, we had to show knitting and give patterns and basically turn people onto the kind of knitting we find so compelling.

*What do you wish you'd known about the industry going in? And where do you see the handknitting industry headed
and why?*

I think the market for some designers' work – knitting patterns – is going to be more and more an
online-based business. Especially since Ravelry, it has become so easy to see something someone
else has knitted, desire to knit it yourself, and immediately acquire the pattern through a download. At the same time, we think there will always be a place for books or other collections of multiple designs by a single designer or from the point of view of an author/designer. There is something
about the object of a book, and the ability to leaf through a related group of patterns, that is irre-
sistible to us despite the thousands of individual patterns available online. Designers now have to
negotiate these two worlds of traditional publishing and online publishing, and figure out where
their work fits in and the best way to present their work to knitters. The yarn manufacturers are
starting to recognize this change in the delivery system for "pattern support" for their yarns. I
think we will see more and more individual pattern sales, but that this will make designers with a
very distinctive body of work or authors with a strong point of view stand out more than they did
before, when pattern books were the only way.

*What does the blog provide you in terms of interaction with readers, skill-honing, friendship, etc...? What other
forms of social media do you use, if any?*

The blog is still like a clubhouse for us. We love the comments, we love the emails with readers, the
information and humor they bring us. We love being able to get up in the morning and blog. It has
never gotten old or seemed like a job.

Ann is on a real social-media kick these days. She's Facebooking and also Twittering. Kay has a
moribund Facebook page. We both spend a lot of time on Ravelry, which is such a miraculous way
of connecting with other knitters and finding more stuff that we just gotta knit RIGHT NOW.

What are your future goals for knit-related work?

We're going to continue chugging along, knitting and thinking about knitting, following the ideas

that are interesting to us right now, and putting them out there when and how we can.
What's your "brand" all about? or, how do you explain what you do to non-knitters?

We write about knitting, and it's funny. That's about all you can say to non-knitters. The analogy that always seems best to explain it to a non-knitter is cookbooks. Before Julia Child, cookbooks were just recipe books. Now cookbooks are lots of different things, but they clearly are more than lists of ingredients and instructions, and they usually bear the author's distinctive voice, approach, and style; the recipes almost become secondary. We write knitting books with a point of view and a personality. Our books are as concerned with the creative impulse, the question of "why do people find knitting so compelling" – as they are about particular patterns. We are always finding new things to knit, obsessions that are long- or short-term. We love knitting and we are always trying to help other people see what we love about it.

What are your dealbreakers in terms of contracts, projects, etc? What won't you do, or sign?

I don't think I could possibly list what we wouldn't do or sign. But in terms of projects, books or magazine columns or otherwise, we have never done something just to do it. We've always had something we wanted to say or accomplish through the particular book or other project. In this sense our books and other writing have a lot in common with the blog; they flow from that impulse to communicate with like-minded knitters out there.

JILLIAN MORENO

Website: http://knittingfrau.blogspot.com
Twitter: @jillianmoreno

Who are you, Jillian Moreno? Apart from being my fairy knitmother, that is…

I started out at Interweave Press in the 1990's and was part of the launch team for Interweave Knits. Also at Interweave, I worked in new product development, marketing and publishing, and then started designing knitting patterns in 2000. I designed for Knitty in the very first issue and have been working with Amy since as a designer, and as staff since 2005.

Amy and I co-authored two books – *Big Girl Knits* and *More Big Girl Knits* (both from Potter Craft) – and I have had many designs published in books and mags. I started the Curvy Knits pattern series with Classic Elite, and designed the series for two years.

Currently most of my work is with Knitty.com wearing a long list of hats – Editor, Knittyspin; Advertising Manager; Catalyst (my favorite job title ever), and Book Review Editor.

Where do you see the handknitting/design industry heading?

Indieland, maybe we should have a theme park.

Designers have to be supremely organized and have a huge output to make a living working exclusively with magazines, books and yarn companies – the money just isn't there. The biggest shifters for independent publishing are Knitty and Ravelry for patterns. Knitty first gave independent designers a showcase, and Ravelry gave designers a venue to sell patterns. Cat Bordhi has done fantastic things for independent book publishing with her brilliant visionary retreats. I think the latest wave of on-line classes are genius too. Stefanie Japel seems to have planted that seed and lots of other designers are following.

All of these things put all of the control (and cost) into a designer's own hands, with none of the constraints that yarn companies, magazines, publishers and shops have.

Independent publishing has made the designing world friendlier. There's an awful feeling of competition and isolation when working with big companies.

What do you wish someone had told you when you first started off as a designer? How did you get into the business?

I initially started designing as part of the team the launched Interweave Knits, as part of the staff projects. I started designing more after choosing to stay home with my kids, to keep my sanity more than anything. I knew nothing about the design side when I started designing. I knew about the business side from my job at Interweave.

What I wish someone had told me at the beginning: take classes, ask questions, don't sell yourself short. When an editor says follow your ideas – they have some strict parameters they aren't telling you about that they will change your pattern to fit – number of pages to use per pattern, pattern complexity, types and amounts of yarn.

How does your non-design work (i.e. editing Knittyspin, etc) inform your pattern design? Do you have time to design much now?

I love seeing what other designers are doing. Looking at submissions and talking to other designers keeps me excited about designing. I only design a little now, I hit a design wall last year, just burned out. I didn't knit at all for a while and now I'm happily learning new techniques by knitting other designers' patterns and just enjoying it all.

I also spend most of my fibery time spinning and puzzling out that which goes into the making of yarn.

What role does the internet play in knit design work these days compared to other more "traditional" information sources? Do you see a special benefit in social media, for example? How do you use social media?

The internet is the most fantastic tool for designers. It allows designers to easily have their own companies, selling patterns, e-books, holding classes. It's created a community for designers that wasn't there before – there's such a feeling of support whether to answer a question or offer a kindness when something goes awry.

Using social media is a great marketing tool, but it's work. You need to choose which outlets you'll actually use. It's worse to have a blog or a Facebook page for your business and never update it than to not have one at all.

What do you see as the most influential traits/activities when it comes to being a successful designer? What do great designers have in common, or have that sets them apart from lesser ones?

Originality – following their own vision; organization – being able to get the work done; passion – a curiosity to explore, a burning desire figure ideas out and make them work; common sense – knowing when to outsource, ask for help, or just walk away.

See and be seen especially when you're new both on line and in print. It's amazing how quickly a designer can become recognized.

What are your current career goals? How have they changed and why?

Individual pattern sales – I'm getting back to designing on my own time frame. I really enjoyed working for yarn companies and writing the books. I learned that I could really do anything I set my mind to, and I learned where I still need to learn.

Mostly it comes down to time, I'm a stay home mom, I have a part time (or more) job with Knitty. com. Designing on someone else's timeline didn't work for me. I'm dreaming about a couple of things – patterns for handspun yarns and totally customizable knitting patterns.

What advice would you give a new designer? What advice would you give someone who's been around a while but needs a kickstart?
Be honest with yourself. What do you want to do? What excites you? Designing is work, it's a job, and like all jobs, some days it flat out sucks. If on the good days what you're designing and who you're working for doesn't compel you to get out of bed and get started, or to carve out time to work, you need to rethink because you're headed for burnout.

It is hard to turn a hobby no matter how passionate you are about it into a job, it's very easy to lose sight of what led you there in the first place. Don't forget to knit just for joy.

What are your pet peeves as an editor?

Not following guidelines, being out of contact, not having a range of sizes. Just not doing it – we had a designer for *More Big Girl Knits* just not send in her work, all along saying – it's coming, it's coming, then she just dropped out of contact. I think it was a month before the photo shoot. We had to scramble.

What stands out as good or great when you get a design submission?

Is it exciting? Will people want to knit it? Is it knittable? For Knittyspin, the photography is very important.

We all look at the same websites, catalogs, fashion and design magazines, Japanese knitting magazines, couture shows – there is a big difference between being inspired by or using as a jumping off point a sweater you saw in Anthropologie for a design than flat out copying it and claiming it as original.

What happens when all the superficial knitting fans get bored and fall away?

The internet compresses time. I think it's kept knitting popular at a higher level than it would have been otherwise. The concept of viral patterns wouldn't exist, and those alone keep the craft alive. Online communities like Ravelry let the faithful and obsessed find and hold each other close, and the casual knitters can come and go. The internet provides the free, too. Before the internet there was a higher cost to keeping your knitting fix – purchasing magazines and books, spending the time/gas to go out to find other knitters. Now you can use the internet at any level as your enthusiasm ebbs and flows.

Pattern sizing. Talk to me.

Sizing has become political in knitting. There was a time not too long ago when there was nothing, or not much stylish, available above a 36"-38" finished bust, that's why Amy and I published Big Girl Knits. Now more than 50% of patterns that I see go above 50". The reality is not every pattern will work structurally at all sizes big or small, patterns would have to be much more complexly written and still the larger sizes wouldn't look exactly the same, which would lead to longer patterns, and fewer patterns in each magazine issue , book or pattern booklet. Then knitters would complain that 1) the patterns are too complex to follow 2) there are not enough patterns in the magazine/booklet/book. Another option would to make all the garment patterns so simple in style that they are easy to size up and down, and no one would be happy with a magazine full of drop shouldered boxes.

I see it in a couple of ways – look at how many more options there are now for plus sized patterns, every single magazine, nearly every single knitting media outlet, responded to the need for bigger sizing, and for articles on customizing patterns. To me that's incredible. Did anyone say thanks? There's very little appreciating going on, only asking for more.

Here's the part where I'll get booed off the stage. If you do not learn to adjust patterns in some way for your body no matter your size, you as a knitter are at the mercy of the media (all the magazines, books, booklets, single patterns), you are letting them tell you what you can wear. Take control of your knitting like you do the rest of your life. Not only am I fat, I'm short and have short arms. There are no or few patterns for short women or for short arms, and very few patterns that tell you where or how to adjust for that.

There are no perfect patterns for anyone at any size, full stop. And it is not economically feasible for the knitting media to keep adding sizes or specifics to every pattern. I would love a magazine that's called: Short/ Stumpy Armed/ Fat- with big boobs and butt, but I do have a waist – though not as much as I imagine/Mostly Cable, but Some Lace/Only using the yarn I currently have in my stash/ Really quick knits that look totally complex/and Every Pattern Would Look Freaking Fantastic On Me Every Time without Doing Math.

If knitters keep clamoring for the patterns that can't exist, they are no longer advocating for themselves, they are victimizing themselves.

MELANIE FALICK

Website: http://www.melaniefalickbooks.com
Twitter: @ STC_Craft

How did you get your start in the industry? What do you wish you'd known going in?

In the early 1990s I was doing a lot of freelance writing and editing. I started knitting during my free time and decided that I wanted to work in craft publishing, so began pursuing editing and writing opportunities in that area. A big break came when I went to the first Stitches and met some people from Rowan who were organizing knitting-themed trips in the UK. I ended up going on a trip to the Shetland Islands and Outer Hebrides and writing articles for Vogue Knitting, Knitter's, Fiberarts, and the Rowan magazine. I can't really think of anything I wish I had known going in. I was following my bliss and felt really lucky.

How have the positions you've held over the years shaped your opinion of the industry, and where it's headed? What overall business-related trends stand out to you?

All of my experience has been in the publishing end of the industry, which has probably changed most dramatically in the last five or so years because of the surge in popularity of knitting and the DIY movement in general and the emergence of blogs, Ravelry, online magazines, the selling and giving away of patterns via PDF downloads, etc. Basically, the internet has both given us an opportunity to grow and created a lot more competition. At this point, publishers really need to rethink the way we work and make changes to adapt to the marketplace.

As the author of Knitting in America/America Knits [author's note: same book, different titles on different editions]*, you've seen some of the top designers at work in their own surroundings, which is not something an editor normally gets to see – what really stood out for you about the successful designers you profiled compared to others you've worked with over the years? Did it inform your editorship at Interweave Knits?*

I can't really compare designers whose homes I've visited and with whom I've had the opportunity to speak in-depth (like those profiled in *Knitting in America*) with others I've worked with but haven't gotten to know as well. When I was working on *Knitting in America*, I recognized that it was a unique and special opportunity. I feel bonded to many of the people who participated in that process and have learned a lot from them. I have always been interested in the person behind the designs and the culture behind the stitches, and that is definitely something I continued to explore as the editor of Knits.

You really set the style for Interweave Knits early on. What did you want to see from Knits that you weren't getting in the magazines that were already on the market?

I think I may have helped to break the mold of what a knitting magazine was "supposed to be." I tried to create a smart magazine with beautiful designs, strong technical content, and interesting writing, all of which reflected the richness of the knitting culture.

Do you come from a visual arts background? It seems that all your books – not just the ones you've written but also the ones you publish at Melanie Falick Books/STC Craft – have a very distinctive visual style.

Whether I'm writing or editing a book, I always need to have a vision for it when I start. If I can't envision it in my head at least in a general way, then I can't imagine committing to making it. So, while I don't have a formal education in visual arts, I do seem to have a visual sensitivity.

What do you wish designers (or even the general public) knew about knitting book production? How long does it take to create a successful knitting book, start to shelf?

Knitting book production is difficult and requires a huge amount of time from a team of talented, dedicated professionals. At STC Craft, typically we give our authors 9-12 months to write the manuscript and then it takes about another 9 months for us to edit, create photography, design, and then send all of the materials to the printer and get them back in book form. We take longer than some other publishers, in part because we print most of our books in Asia, so it takes a long time for them to be shipped to the States after they are printed. We are definitely looking at ways to shorten the process without sacrificing quality. Sometimes I refer to what we do at STC Craft as "boutique publishing" since we devote so much attention to details, which takes a lot of time.

Where do you see the publishing industry headed as regards knitting/crafts?

The publishing industry, including the knitting/crafts segment of it, is definitely focused on learning how to embrace digital technology.

Have you seen an evolution over time in terms of designers' rights? How have things changed in the past decade? Do more authors and designers ask to keep their rights to patterns, and so on, or...?

I have heard designers talking about keeping the rights to their patterns recently, although it hasn't become a big issue with our authors thus far. I'm not sure how our contract compares to others.

What makes a designer stand out to you from the crowd? What makes you sit up and take notice, editorially or professionally?

A designer stands our when the designs s/he creates are unique and well-executed, when patterns are well written, when s/he is able to meet deadlines, and s/he is a pleasant person with whom to work. These days, if a designer wants to write a book, it is more important than ever that s/he has an established marketing platform and is committed to promoting the work long-term.

How do you (and your staff at MFB/STC) use social media? Has the internet changed how the public interacts with you, the content publisher?

We have a blog, we tweet, and we have a fan group on Facebook, which means that the public has easier access to us than ever. I am more involved in the blog than anything else, but I am trying to find time to learn how to work with the other forms of social media. To sell books, we need to reach the public in these ways; the challenge is to figure out how to do it in an interesting, graceful way, so people are happy to hear from us.

JANET SZABO

Website: http://bigskyknitting.com

Where do you see the handknitting-and-crochet/design industry heading?
I'm really not sure. I think I would have a better handle on it were it not for this economic meltdown that has muddied the waters so dramatically. I do think that modes of information delivery are changing and will continue to change. There will always be a segment of the population that wants hard copy (even after I offered a digital delivery option for my cables newsletter Twists and Turns®, more than half the subscribers chose to stick with the hard copy), but more and more knitters want information electronically.

I've also seen a shift toward not wanting to pay for information. Knitters will always seek out a website or YouTube video that has the information they want before they will pay for it. The challenge is to figure out what kinds of information don't package well that way and market those products.

What do you wish someone had told you when you first started off as a designer? How did you get into the business?

Well, anything anyone would have told me 15 years ago is actually useless information to me now because it's so out-of-date and the industry has changed so much.

I had NO plans to become a knitting designer. I worked for a software company in Baltimore in the early 90s doing tech support and training classes. When we moved to Montana in 1993, I was offered a similar job here, with a pay of $7 an hour – less than half of what I had been making in Baltimore. And it's not cheap to live in Montana. My husband preferred that I not put our one year-old daughter in daycare just to go to work and bring home $300 a month. He was the one who suggested I try to make money from my knitting ("because you're always knitting"). It started with the finishing book, then the Master Knitting program, and then the designing, and went from there.

Do you earn most of your income from design work or do you do other things as well?

I earn the *least* amount of money from my design work. The majority of my income comes from book sales, followed by teaching, followed by designing and pattern sales. Last year, for example, it was about 60% books, 20% teaching, 10% from the newsletter, and 10% from pattern sales.

How does your non-design work inform your pattern design?

Well, the biggest thing is that writing books about cables really stretches my cabling technique boundaries, and the things I learn along the way tend to show up in my designs. It's one thing to

write about a really cool cabling technique, but that technique is more useful to knitters if they can see it applied in a knitting project.

What role does the internet play in knit design work these days compared to other more "traditional" information sources? Do you see a special benefit in social media, for example? How do you use social media in your business?

Social media is rather a necessary evil. Knitters have come to expect easy access to designers (especially indie designers), so having a blog, or a Twitter/Facebook account are almost requirements. I find, though, that they take away a lot of time that I could spend designing.

What do you see as the most influential traits/activities when it comes to being a successful designer? What do great designers have in common, or have that sets them apart from lesser ones?

I think what sets great designers apart from lesser ones is a commitment to their craft (and I mean craft in the most complimentary terms) – a willingness to constantly push the knitting boundaries, to constantly hone their skills, and to behave in a professional manner. This recent explosion of everyone calling themselves a "designer" has really diluted the value of that title, sadly. It took a number of years of work for me to feel comfortable calling myself a designer, because I felt I had to work hard to be worthy of being called one. Is someone who designs and writes the pattern for a simple scarf the same as someone who designs and writes a complicated cabled sweater in 10 sizes? While I think it's important to encourage all knitters to explore designing their own stuff, I see a difference between "designer" (with a small d) and "Designer" (with a capital D). And that makes me sound like a snob.

What are your current career goals? How have they changed and why?

My current career goals are to finish the second and third cabling books, and then I might go off and find something else to do. I am getting a little tired of having to justify (constantly) the fact that I charge for the knitting information that is in my head. I've always said that when this isn't fun or profitable any more, I'll do something different.

What advice would you give a new designer? What advice would you give someone who's been around a while but needs a kickstart?

I would tell new designers that they will spend less time knitting than they ever thought possible, and more time on all the other "stuff" that goes along with any small business. Hard work and talent don't guarantee success anymore (unfortunately), and they probably shouldn't quit their day job if they have one. I don't know that I would go the "direct-to-knitter" route if I were doing it again, although it has worked out well for me.

Self-publishing versus working with big publishers, bookwise?

Oh, my goodness. It's hard for me to speak with any authority to the subject of working with big publishers. My only experience with them came in shopping around my finishing book. I sent the proposal to half a dozen book publishers, and got lots of pink slips. Someone fairly high up at [publisher name redacted] actually *called* my house one day and expressed interest in the idea, but said that they had just hired a new acquisitions editor and that she would have the final say. Sure enough, about two weeks later I got a letter from said acquisitions editor panning the idea. I was so frustrated at that point (with nothing to lose) that I called *her* and asked for some feedback. If she had said, "You suck at writing, find something else," I would have given up right there.

She said, "I am a knitter, and I hate to finish sweaters. Why on earth would I pay money for a book on finishing techniques?" When I suggested that perhaps knitters hated finishing because no one had ever shown them how to do it properly, she snorted and said, "It's just not a sexy knitting topic.

We're not interested." The "I Hate to Finish Sweaters" book is titled in her honor. She actually did me a huge favor, now that I look back on it, because I decided then and there that if any books were going to be written and published with my name on them, I was going to do it myself.

And I haven't changed my mind about that part. How many publishers out there would have let me write the kind of books I write? Not many.

Can you tell me more about your newsletter? (Twists and Turns®)

I started traveling and teaching back in the late 90s and discovered I really liked it. However, I had a 2-year-old and a 7-year-old at home, and it was a logistical nightmare, even with a very support-ive husband. I thought about how I could keep "teaching" and decided it could come in the form of a newsletter with cable designs and cabling articles. I taught at Stitches East in the fall of 1999 and floated the idea to students in my classes. I got enough positive feedback about the idea that I started it in January 2000.

I am really proud of the fact that I have published it – on schedule, four times a year – for ten years. Sometimes I look back and think, "Wow, when did I have time to design and knit all that stuff?" I am also proud of the fact that I was able to provide a place where newbie designers could get their feet wet without the pressure of designing for the big magazines.

The weird thing about the newsletter, though – and part of the reason I decided that ten years is enough – is that it never grew beyond a certain point. I've always had the same number of sub-scribers at any given time, although I've had almost ten times that number in total number of sub-scribers over the past ten years. Perhaps if I had spent more time assessing the demographics of my subscriber base I might have an answer to that puzzle.

The one thing I am concerned about is "Will I still be able to churn out designs if I don't have a self-imposed deadline every three months?" On the other hand, I won't be limited to designing things with cables any more. So we'll just have to see how that works out. I am pretty self-disci-plined and if I say I am going to put out one new pattern a month, I am pretty sure I'll be able to stick with that schedule.

Any other advice to impart?

The best piece of advice? Hire a good tech editor.

MELISSA WEHRLE

Website: http://www.neoknits.com
Twitter: @neoknits

Where do you see the handknitting-and-crochet/design industry heading?

It is hard to say exactly where the handknitting industry is going, but I do know that it will not suffer the same fate as in the 80s. The internet has helped foster a knitting community online and in real life. Even if no one in your immediate area is a hand knitter, it is easy enough to connect with others through the internet. Knitting is no longer a solitary activity that can easily be put aside, it is a group activity where opinions and help can be found at any hour of the day. Until I joined my first knitting group, I used to knit maybe one sweater a year. After joining the group, I felt motivated to show off my progress and to actually finish things in a timely manner. I was also inspired by what others were knitting and would learn about new things, techniques, and patterns. When Ravelry came along, I met even more knitting friends right in my neighborhood, something that would have been very hard to do on my own.

One other thing that is certain is the future of the industry is definitely a digital one. What started with indie designers offering instant downloads has grown into fully digital magazines like Twist Collective. We will begin to see more and more mainstream publishers get on the ball with digital media and publishing. Of course there is the obvious, with digital magazine subscriptions or downloadable patterns, but there is so much more to explore such as podcasts, videos, blogs – even apps on smartphones.

I think what surprises me about the push toward digital media is some of the more established designers' hesitation to use it as a promotional tool. Many worry about knitters sharing PDF files. Some don't feel the need to keep a blog, use Facebook, Ravelry, or Twitter and think it is just a waste of time. I can understand that change is hard, but with new talent flooding the market at a very fast pace due to the internet, competition is too fierce to ignore the digital world.

What do you wish someone had told you when you first started off as a designer? How did you get into the business?

I wish someone had told me that I didn't have to accept every offer that came across the table and that it is OK to negotiate contract and fees. When you are a new designer, it's really exciting to see your name in print and sometimes that excitement gets in the way of good business sense. You shouldn't have to sell away your rights and hard work for nothing! You also don't have to accept everything that comes your way from a scheduling point of view. If you accept two projects both due the same time and only have four weeks, you're going to find handknitting design to become very stressful, very quickly.

I truly got into the business when I decided to self publish my first pattern. I had been published in a book a few years before, but did not really have much interest in pursuing it further at that time. The amazing thing about my lack of interest or maybe even lack of confidence was I had attended design school for knitwear design! It just seemed too hard to write a knitting pattern on my own. After my first pattern was published in *Stitch N' Bitch Nation* (Lucky Clover Wrap), I started a blog in reaction to a knit-a-long going on at the time. I was still mainly writing about my own personal knitting projects, though.

One day I had decided that I wanted a sweater and couldn't find a pattern for it. So I designed the Grannie Smith cardigan for myself, never really thinking that others would have any interest in purchasing the pattern. I put pictures of that first design up on my blog to get reaction and to see if anyone would be interested in the pattern. Turns out knitters were very interested, and that pattern is still a best seller to this day.

With that one self-published pattern under my belt, I was then contacted by Sundara of Sundara Yarns to design something with her yarn. She was just beginning and her yarns were beautiful, so I jumped at the chance. I gained quite a bit of nice exposure from that partnership.

From there, I got involved with One Planet Yarn and Fiber, an online yarn store that had 3 exclusive lines of yarn. I became their Creative Director and oversaw all of the other designers and helped build up our own pattern library for the yarn brands they held exclusively. I also got up the courage to start submitting to magazines, books, and began publishing more designs on my own.

Do you earn most of your income from design work or do you do other things as well?

Most of my income comes from my full time job as a sweater designer in the industry, which is machine, not hand- knitting related. The split is about 95/5. Since my full time job is design related, it informs my pattern design in many ways. I am constantly surrounded by yarn, stitch, and trend information and it constantly shapes how I approach my knitting design. It inspires me in so many ways and I am able to file all the little details away for future hand knit designs.

Sometimes the constant influx of information can be a little overwhelming though. It's very easy to get a little ahead of the curve and be too forward. It's also really easy to do trendy, much harder to do wearable for several seasons. You just have to know how to filter out the good from the bad, take pieces here and there, and then fine tune it all into something you hope other knitters will want to take the time to knit. I find that hand knit design is different from mass market design in the area of trend vs. timeless design. When you spend so much time making a hand knit sweater, which sometimes stretches to the next season for one reason or another, timeless design is very important. If it's so super trendy that in a year you won't want to wear it anymore, that isn't really a good use of the knitters' time or money.

What role does the internet play in knit design work these days?

I think the internet plays a huge role in design work these days. Anyone with a computer anywhere in the world is able to access you and your designs. When self-publishing, you are also able to publish instantly. The wait period is only as long as it takes you to knit, write up and tech edit the design. And on the knitter's end, the internet provides instant gratification with PDF downloads. There is no need to wait for that next book or magazine to be published or the pattern to arrive in the mail. They can cast on for a new project that very second.

With the help of the internet, it's very easy to create an instant design business. Getting into print to get your name out there isn't the only option anymore. All you need is a blog, post a few designs, and set up pattern downloads. Or you don't even need the blog now, with Ravelry's pattern store feature. The internet has really leveled the playing field when it comes to individuals trying to compete for a piece of the pie. Designers can play by their own rules and not be subject to contracts and losing rights to their designs. Of course just because it is that easy to become a designer doesn't mean you don't still have to work hard to be successful. Being represented in traditional print media reaches a captive audience that has been built up over time. Starting out fresh and on your own is just that – a clean slate.

When looking at traditional information sources, their actions speak louder than words when determining how important the internet is in the design business. More and more print magazines are going digital, have websites, video tutorials, sell patterns online, have blogs, etc. The internet is a crucial part of the business and the need for that internet presence is becoming more important that ever.

Social media is a very helpful tool in promoting my business. Personally, I use Twitter, Ravelry and I have a blog. It allows my readers and followers to get to know me a little better and that I am more than just a name on a sweater design. I have a family, I do stuff, I have other interests and I have feelings. The internet has a way of desensitizing people to the human behind the keyboard, so I like to think that a little "getting to know you" goes a long way. It's also a good way to keep people tuned in to what you are doing and fill in the gaps between new pattern releases.

What do you see as the most influential traits/activities when it comes to being a successful designer? What do great designers have in common, or have that sets them apart from lesser ones?

Determination, patience, professionalism, and attention to detail are all important traits to have if you are going to be successful. It takes a while to build up your portfolio, product, and name. Even if you hit on something big right out of the box, it needs to be followed up with something else equally as engaging. One hit wonders can happen in the knitting world too!

Knowing how to write a clear pattern, make sure the garment fits as it should, and a good technical background in knitwear never hurts either. One poorly-written or -fitting pattern can end a designer's career quicker than anything.

It's really hard work getting something ready to be published, and it doesn't end there. With designers being so accessible via the internet, questions are now sent directly to the designer instead of the magazine or book company that originally published the work. If the pattern is self-published, pattern support is most definitely a designer's responsibility.

Great designers seem to have a few things in common. First, they have a definite style and flow to their work that sets them apart. The easier it is for knitters to pin point their style, the easier it is to gain followers through repeat exposure and familiarity. The designer knows who they are designing for and they know them well.
Great designers also put out new work in a timely manner and keep knitters entertained with blog posts or updates on social media sites. People have short attention spans and once a designer goes off the radar, it's harder to get back in the game.

What are your current career goals? How have they changed and why?

I would really like to be able to support myself through my hand knit design, but I realize it will still need to be supplemented with some other side project. It's pretty hard to eke out a living in the hand knit world, and there are only so many hours in a day. Without the help of sample knitters, there is only so much one designer can possibly accomplish.

I don't have any clear cut goals for the future, but I would absolutely love to have my own yarn line, one that I could have creative control over. Or maybe an online yarn store.

I always thought that I'd just be a designer in the industry 'til I retire, but I realized very quickly that maybe it's not for me. The industry is very stressful and sometimes very uncreative. Hand knit design is my escape from all the craziness and allows me control over design, yarns, and color. The biggest problem that is holding me back is the very big difference in my industry pay vs. my hand knit design pay. While supporting myself with hand knit design is my goal, moving back in with my parents with no health insurance isn't my idea of fun either. It will take careful planning, time and hard work to get to a place where I can feel comfortable financially leaving my full-time gig.

What advice would you give a new designer? What advice would you give someone who's been around a while but needs a kickstart?

New designer: Don't feel like you need to accept every offer that comes across your desk. If the pay is too low, don't waste your time or figure it's a good exchange for exposure. If it's every going to get any easier for a designer to make a living at this, we all need to stick together for one another and for ourselves. Don't be taken advantage of and don't be afraid they won't want to work with you again if you speak up. If they like your work, they like your work no matter what.

To the old school knitter: The internet is your friend! PDFs are not the enemy. Twitter is not going to steal your soul. Trust in the digital revolution, your customer base will grow and everyone will be happy! Mainly you! It's also helpful to take the time to add your old designs to the Ravelry database. It is a lot of work, but worth it when your designs are "rediscovered" by new knitters.

ADINA KLEIN
Creative director, Tahki Stacy Charles

Is being a creative director like being a magazine editor, but for only one yarn line instead of many? What are your day to day duties and responsibilities?

NOOOOO. Well yes and no. Let's start with no first. When you are an editor of a "fashion knitting magazine," what you are selling is a trend and when you are creative director of a yarn company what you are selling is yarn. As an editor you choose garments that support the fashion story you are trying to tell. For example "a feminine story": you'll want lace shawls, and ruffled cardigans and cute embellished tops and fingerless gloves. Yarn amounts don't concern you, skill level – though you want to maintain a balance for your readers – doesn't concern you. Fiber type doesn't concern you: if one yarn company doesn't have the pink you are looking for, you go to another one. Sometimes you'll include a statement piece that few people will actually make but it inspirational and visually exciting will tie all the looks on the other pages together. With a yarn company, basically what you are trying to sell is yarn. If you're lucky you can weave a fashion story together with styling and photography but basically that's not what is supposed to be important. Selling yarn is important.

There is the age-old question among yarn execs as to whether or not the patterns sell the yarn or the yarns sell the pattern. If you look at Debbie Bliss, you could say that her whole aesthetic from garment design to photography to page layouts of her books is what helped build her yarn line. For a company like TSC, and most yarn companies, creating a pattern line is basically a massive, expensive pain in the ass. They become little magazine publishers. They don't have a staff of technical editors, they don't have a staff of people waiting by the phone or computer to answer consumer complaints, so they don't want sweaters that are too hard, that are alienating-ly fashion forward, that have a limited appeal in sizing.

When I begin the season, we come up with a list of yarns that are going forward from last season and usually little snippets of new yarns which are in the development phase. Budgets are as tight as they've ever been, so then we decide how many garments per yarn should get made, how and if we are going to make a free pattern for the internet and (here's what I hate almost more that any other part of working for a yarn company): WHAT THE PROMO SWEATER IS GOING TO BE.

What is a promo sweater, you may ask? It's the sweater that yarn companies offer to the retailers either for a nominal fee or for free if they buy x amount of bags of a certain yarn. These sweaters can't use a lot of yarn because the company doesn't want to pay too much to have them produced, they can't be too hard to make because they are sent to India to be made, and they have to look half way decent hanging on a hanger in a store. When my budgets have been cut and I only have 3 sweaters to sell a yarn, and one basically has to be a t-shirt, it limits my ability to tell any sort of story.

The other gruesome part of working for a yarn company is that you are basically killing yourself for the yarn rep. Not the retailer, not the knitter, the rep. The rep is basically a traveling salesperson who has a territory of yarn shops to which he or she sells. There are some amazing reps out there. And there some not so amazing reps. Some reps wouldn't know a purl stitch from a pearl necklace. Its the reps who represent all your hard work. They are the ones who take it to the retailer and have to get the shop store excited about your yarns and patterns. By the time TNNA has come most of the yarn shops have already put in their orders for the season. So you have to create a line of sweaters that are easily explainable by a third party who may not know a much about yarn besides what you tell them.

Another thing that is different is budget. On a grucling day for a magazine shoot, you shoot maybe 15 shots. You have 2 models. You have a creative director, you have me the fashion director/editor, you have a stylist and styling assistant. You have catering. You have a location. You shoot one or two stories. On my shoots we do 25 to 30 shots a day, with no help, with 1 model. To break up the look of the books I have divided the books so that on one day we'll shoot half of one book with one model in one location and then on another day shoot the second half. (Keeping in mind that a model on any given day will be in 3 or 4 different books).

At a magazine, (and this part I prefer) the creative director, not the editor in chief, gets to see all the photos, does the layouts, and puts in the graphics. The editor has final say but really isn't involved in the spreads of the magazine. So when I am shooting for TSC I am the editor in chief and the creative director, I have to keep in mind what will be on the facing page – if the color is right, if there's a cropped shot on the left hand side, do I want a full body pose on the right? I also often have to cram more than one or two garments per page, so I have to figure out how they'll work together even before I see a single picture. I edit all the images, work with a graphics person to lay out the spreads, pick the type, the color etc. A magazine prints hundreds of thousands of copies. I'm lucky if we print 3000.

And again, the reps. The reps are the reason for your deadline. Everything centers around getting the "look books" to the reps as fast as possible so they can be on the road sooner than the other yarn companies so they can get to the retailers before they've spent all their money on the competition's yarns.

Do you work strictly with an in-house team of designers, or do you use freelancers as well? If you do use freelancers or independent designers, how do you find them/convince them to work for TSC?

I'm proud to say that TSC is one of the few companies that still hires "real" designers. Yes we have a few "house designers" who have been loyal to the company for years and we give them a certain amount of work per season and we have some knitters who make us simple stuff that we don't need a "real designer" to make. Sadly, and you'd think it was the opposite (and it SHOULD BE THE OPPOSITE), we can't pay as much as magazine rates. I'm lucky enough to have strong relationships with industry designers who will work for me at the rates we can provide. And they get designer credit. And through the newsletters I try to profile them. And – here I am tooting my own horn again – I provide them with beautifully styled, well-photographed images of their work for their portfolios. There are some big name companies that pay much more for designs (which they should), but they don't give designer credit and the designer may never know where their sweater or afghan will wind up.

Other companies that have name designers as their creative directors spec and swatch hundreds and hundreds of sweaters and have them knit in India. I can't do that. And I don't want to do that. I believe that the knitwear designer is the most important and most underpaid part of the yarn industry. I have no desire to knit for a living. I admire people who do.

How did you get into the industry? What do you wish you'd known going in?

LOOOOOONG story. Basically I was a film student/writing major. I got out of college and was an assistant feature film editor. I planned to be the Woody Allen of the 90s, I had been working on back to back low budget films, and said I was going to take a break and write a screenplay which was called "Knit 1 Purl 2." It was a teen romance about knitting. To keep me out of trouble, I got a job working for Melissa Matthay at the Yarn Company in NYC. Melissa Matthay was and is one of the old school yarn shop owners with a cigarette hanging out of her mouth and a tape measure around her neck. Rowan was the only company creating patterns you'd be caught dead wearing, and basically a customer would come in and we'd combine yarns and design sweaters for customers on the spot. Melanie Falick was launching her "Knitting in America" book at the shop and she asked to read my screenplay and we became friends. My film got optioned and I got married and divorced to a sound editor and my mom got cancer among other things. And no one was into teen romances at that time, and no one knew what knitting was at that time, and the film was floundering and my husband was a drunk, and Melanie became editor of Interweave Knits and I sent her an email congratulating her and... before I could hit send she called me, frantic for help.

I also somehow got involved with the doing the doggy fashion show at the NYC knit-out. And I was way into knitting then. I went to all the Stitches shows and befriended all the designer/teachers and the vendors, and at that time the Big Apple Knitting Guild was very popular with the NYC-based knitters such as Lily Chin, among others. There was a group that bought a lot of cashmere at School Products etc, and hung out at Barnes and Noble. It was a good escape for me from my bonkers husband and I took every hard core knitting class available. I went to Doily Camp. Ann Feitelson's Fair Isle class, Horst Schultz had me shaking in my boots, Shirley Paden's design class, etc.

One day I got a phone call from David Blumenthal to come in and meet him. I thought he wanted to talk to me about the knit out or something. I sat in his office and he asked for my resume, and I was like "why?" Lily had recommended me to be his personal assistant. And I said I'd make the worst secretary in the world, I'm sloppy, I can't type, and I talk back, so he hired me as design editor. Then my mom died, it was awful and I got an offer to help a woman open a fancy yarn shop (we'll skip that era), and after that I wrote 2 books for Potter Craft for Lion Brand and started freelancing as a stylist for Soho Publishing. They were in the process of making the deal with Lion Brand for knit.1 magazine, and I was familiar with all the yarn etc. It took me 3 years to get promoted to editor in chief of VK but that's basically my story.

What do I wish I knew going in? NOT TO DO IT. Really. I have hard time with hobbies. They tend to take over my life. I could have been a filmmaker who knitted sweaters every once in a while. In the beginning of my career I thought "this is amazing": I believed I was working in an industry that empowered women, I am a nice Jewish girl and I loved the idea that I was helping to perpetuate a tradition passed to me from generations before me.

I thought of the yarn shop as the public "grandma": a community. I thought a fashion editor for a "normal" fashion magazine just gets clothes and makes pictures from what other designers have thought up. I got to come up with ideas of the sweaters. I got to collaborate with some of my heroes in this business.

Granted this recession has really kicked my butt: I lost my dream job, etc. But I feel like (and it's not just our industry), that the world thinks that being able to have a job that lets you be creative should be reward enough. As a creative person, you put your whole being into what you do and you are not compensated because you are an "artist."

I attended a lecture by a quilt artist about a year ago and she said people often ask her how long it takes her to make a quilt and she gets really pissed off because it took her 50+ years to get to the point where she knew all the things: technically, artistically, financially etc. to make the quilt. My boss thinks he flatters me when he says "Oh Adina, you can do that in your sleep" when I come up with a viable way to create pattern books that I am proud of on no budget (using my sister's closet for styling), but it's taken my entire life to have the eye to find the shot, and years of relationships with incredibly talented designers who love me because I make their work look better to work at discounted rates, and my years of training as a filmmaker to be able to organize a set.
My mom used to say that there were 4 anchovies in the whole world. That someone would pick them off their Greek salad and they'd wind up on someone else's pizza. I always say that that us YIPS (yarn industry professionals) are the anchovies of the business. There are very few of us who are fluent in yarn and patterns that should be valued and compensated generously, but are not.

A few years ago you weren't very impressed with online pattern sales, etc. Has your mind changed at all?

Here's what I think.... I get it. I get why a person would download a pattern. It's immediate. It's more environmental. I am the first one to admit that I hate buying CDs when I can download the same thing on iTunes. I don't need another plastic thing in my apartment.

These are all the reasons I hate it:

1. It obliterates the need for an editor, an art director, a photographer, a stylist. It takes the fashion out of knitting. It takes the fantasy out of knitting. It's pretty much destroyed my career.

2. Unless you are tech savvy and want to spend a large part of your working hours working on your website, your blog, your Twitter, etc. you can't be a success as a designer these days. My heroes in this business are eating beans and foreclosing on their homes or abandoning their careers because they simply don't give a damn about the internet. They are designers. They don't want to be blogging, they want to be designing. They don't want to be answering questions from idiot knitters 24 hours a day. Inferior designers who are tech savvy or who have tech savvy boyfriends or sisters or whatever are making money hand over fist and the people who created the foundation of this industry are being left in the dust.

3. It has dumbed down the standards of knitwear design. Why do you think VK has fewer and fewer sweaters? Because the shawls and scarves and socks are what the Ravelers etc. want to make. They don't have to fit, they don't reflect a point of view or a trend, they aren't daring. They are what sells.

4. Needless to say, these kind of designs sell fewer and fewer balls of yarn, which has an impact on the yarn industry as a whole. If knitters are making accessories on size 1 needles, or knitting from their stash, the yarn companies are making less money and buying fewer ads, which gives the magazines smaller budgets, which forces them – in turn – to publish sock patterns, and the cycle repeats itself.

5. If you are a small (and you wouldn't believe how small these companies have gotten) "big name company" like Classic Elite, TSC etc., you can't afford a technical staff to support e-commerce for its patterns. Not to mention the "high end" yarn companies are terrorized by the retailers and are threatened if they give stuff away for free. We need to create pattern books to sell the yarn, but we need the retailers to buy the pattern books to pay for our expenses. They won't buy them if we're giving them away for free on the internet or selling them on e-commerce sites. Again, worse than me, the designer suffers, because rather than paying for new designs, the yarn companies are forced to dig into their archives to give away patterns the shops can't sell. Which means no new revenue for the designers, and no job for creative directors.

People say to me all the time "you should blog" or "start your own magazine" etc, but the fact of the matter is I hate being a single woman. I hate having to deal with the garbage and the printer ink and I really liked putting on a skirt and some lipstick and going to work. I don't have any desire to run a business out of my home, I have a one bedroom apartment. Great for the suburban mom who's a brilliant designer, great for the homebody. My cousin is editor in chief of NY maga-zine. And when I got promoted to editor in chief of VK, he asked me what he thought my main job responsibility was and I said that I thought it was the same as being director of a film. You have all these extremely talented people who are the best at what they do and your job is to harness their talents to achieve your vision. I love the process of creative collaboration...self-publishing has made that obsolete.

It's made everyone Anna Wintour. I understand bucking authority. But I love points of view...I loved reading VK and seeing what fashion knitting was and seeing what the crafty knitters were knitting at IK. Self-publishing has made everybody an expert with no expertise.

On the flip side, I appreciate that designers are under-compensated and should be able to get additional revenue from their patterns.. I think they should be making 10 times more than what they are. I think that Twist Collective in some ways is on the right track from what I know about them. They create editorial content, they shoot cohesive stories), the articles are free and then you can buy whatever pattern you want and the money goes back to the designer.

I'd love to do something similar, but don't have the energy to find an IT person. I want a staff, an office, someone else to deal with the copy machine jamming. My own life is heinous enough.

What are the traits of a good designer? What about a truly great one?

Now that I have the job I have the definition of a great designer has changed, sadly. The two best designers in the business, whose work brings me joy and reminds me why I do what I do, are, on paper, the worst possible designers for the job I do now. However, I fight to the death to work with them and will quit before I can't use them. A great designer...

- Understands fashion and trends, but also understands that a sweater is an investment in time and money and is not disposable.
- Truly loves the acrobatics of knitting techniques: will use the magic of knitting to create three-dimensional garments that flatter all women and empower knitters to feel like they are technical divas.
- Works within the confines of the assignment...if the design is for a magazine, skill level need not apply, if the design is for a yarn company they must create a sweater that can be sized easily, whose directions can be written by 2nd tier pattern writers.
- Provides sweaters that look like what they were assigned, be it their own sketch or a maga-zine swipe.
- That communicates with the editor/creative director if a yarn is not working, if a color is not working, if the only way to achieve a look will require extra yarn, advanced skills, etc.
- (and this sounds silly): meets deadlines, provides clear patterns, isn't a diva.

What advice would you give someone starting out in the design field today?

Go to law school! Work at McDonalds! Become a trophy wife or husband! Here's the thing...a designer needs to establish a name for herself and the best way is getting published in a magazine. The money is not going to come from that, the money is going to come from establishing relationships with yarn companies and "low end" publishers like DRG and Annie's Attic, "Leisure Arts" etc.

Not so much in my present position, but as editor of a magazine you are looking for a submission that has a nice sketch, a swatch and usually a "swipe" of a look from a magazine of what you are aiming for. Label everything. Put your name and email on a tag on swatches, and label the swatch next to your sketch. If you are new, including photos of finished work is important.

If your sweater gets picked and you get the job, be as unobnoxious as possible – I have horror stories up the gazoo which I will elaborate upon. Often you may disagree with a color combination, or you have a creative question that you can answer yourself. Leave the editors alone, at least in the beginning. For the first few assignments, bite your lip if you disagree about color or silhouette, do the job impeccably and on time. Then again, if you can save an editor from embarrassing herself, make sure she knows the yarn is chartreuse when you thought it would be brown. If you need to do something like double a lace weight mohair, make sure it is okay before you start. If there are buttons, either provide them or clearly mark the button holes. Send back the used yarn labels and the unfinished balls plus extra yarn. Ask for a pattern template from whomever is hiring you so can conform your pattern to the company's stylesheet.

On the business end: Make copies of all your submissions and date them. Send to as many people as possible. If in the unlikely event 2 companies chose the same project, modify it.

Also, the only way to make any real money as a designer is to find knitters. If you consider the fact you're only going to make 500-800 bucks a sweater it's hard to find someone to knit for you. Find them anyway. Make sure you get a gauge swatch from them. I'd recommend doing all the finishing yourself.

Get yourself a portfolio and a suitcase with wheels and attend TNNA and walk the show...ask companies for yarn samples. DON'T PAY FOR YARN, IT IS ONE OF THE FEW PERKS OF THIS AWFUL INDUSTRY.

Find a mentor...work in a yarn shop and get a following...start a blog. Don't get too big for your britches, you people are a dime a dozen.

Can you speak on the importance of developing and maintaining relationships in the industry? Is it the best way to land jobs or...?

See above. If you can develop a relationship with a YIP, great. If you find yourself near an LYS that has great relationships with yarn companies and you design for them, they can promote you. Sadly, you should blog, go on Ravelry etc. Contact Knitty.com. Write every yarn company and ask for yarn and knit patterns on spec. Don't piss people off....sing the praises of people who've helped you. Send thank you notes. Again, invest in going to TNNA and make business cards. Learn how to digitize your own schematics. Respect your elders.

Bad behavior in the industry – any horror stories so designers know what NOT to do?

There's a threshold of drama that I will allow for my long time designers who are notoriously late, or whose patterns are indecipherable, but they've been in the business for a zillion years and they deserve the diva treatment.

I had freelance gig for a yarn company, the woman emailed literally 4 times a day to make acrylic afghans. She insisted that I send her countless skeins of yarns, and she called incessantly, and sent one ugly swatch after another as the deadline approached. Meanwhile I had about 12 other projects I was juggling for the same shoot and had cemented the colors for those projects, after the 9 zillionth email and swatch, I said just use these colors, my hands are tied and she said she'd refuse to do the afghan.

I had a who went MIA after having been assigned 8 projects. I called and emailed her for weeks. When I finally got a hold of her, two weeks before the deadline she told me she had a "nervous breakdown" and had started nothing. Now, I am the most sympathetic person in the world when it comes to mental problems, but the fact is, she had had the yarn for months and let me know 2 weeks before the shoot. I had to postpone photography, during which time my start model "got engaged to an Italian" and literally gained 15 pounds.

I've had projects shown up on set with the needles still in them.

I could go on.

In retrospect these stories are little war wounds and make for good cocktail party conversation but while they are going on they make your life extremely stressful and often cost your company a lot of money. Truthfully I don't think I've ever had a shoot where all the sweaters arrived in a timely non-dramatic manner. That doesn't give designers permission to slack on deadlines. But stuff happens. Knitting and designing is intense personal labor. And I doubt there's an editor in chief or creative director out there who isn't sympathetic. So if you are having a nervous breakdown, or you can't get the sweater done for any reason COMMUNICATE this information as soon as possible to the people who need to know so they can make contingency plans.

KARIN STROM

Editor in chief, Yarn Market News

Website: http://yarnmarketnews.com

How did you get into the business?

I've been in the yarn industry on and off for, um, let's just say, many years. I got the textile bug early. I've been collecting ethnic textiles since I was about eight years old. My father traveled a lot on business. He brought me an embroidered vest from Lebanon and I was hooked – I requested textile-related gifts from wherever he went. And, yes, my grandmother was an avid crocheter, knitter and taught me both. My cousin and I loved making huge multicolored pompoms with her leftover yarns. But the craft gene skipped a generation – my mother was a talented painter – but hated doing "hand crafts." And when I first got into the crafts industry, my parents were amazed that I could make money from my "hobby" – thankfully, times have changed!

My first job was with the National Park Service demonstrating spinning and weaving at a restored colonial village, in period costume! At the time I was also making one-of-a-kind crocheted garments, which I sold in boutiques and galleries. I used a lot of Tahki yarns, which eventually led to a job at Tahki. I owe much to Diane Friedman for training me so well! I learned all about sourcing yarn, choosing color palettes, working with magazine editors, knit and crochet designers, and much more. My next job was as editor of the Woman's Day craft and needlework special issues. I also worked as fashion director of Reynolds/JCA.

My career diverted in some other directions for several years – I was a photo stylist, marketing director, author. But when I heard that Soho Publishing was thinking about reviving Yarn Market News in 2005, I knew I was their gal. I just had to convince them that I had the exact right skill set and experience to do the job. And it's been a perfect fit. I love being editor in chief of YMN and I get such amazing feedback from LYS owners, designers and industry members, so I know it's valuable to folks in the industry.

What do you wish someone had told you when you first started off in this industry?

"You'll never make a lot of money"! (But you will meet amazing, supportive people and have opportunities to travel and have a career with a lot of flexibility that lasts a lifetime.)

What do you see as the most influential traits/activities when it comes to being a successful designer? What do great designers have in common, or have that sets them apart from lesser ones?

I've been watching the Olympics this week, so please excuse a figure skating analogy. I have been so struck by the grit and determination it takes to get to that level and I do think there are some lessons to be learned. Success is the result of a combination of talent, technical ability, self-confidence and perseverance. A good coach (or mentor) doesn't hurt.

Luckily, in knitting, there is a much bigger window of time to pursue your passion and as long as you stay fresh and continue to stretch, you can really work forever! You can see this in designers like Deborah Newton and Nicky Epstein who continue to produce very knittable and original designs after twenty or thirty years of designing.

What business traits set apart great designers or companies?

It's not exactly a business trait but think it's the companies and designers who have the instincts to tap into the zeitgeist, anticipate "the next big thing" and translate trends into knittable patterns. All the recent game changers for our industry have really come from smart people who have had an "aha" idea and run with it: Knitty.com – an e-zine, aha! Ravelry – a social network for knitters, aha! Patternfish – an online pattern store, aha! And I know there are other ideas brewing out there even as we speak!

A number of larger yarn companies have hooked up with up and coming designers or have a design director with a strong point of view, which allows them to maintain a level of excitement.

Both as a designer and as a business, you sometimes have to spend money you don't want to spend to invest in your business. It's like that old advertising adage: The most important time to advertise is when business is slow and you feel like you can't afford to advertise.

And I've noticed that smart business people know their limitations and ask for (and hire) help in the areas they aren't strong in.

What advice would you give a new designer?

Don't be afraid to make mistakes. Again, an Olympic reference: it's so inspiring to see those skaters jump right up and continue after they've fallen, with the whole world watching.

Also, beware of burnout. This is a passion-based business and when the passion isn't burning so bright, it can be time to regroup.

What advice would you give someone who's been around a while but needs a kickstart?

For a while it seemed like getting a book contract was the key to getting your name out there. And certainly doing a book is a wonderful way to gain credibility and visibility but as we all know, it's a lot of work for not a lot of money. And there are so many other ways to get attention today. Besides the obvious "get on Facebook" suggestions, I would say partner up with someone. Often two heads are truly better than one, especially if one of them is less outgoing or one has a better business head. For example, a designer might partner with an LYS to develop a pattern line and it could benefit both.

What role does the internet play in knit design work these days compared to other more "traditional" information sources? Do you see a special benefit in social media, for example?

I'm really impressed with how people in our industry are utilizing the internet and social media. Knitting has long been a community builder, but with the advent of social media, it has become even more so. I first saw it in the forums on Knitter's Review and then Ravelry really took off and now Facebook.

For designers, having a website and blog is still the perfect forum not only for introducing their work, but for establishing an identity and making a connection with an audience. The social media act to augment that connection. A caveat would be: just be careful what you say because it's out there for everyone to see.

Another thing that the internet does for designers is it can lessen the isolation factor. In the past, being an independent designer could be a lonely pursuit. By the very nature of it, you spend lots of hours alone, knitting, thinking, worrying. Social media has alleviated some of that – you can be instantly in touch with others in the same boat. And of course the Internet offers instant inspiration and the ability to research...

Do you think the "up/down" knitting cycle is shortening up a bit? We've been on a sustained kick for a while – does the internet get credit for that?)

I think, like anything, there will always be cycles but I can't imagine that yarn crafts will drop off completely like they did after the knitting boom of the 80s. And, yes, I agree that the internet is in part responsible for that. It has created an endless online gallery of ideas. And there is a certain healthy competitiveness that is fostered by seeing what other people are doing that has contributed to the interest in learning new and more complex techniques.

I do have to put in a little plug for print media and say that the quality of what's being published has also risen with the tide.

Where do you see the handknitting/design industry heading?

There is so much good energy in this business. As long as designers keep cranking out great patterns and yarn companies and dyers keep producing wonderful yarns, things will continue to thrive. When the economy fell apart last year, a lot of us were concerned how it would affect this industry. It has certainly influenced people's buying habits and shops in many areas are struggling, but the stores that are keeping on top of trends, creating a sense of community and continue to create ways to get people in the doors are doing well and growing.

What are the top challenges for our industry right now?

Keep the LYS strong so knitters have a physical place to go to see yarns, sample garments, learn techniques, meet designers.

What are your pet peeves as an editor?

I almost always give writers a second chance. Sometimes we'll get a manuscript in that needs a lot of work to get it to the place where it's ready for primetime. So the article that comes out in print is often quite different from what was submitted. A good writer will read this final version and learn about what a YMN article should read like and usually the next submission will be more on target.

We have editorial guidelines that are pretty clear and do expect writers to at least read them...and do a spell-check before they submit something. A big pet peeve of the art department is [submitting] low-res photographs.

All that being said, if an author really understands this industry and has something to say that can benefit YMN readers and has a passion for the yarn business, we can tinker with what is submitted and make it work.

What are your current career goals? How have they changed and why?

I really like my position as an observer of the industry I love. I get to meet people from every corner of this business from mill owners to brand new designers. And I don't have to edit patterns...

CHARLOTTE QUIGGLE

Charlotte is an experienced tech editor and designer.

You work with a large number of publishers' and designers' stylesheets — how have you seen them evolve over time? What are the beginning steps to establishing your own stylesheet and working with it, as a designer?

Some publishers distinguish between *designer guidelines* and *stylesheets* that are used by technical editors and proofreaders. The stylesheets encompass all the information included in the designer guidelines, but detail the specific language/punctuation/grammar conventions that must be followed. That's *way* too much information for the designer who is usually just told to follow an existing pattern as a template. If she does that to the best of her ability, then there is minimal work for the tech editor to revise the text to adhere to the stylesheet. If, however, she does *not* write her pattern using a publisher's current pattern as a template, it takes a lot of time to whip into basic shape before ever starting "tech editing".

Designers should establish their *own* stylesheets for their self-published patterns and adhere to them. They should follow the publisher's guidelines when writing a pattern for outside publication. Recent changes to many publishers' designer guidelines include requirements that:

- all patterns be sent digitally, including graphics.
- lengths be expressed in imperial and metric measurements
- designer follow established standards for grading patterns (often the CYC standards, but not necessarily).
- resulting stitch counts are given following all shaping rows/rounds.
- specific shaping instructions be given. For example, rather than saying: "Dec 1 st each end on next, then every other row twice, then every 4 rows 6 times", the designer should write out a sample dec row, then say how many times it is repeated. Example: Dec row (RS): K1, k2tog, work in pat to last 3 sts, k2tog, k1. Rep Dec row [every other row] twice, then [every row] 6 times – 15 (17, 19, 21) sts. The reason for this is that it establishes that there is a selvedge st (or not, as the case may be), and that the decreases are to be directional, either with or against the slope.
- the designer provide schematics for all garments (as appropriate – socks need not apply) that include many more measurements than most currently give (see below). Schematics aid the knitter not only when working the size as published, but also customizing a pattern to fit her own body measurements.
- the designer provide charts for all but the simplest of stitch patterns.
- any stitch pattern be expressed as a multiple of X sts + Y.
- that all contact information be included on each pattern page (including email). **Very important and often neglected.**

How can designers make YOUR job easier?

She should follow the designer guidelines provided by the publisher. If a given publisher or yarn company does *not* send the designer written guidelines, she should find a recent pattern published by the publisher/yarn company and use that as a template for use of abbreviations, language, order of pattern elements, etc..

If she is sending me a self-published pattern to be tech edited, she should provide me with the style sheet for her patterns. That eliminates a lot of the back-and-forth that occurs with sloppily written patterns.

She should provide *all* st/row gauge information, not just St st. If there are multiple stitch patterns used in a garment, she should provide st/row gauge for each stitch pattern so that the tech editor can successfully check the accuracy of the schematics.

The sample should be worked to those gauges.

She should give yardage of yarn used for sample garment (including swatch) so that it is possible to check the accuracy of the required yarn amounts for other sizes. (Some wonderful designers provide the tech editor with their calculations for yardage – this is *extremely* helpful!)

She should provide all appropriate information re: the yarn used (if it's not a generic pattern). Just giving the yarn name means that I have to go to the yarn company's website to get the information. Necessary information includes: yarn company name; yarn name; fiber content; some sort of weight designation (either lace, fingering, sport, DK, worsted, Aran, bulky, super-bulky or CYC yarn weight designation, as desired [or required]); yardage/weight of the put-up; # of balls/skeins used in the sample colors. There are a lot of knitters who want to use *exactly* the yarn and color used in the sample. For those who want to substitute yarns, knowing the yardage per 50g and fiber content of the sample yarn helps them find an appropriate substitute that will have similar properties.

She should know how to grade a garment pattern properly and provide 4-7 sizes, depending on the suitability of the design for up/down-sizing. Many designers don't have the foggiest idea of how the human body is constructed and how different parts of a garment are differently-proportional as the garment increases in size. If proper measurements aren't used, all the shaping instructions are wrong and have to be re-done.

Some tech editors will grade patterns for designers and some publications (e.g. Vogue Knitting) *insist* on doing their own pattern grading. While I can (and have) graded patterns for designers (and VK), I think that it is not the best way to go for a variety of reasons.

First of all, if I'm generating numbers/measurements as the tech editor, there is no one to check *my* work. And that's just *crazy*. Tech editors are just as likely to make a typo/math error in original grading as the designer is and it's much harder to catch one's own error. Secondly, and more importantly, I consider grading to be an integral part of the design process. While a particular design may very well work as a "custom" or sample size, it may not work at all in other sizes or the size jumps end up being so great that they are impractical for use by many knitters. When a designer chooses a stitch pattern, she has to be thinking ahead to how she is going to up-/down-size a pattern using the pattern repeat and placement. It's often *very* difficult to grade a pattern that uses a very large pattern repeat that is centered both front and back and meets at the sides.

The same is true of a pattern that uses panels of patterns (e.g. an Aran-style pattern). Is the designer going to increase a plain pattern field (seed stitch, double moss, whatever) at the side edges when upsizing? If yes, as the sweater gets larger, will the proportions of the main set of panels get out of whack with that side section? Or is she going to increase the number of stitches *between* the panels themselves, and if so, between which ones? Or is she better off adding panels to some sizes? Increasing the size of each panel so that they are proportional?

How does the placement of the stitch patterns integrate with the shaping (waist, armholes, neck, shoulders, etc) for the various sizes? Do they end appropriately at focal points (necks) and horizontal edges (shoulders) so that they are mirrored (if necessary) across the shoulder seams?

It's all part of the design process and *she's* the designer, the tech editor is NOT.

- I like to know the intended ease of the garment at different fitting locations. (Rarely given, but this is a wish list! [grin])

- Stitch counts should be given following each shaping instruction. That's helpful for both the tech editor and the knitter.

- She should provide complete schematics for the project. When stitch counts appear to be off, it is helpful to have schematics to check the measurements against. A schematic is also my first tip-off as to whether the designer understands proper grading.

- She should use standard terminology where appropriate. She should not make up her own unique abbreviations. (Her "standard" abbreviations should be included in her stylesheet.)

- When charting, she should use commonly accepted symbols in her charts and not make up her own. While there are several different symbols for the some maneuvers, she should be consistent in deciding which ones to use in her patterns.

- I prefer all stitch patterns to be broken out and written out separately. Where there are multiple stitch patterns in a given row, it is MIND NUMBING to try to separate out the different patterns, both for the tech editor and the knitter. Judicious suggested use of markers is helpful.

- She should thoroughly understand the results of different maneuvers. For example, not all left-leaning decreases are the same. K2tog-tbl and p2tog-tbl are very different from ssk/ssp, especially when stacked/mirrored decreases are being used. It's a pain to have to explain this to a designer and ask whether she really *intends* for some of the decreases to be twisted. When shaping in a Fair Isle pattern, she should know that it is usually better to have the decreases angle *against* the slope to maintain the pattern. I could go on and on…

- Where the designer feels that it might be helpful to give the tech editor insight into her thinking, side notes to the tech editor are very much appreciated. For example, a recent lace shawl designer used symbols for both ssk and skp in his chart and *explained why* in a side note to me, the tech editor.

What separates the good from the great in terms of writing patterns? Would you prefer someone overexplain and allow you to edit down, or write it the way they want to and expect that you'll "fill in the blanks," such as it is?

I prefer succinct, well-written patterns that give the knitter (and me as tech editor) the information necessary to work a given project. So, I don't like to get a 20-page pattern where everything is over-explained. I particularly dislike patterns that tell a knitter "Now you are going to do this, now you are going to do that, when you're done with that, do this while doing this at the same time." I don't like the use of the 2nd person in a pattern and don't think that a well-written pattern is a conversation, it's a recipe. All that "talky" stuff tends to overwhelm the actual instructions and the pattern gets more difficult to read.

On the other hand, I'm not a mind-reader either and I prefer *not* to have to fill in many blanks.

Both situations take a lot of editing time and requiring back-and-forth emails to establish what exactly the designer is trying to achieve. Sometimes the designer's stylesheet will address some of this and can cut down on questions. If she *really* feels that it's necessary to explain every last thing to her customers, I'd like to know that going in. If, however, she feels that her customers all know that when she says: "Dec 1 st each edge 7 times" she really means to do it every RS row with mirrored decreases and inside of a selvedge stitch, then I should know that as well.

I prefer patterns that are written with rows/rounds on separate lines rather than in paragraph form. I think that it's easier for the knitter to tick off the rows/rounds as she's worked them if they are separated. White space is good! Paragraph format also gets increasingly difficult to read (and edit!) when there are 5-7 sizes and both imperial and metric measurements given.

I don't think that sweaters should ever say: "Work Left Front as for Right Front, reversing all shaping." The designer should write out shaping for each front for the knitter – more than one knitter have worked 2 Right Fronts in error!

I prefer most "notes" to the knitter to be segregated in a "Pattern Notes" section at the beginning of a pattern rather than sprinkled throughout the pattern text. If a project uses an innovative construction, it's good to explain that construction briefly in the notes so that the knitter understands it before jumping into her knitting. It's also useful to include basic construction methods in pattern notes, e.g., "This sock is worked from the toe-up, starting with a Turkish cast-on and increasing at each side of the toe; the heel is a short-row heel; the cuff ends with a picot bind-off."

I expect that the designer has already proofed her entire pattern and double-checked her math. Yes, it's possible (likely!) for errors/typos to creep in, but they should be few and far between.

See also everything above.

Consistency. Explain it in terms of tech editing. Why is it important? And for whose benefit is it to have consistency?

Consistent language, use of abbreviations, symbols, etc establish the "voice" of the self-publishing designer and set her apart as a professional with a line of patterns that will become familiar to her customers. Maintaining that consistency across patterns also helps the designer write a better pattern because she's *thought* about how she prefers to express certain things and adheres to her style. That said, that written style will probably evolve over time and that's good! Rigidity is never good.

As Emerson said, "A foolish consistency is the hobgoblin of little minds…"

Patterns that are submitted to publishers all have to be consistent within the publication – that's why it's important to follow the publisher's designer guidelines and write a pattern that mimics that publisher's established style. My assumption is that publishers maintain consistency across all patterns following their own established style because they have years of experience in what language/presentation style works best and generates the fewest reader queries; they revise their style as knitters' expectations change.

If a designer pays no attention to the publishers' preferred style, it is up to the tech editor to re-write the pattern. Not only does that take time (sometimes a lot of it!) but it is also more likely that the tech editor will introduce an error when re-writing than if she is just editing lightly while she checks the pattern.

If you were teaching a pattern writing class, what would you emphasize above all else?

A designer should study other peoples'/publications' patterns – the language, the format, the presentation of information, the schematics, the charts, everything. She should notice how other patterns are presented differently from her own and analyze whether perhaps another method is better or worse. Based on that analysis, the designer should establish her *own* style or revise it.

Such an analysis also makes it a lot easier for a designer to mimic a publisher's pattern style when necessary because she can immediately pinpoint the differences between her own style and the publisher's.

Tips and tricks for writing patterns?

- Work large swatches of each stitch pattern used to establish gauge for each. If necessary, work a swatch with the stitches in sequence (be it horizontal or vertical).

- Work out "interesting" construction/shaping before doing anything else – that's what swatching is for. Resist designing "on the needles". (Yes, we all do it on occasion, but that's usually because we haven't thought through the potential problems ahead of time).

- Create a preliminary schematic that includes all measurements for all sizes (need not be to the 1/4" at this point).
- Chart out/do a spreadsheet/or whatever works to determine how the grading is going to affect the placement of the stitch patterns for the different sizes to "prove" the end results. The designer doesn't want to design something that isn't "grade-able" or should already know how she's going to solve the grading challenges.

- Write the pattern *before* casting on for the sample. That includes most elements of grading. While this initial draft doesn't need to be in final form (it can be just sequential notes), the more formal it is, the more clearly the designer is able to think about and anticipate what she's doing.

- Some words to the wise: **Keep good notes**. We all forget some of the specifics of what we did with a particular design. In the case of a pattern being edited for an outside publisher, the tech editor will probably be working on the designer's pattern MONTHS after she has turned it in and put it out of her mind. If the tech editor emails with questions, it is because there's something confusing about the pattern text that she can't figure out. It's a big problem when the designer says "Oh, that was so long ago, I don't have a clue." The same is true when a publisher's customer service department has to go back to the designer a few years later to double-check a possible error. "No notes" means "no help," which doesn't endear the designer to that publisher.

Give us the lowdown for designers on shopping for a tech editor...

Qualities of a good tech editor include:

- attention to detail
- comfortable with elementary math (including basic algebra and geometry)
- excellent language skills, both in English and "knitter-ese"; firm grasp of proper grammar (she usually functions as the proofreader as well)
- ability to "mind-knit"
- knows virtually all knit techniques, construction methods and fiber/yarn properties
- good communication skills; ability to explain a problem in a pattern to the designer in a clear manner and propose a clean solution.
- sufficient computer skills to be able to work across different software/OS platforms as necessary
- sense of humor and ability to play well with others

Schematics, charts, illustrations, photos? Can you talk more about the importance of these, how you recommend including them and when?

Photos—are we talking for the benefit of the tech editor here? Or the knitter? Certain types of photos are useful for the tech editor that might be unnecessary to include in the final pattern. If I'm not seeing the physical sample, I like a picture of the project front and back, sleeves if appropriate. Close-ups of the critical elements (sometimes seams – is there a selvedge stitch?), shaping areas (are decreases worked along or against the slope?), stitch patterns (do the instructions give the correct direction of the cable turn?), etc. Absent the sample, more photos/scans of the project are better than fewer.

For the knitter: Clear photos that focus on the garment and don't attempt to be "fashion-y". Close-ups of design details as appropriate. Schematics are critical for all sweaters/dresses/

jackets/pants/etc. Sweater measurements included should be (at minimum):

- Bottom width if worked flat (circumference if in the round)
- Waist width/circumference if body has shaping
- Chest width/circumference if different from bottom
- Total length
- Length to armhole
- Armhole depth
- Shoulder drop (as necessary)
- Neck depth (front and back as appropriate)
- Neck width
- Shoulder width
- Cuff width (circumference)
- Sleeve width (circumference) at underarm
- Top sleeve/cap width, as appropriate
- Length to underarm
- Sleeve cap depth

I recommend that charts be included for all the but the simplest of stitch patterns, i.e. for anything that is more than a 5-st, 4-row repeat. There's a bit of flexibility here, but it's usually better to opt for including a chart rather than against. The more complex a pattern is, the more many knitters rely on a visual representation of the pattern in preference for written out text. If room permits,

both should be included, but there are times when a chart is preferable to text, e.g. a complex lace pattern over a shawl.

Finally, although self-published downloadable PDFs do not have the same space limitations that hard copy patterns do, many knitters do not want to print out an unnecessarily long pattern – it's annoying! The pattern should only be as long as it needs to be to get the job done.
It is not critical that a self-published pattern *teach* the knitter to work all maneuvers used in the pattern. That *may* be a choice made by some designers (i.e. the pattern as pedagogical tool), but it is not necessary these days where other teaching resources abound, i.e. books, magazines, videos and tutorials on the net, Ravelry, etc. It can be sufficient to insert links to one's own website/blog or refer the knitter to other resources. Even basic abbreviations that are standard to most knitters can be on a website rather than in the pattern itself, if space is a concern. After all, in many cases, the knitter downloaded the pattern PDF, and should know how to use the internet to her advantage. If the designer *does* choose to educate her customers, the explanatory text/diagrams should be segregated in the pattern, preferably at the end. That way, those experienced knitters who have no need for all that "extra" stuff can print out the pattern alone and exclude the educational parts.

Tell us some horror stories so we know what NOT to do as designers.

Horror stories? I try *not* to remember them! I usually kvetch to another tech editor when I'm in the middle of a horror pattern, then pull up my pants, get the job done and forget about it, hoping that I never encounter that designer again.

I've found that poorly-written patterns are just as likely to come from experienced designers as from "newbies". Some new designers are meticulous in following a publisher's designer guidelines and many long-term designers frustratingly never even look at them.

The worst "horrors" are the unfixable ones, i.e. errors in the sample garment itself, not in the pattern. The cable that is turned incorrectly, missed rows in a Fair Isle pattern, the mis-sized garment that won't fit a normal human being (huge baggy necks, elephantine sleeves), the child's pullover that won't go over *any* child's head, even crappy finishing that can't be hidden. I've encountered all of the above. Some require extensive Photoshop-ping (where possible). Others may be salvageable in some way, such as sleeves are cut off and cuffs re-knit before the photoshoot. But most such projects just get killed.

Your training – how did you come to this profession?

I've knit forever (well, since I was 7). Math comes very easily to me, as does writing. I worked for years in magazine publishing (TIME Magazine) and feel comfortable working in that kind of deadline environment and understand publishers' production needs.

I've read almost every knitting book ever published cover-to-cover. Yes, seriously! I'm a book junky. You name the book, I own it, from Thérèse de Dillmont's Encyclopedia and the Weldon's books to books published in the last month. Starmore books – got 'em all…and signed! Knitting books in Japanese, German, Estonian, Russian, Latvian, Turkish, Spanish, Portuguese, Icelandic, French, Italian, Swedish, Norwegian, Danish and Dutch fill my shelves.

I read patterns for enjoyment (who needs to knit the darn sweater/shawl/sock/coat/bag/afghan when I already have a few hundred of them that are quite useful – I can knit so many more of them in my mind!), so I speak fluent pattern-ese.

I've taken *jillions* of workshops over the years with people like Kathryn Alexander, Beth Brown-Reinsel, Nancy Bush, Nilda Callanaupa, Lily Chin, Katherine Cobey, Kaffe Fassett, Catherine Lowe, Lucy Neatby, Shirley Paden, Mary Walker Phillips, Joan Schrouder, Horst Schulz, Alice Starmore, Sandy Terp, Barbara G. Walker, and Rebekah Younger, among many, many others. There is no hand-knitting technique that I can think of that I haven't worked in a project. I learned to machine knit at the Fashion Institute of Technology in NYC (many machine knitting tricks translate neatly to hand-knitting) and spin (knowledge of yarn construction/fiber properties is important for successful garment design).

After designing for myself for years, then knitting some samples for Lily Chin, I figured that I could design professionally – I've been published in Vogue Knitting, knit.1, IK, Knitter's and by various yarn companies.

I didn't enjoy designing for publication as much as I thought I would, but I found that I *did* enjoy editing patterns when asked to. So I quit designing and started tech editing full time instead. (I have little interest in Self-publishing my own work).

So now I've tech edited 31 knitting books, tech edited for 4 different magazines and 4 yarn companies, and worked with over a dozen Self-publishing designers.

What else do we need to tell designers to make the world a happier and more effective place?

Creative design skills are very different from pattern-writing skills. Ideally, each skill set should be mastered. Some designers are wildly creative but can't write a decent pattern; other designers offer more "everyday" designs but write excellent patterns. The successful designer will continually explore new things creatively and at the same time strive to communicate that vision clearly to the knitter, enabling her to make an interesting garment that will fit.

One last note that doesn't fit anywhere: There is a real need for designers who focus on plus-size knitters **ONLY**. I'm not talking about being taking a design from an XS to a 4XL, but rather designing only for the larger lady, so that the initial design decisions (yarn choice, placement of pattern, color choices, internal shaping options) are made appropriately from the get-go. This would mean designing for the variety of shapes that plus-size women come in – fitting standards for these women is sorely lacking.

LOUISA HARDING

Website: http://louisaharding.co.uk

Relative to other designers, you exercise a lot of control over your patterns, pattern book and imagery/photographs, since you do it all in-house. Was this a conscious decision? What led you to it?

I have been very fortunate. During my career at Rowan I was able to pick up all the skills necessary to feel confident to act as creative director when it comes to the imaging, publications, and photography associated with my yarn collection.
I attended my first photography shoot as a stylist's assistant to Kim Hargreaves on a Kaffe Fassett shoot. My job at Rowan eventually led to me being appointed the brand coordinator and designer for the Jaeger Handknits brand, choosing models, locations, styling and working on the layouts for publications. This role was part of the job description and to keep costs at a minimum, however it was a fantastic opportunity.

Once you have had creative control over your work it is very difficult to have it removed. I have very defined ideas of how I want my work to be viewed. As a designer you often design a whole look in your head that fits to your creative inspiration – to me the knitwear is just part of that. Over the last 20 years publishers and yarn companies have come to respect my views and allow me to have creative input, it is a very nice position to be in and one I realize is very privileged.

Where do you see the knitting industry headed?

I think that the knitting industry has reinvented itself quite significantly over the past 10 years. It has had to respond to knitters who have really grasped the idea of community, not just on a local level through their LYS and knitting groups, but on a global level with online communities such as Ravelry. The internet has meant that knitters can talk, knit and share experiences. Where once knitters worked very much in isolation, they are very proud of their work and want to show it off, and believe in sharing their experiences of working with yarns and the companies that produce them. I believe that in our fast-paced throwaway society that knitters and other artistic people are channeling into their creative genes, we all feel so accomplished when we have created and finished a project. I feel that more designers' work will become accessible through the internet and I see it as one of my roles as a designer to ensure that I source interesting yarns for knitters/designers to 'play' with. With regards to yarn development, we have to ensure that we act responsibly and ethically, and this doesn't just mean only using hand dyed organic yarns but also embracing new technology.

How were you trained/how did you enter the knit design field? What do you wish you'd known before starting?

Somehow all the levels of my education have led me to the path of designer.
At school (up to 16) I studied Art and Printed Textiles, at sixth form (16 - 18) I studied Dress (pattern cutting and fashion design) and more art. From 18-19 I studied an art foundation course at Camberwell College of Art, this course involved looking at every area of art, graphics, printmaking, sculpture, wood and metalwork, jewelry, life drawing, fine art – painting with oils as well as textiles. The foundation course was a taster year. As a result, in 1986 I decided to specialize in Textiles for Fashion, embarking on a BA Hons degree at Brighton University. This course was over 4 years, the third year spent in industrial placements (internships). It was during my third year that I spent 3 months working for Rowan Yarns. I finished my degree, Rowan sponsored my final collection and in December 1990, I went to work for them.

I worked for Rowan for 11 years. After that, I freelanced for 4 years, then in 2005 I was offered the opportunity of introducing my own line of yarns and publications. Many people may only know me through my yarn line but there have been many years behind that learning all the skills that have brought me to this point.

Patience is a virtue, very underrated in today's world, but patience, time, self belief and doing every project to the very best of your ability are the most important factors you need to become a successful designer.

On a similar topic: what bits of advice would you offer a new designer today?

Becoming a successful designer does not happen without an awful lot of hard work. Most importantly, you have to get your work noticed. This is only achieved by learning your craft, networking and sending images off of your work.

Learning your craft is essential, just because you can knit does not make you a designer, do you understand the math involved in design, how knitted stitches, fabrics and garments are constructed? Develop your own personal style, your unique selling point which is different from other designers. When you network and send away your design work, even if your work is rejected, ask why, ask for constructive criticism, and resubmit. If you have been given a brief to work within, then that brief is given for a reason. You may believe you produce the best designs but if no one sees them how will they ever know you are there, you are your 'brand'. Being a commercial designer and selling your work is a way of enjoyably earning a living – not 'selling out'.

What's it like having your own yarn line? How did it come about, and how does it affect your design work when you have the ability to develop your own "perfect" yarns?

In an earlier answer I said how important it is to network, talking to industry people and letting them know you are available for work is invaluable. In 2004 at TNNA I made contact with lots of industry people handing out my business card and letting magazines and publishers etc know that I was looking for freelance work. The following March (2005) I was approached by a US yarn distributor (Knitting Fever) who knew of my work at Rowan as they had been the distributors in the US for the Jaeger Handknits brand; they also had seen the Miss Bea publications. I was asked to visit with them in New York and asked if I would be interested in developing my own yarn line with design publications to support the yarns. This sounded like a fabulous opportunity, which it was. However, there are always obstacles to overcome. If I said yes to this offer, the collection had to be put together in less than three months to be showcased in June 2005 at TNNA, and I had to give them a decision before I left New York the following day. Needless to say I spent a long time discussing the implications with my husband, as at the time our children were 4 and 5. We knew that if I declined this offer the opportunity would never present itself again, so with Stephen's support we took the jump.

As I had the experience as the designer and brand coordinator of the Jaeger Handknits brand I had knowledge in developing yarns for the handknitting market. There is a yarn manufacturer's show in Florence, Italy twice a year called Pitti Filatti, this is where all the new season's yarn collections are showcased, not just to handknit designers but also to ready-to-wear designers from the 'designer' level down to the high street. I had already contacts with many of these suppliers and so the transition to choosing yarn to represent my own line was natural.

The aspect of developing a yarn for your own named brand which is fundamental to me is that the yarns I choose are yarns that I would knit with and wear, and that are affordable. I did not want to replicate yarns from any other existing yarn brands. I wanted to develop yarns that had a definite signature which I have been very conscious to exploit, this being the femininity of my yarn choices, shades, photography and overall brand identity.

Because of my years of experience I know how a yarn will drape, show stitch detail, stretch on a female form and that influences the fibers that make up the yarns. I love viscose (bamboo/corn) in yarns, as this is a heavy fiber and will give a yarn drape. Linen gives a yarn crispness, a overly textured yarn will not show any stitch detail, and a ribbon yarn (although knitted on large needles) will create a flat fabric, unlike a round spun wool... a much more flattering female silhouette.

What did you learn as an in-house designer at Rowan that's helped you as your career has developed?

Everything. You can learn all the theory about design and running a business at college but working in a company is the best education you can get. I consider my time at Rowan as an apprenticeship to running my business today.

*And on a pure curiosity level, does working with a large group of talented designers building something like a Rowan mag push **you** forward as well? I know that in other matters having people around who are as good or better than you tends to push you to do better!*

I have a huge respect for all hand knitwear designers and I am very fortunate that I have worked alongside many of them. I have learned so many important and invaluable lessons from each of them. Important to all of us is that we maintain our designer integrity and that our work is unique.

Where do you draw your inspiration from when you're building a booklet of patterns? Do you start at the yarn level or on a more abstract level, thematically?

I always start designing my collections by taking ideas from an inspiration source. It is integral to my creative process to have a starting point to which the collection refers, whether it be a visit to Venice or a classic children's story such as Alice's Adventures In Wonderland. My newest collection is inspired by the East (*Chinoiserie*). Having a design theme ties all the creative elements together from the sourcing of the yarns, selecting of the colors, the stitches used in the patterns, the shape of the garments, to the look and feel of the photography and printed publications. I am incredibly lucky to be able to oversee all these elements, ensuring that my vision is as true to my original inspiration theme as possible.

Has the internet/social media and other technology helped bridge the gap when it comes to opening up a broader audience for your work?

Definitely, I think that communication via the internet has totally open up the world of knitting community. I have a group on Ravelry which I find invaluable. I have knitters who contact me from around the globe: Brazil, Russia, Scandinavia, North America, Europe. They let me know how they creatively respond to my yarns and patterns but also if they have any pattern or distribu-

tion questions. The immediacy of knowledge that you can gain by the use of the internet is revolu-
tionary, it works on all levels: information for knitters, retailers, designers and manufacturers.

Do you use test/sample knitters? Are skilled sample knitters easier to come by in the UK?

Yes, I have 9 ladies who knit for me. They range in ages from young mums to knitters in their twi-
light years. My mother is one of my test knitters. I guess that test knitters in the UK are easier to
find, as there is a selection of ladies who knit who really can't be without anything to occupy their
hands. I am extremely lucky, at least 4 of my knitters are like this and can knit a sweater in a week,
sometimes I do feel like I am contributing to their 'habit'. Some of my ladies just like to knit, so
send me back the garments in pieces to construct and some like to do the whole process and feel
very cheated if I don't send them the buttons to stitch on. I think in the US knitters really value
their time and so if they are knitting they want to be knitting for themselves or for gifts and not to
feed their compulsion!

Anything else to add?

The most important thing that I would like to say is that publishers won't find you no matter how
good your work is without you spending time sending out your work and keeping your profile in
view. In all businesses there is no gain without hard work and determination. I learned my craft
over a period of 15 years working for Rowan and freelancing. Every job you do, everyone you
speak to will impart some knowledge that you will later use. Be true to your own style, don't let
anyone try to compromise your design integrity. If you believe in yourself then others will believe
you too.

NICKY EPSTEIN

Website: http://www.nickyepstein.com

*How did you get into the design business? What do you wish you'd known going in? (And did your previous career
influence how it all happened?)*

I won a design contest from McCall's magazines and offers began coming in from various magazines – I had an art degree and worked as an art director and stylist/wardrobe for TV commer-
cials – I wish I knew how work intensive designing would be, If I had known I might have gone into
something easier, like coal mining!

Where do you see the industry heading? Any differences between the knit and crochet sides of things?

It's very difficult to guess with the internet, e-books etc playing such a big part. Knitting still dominates the fashion scene, with crochet still going strong with afghans, clothing, toys etc.

You've had a long relationship with Sixth&Spring/SoHo. What are the benefits of working with one publisher for so long? Also – how'd you end up with your own imprint there? is there any special benefit to that in terms of what ends up getting published, or...?

15 of my 21 books have been with SoHo. It makes for a comfortable working relationship knowing what to expect, but it should not get too comfortable, so I stay non-exclusive. My imprint came by way of having several best-selling books, so I have final say to content, cover etc. Making money for a publisher is a strong incentive to getting perks.

What's the source of most of your income?

Books are my biggest source of income, but I feel fortunate, because many designers do not always earn any royalties beyond their advance, perhaps because the market is so flooded with books. It is tough to make a decent living by just designing for magazines and yarn companies.

What are your dealbreakers in a contract – what won't you agree to under any circumstances?

- No exclusives on books
- No two book contracts
- Be aware of e-book rights
- Try for escalation clauses
- Rights to garments

I've had to work long and hard to achieve certain clauses that may not be easy for beginners to get, the competition and negotiations are intense.

Do you think living in NYC has an influence on you as a designer?

Most of the knitting magazines were in New York so it helped, in the beginning, that I lived there. Now with the internet, it is not that important, and talent, artistry or sophistication is not a geographical thing. I'm a West Virginia girl, originally, but now I'm a diehard New Yorker.

How do you stay productive? What's your typical work week like?

When I'm working on a book I work 24/7. When I'm not (which is not often), and just designing for magazines, teaching or traveling...24/7! Don't get into this business if you're not dedicated and want to make a living.

You've been in the business for quite a while, and maintained your popularity throughout – to what do you attribute your success?

First, I love what I do – but it is a tough industry and so I've had to keep re-inventing myself and staying on the cutting edge. I have to keep thinking outside of the box, think ahead, and be ready to work with everything from cashmere to acrylic without discrimination.

Is marketing yourself important? How and why? What do you do to stay at the top of everyone's head?

I give interviews, make appearances, go on knitting trips, etc., but the success of my designs and books have gained me a substantial following. Of course winning several publishing awards, having articles written about my work, writing article for Vogue Knitting magazine and having my scarf of the cover of Vogue Magazine's 25th anniversary issue doesn't hurt!

Do you think the internet has tightened up the design cycle / the cycle of knitting popularity?

Yes, knitting has been hot for some time and shows no sign of slowing (thank goodness), and the internet and Ravelry are a big part of it.

You've done a lot of amazing reference books – the 'edge' books, the flowers, Knitted Embellishments, etc. What hole did you see in the market that caused you to write them?

I do books that I would want to own as a knitter/designer. I try to do books, techniques and designs that are unique, and I love sharing them with knitters, and encourage them to exercise their creativity.

Did your background in art influence the intarsia, applique and other colorwork you're known for?

Yes, my art background and wannabe artist yearnings have influenced me. Even in college I did paintings with dimensional flowers!

When did you start selling items on your website (the scarves, the buttons you designed, etc)? What was the impetus behind that?

Just recently. I'm working on a new website and new products. Designing buttons, clasps, scarves etc, seemed the next step in my creative quest, while of course, promoting my knitting books...it's what I love to do.

JOAN MCGOWAN-MICHAEL

Website: http://whiteliesdesigns.com

Where do you see the handknitting-and-crochet/design industry heading?

That's a big question. It seems to me that the pendulum is swinging back from a time when home-made was looked down upon as being something that folks did when they were not affluent enough to afford store-bought to something we do to express our creativity and display our cleverness.

Personally I think that in spite of the current economic upheaval, we are heading toward a place in our industry that will see fewer of the ups and downs of decades past. Think about it; even if a small town loses its local yarn shop for whatever reason, those who want to knit and learn are able to log on to the internet and get the information or even take the classes they need to progress. They can find the supplies they need in the same way as well as the camaraderie. We surely do live in interesting times.

What do you wish someone had told you when you first started off as a designer? How did you get into the business?

I was essentially born knowing I would design, so no matter what anyone told me I would have damned the torpedoes and gone full speed ahead. It's better that nobody told me anything.

I had been in the garment manufacturing industry for many years by the time I came to knitwear design, so I already had a certain professionalism established when I entered this industry. What I would tell a new designer is to behave as professionally as possible, as it is a very small industry overall where everyone tends to know each other. Dot your i's and cross your t's, don't send any

thing in unfinished or done poorly. Let folks know well in advance if you'll have a problem meeting a deadline for any reason, don't just leave them hanging.

Do you earn most of your income from straight up design work or do you do other things as well?

I like to have multiple streams of income in place so that if one thing dries up or is slow, others are there to take over. We do online sales of our patterns and yarns. We also sell jewelry and knit-themed t-shirts and a few tools and books.

We do yarn shows up and down the west coast whenever possible. I still submit designs to books and magazines as well as designing for White Lies Designs. I teach workshops and travel all over to do that. We also do wholesale and show at TNNA. We have four sales reps right now and I'm looking for more. I've written a book and am planning another. In other words, I'm dancing as fast as I can over here.

What role does the internet play in knit design work these days compared to other more "traditional" information sources? Do you see a special benefit in social media, for example?

I wrote *Knitting Lingerie Style* completely by email. That was amazing to me. Everything but the ac-tual photography and the knitting took place online; the conceptualizing, the yarn sourcing, the editing, etc, all online. How 21st century is that?

I like Facebook for its ability to show photos and links so I work my account over there as much as possible. I have a personal page and a fan page for White Lies Designs. I also have a blog where I've begun posting a styling guide featuring White Lies garments styled using pieces from other web pages to make complete outfits from head to toe.

I link everything together and then throw Ravelry into the mix which is like a Facebook for knitters, only better.

What do you see as the most influential traits/activities when it comes to being a successful designer?

I really can't speak for others as I've only my own life as a point of reference, but I just have this stuff that *must* come out of me. I am primarily a creator and there have been times in my life where that creative energy has had nowhere to go, and let me just say that that never goes well. From those times I've learned how to respect my creativity, and White Lies Designs is the manifestation of that

What do great designers have in common?

I have a deep, deep love for fashion and making things and I think that love has helped me to gain success. I think that love/passion/obsession thing is a trait that great designers share.

What are your current career goals? How have they changed and why?

They haven't changed. My vision of getting knitters of all shapes and sizes to make wonderful things to look beautiful in is the primary goal of my business and central to my design aesthetic. More than ever women need to love themselves as they are while the world of media throws unrealistic images at us, demanding that we conform.

Life goes on and no matter what size or shape a woman is. She loves, has children, works for a living, travels, takes care of a home, etc. and she should look and feel great while doing all those things.

Let's talk sizing. You're one of the only designers out there who is not only designing stuff for larger women, but stuff that actually looks amazing. *How did that happen? Was it calculated or...?*

As I said previously, I've spent many years as a professional designer in the manufacturing segment of the clothing industry . Some of that time was spent doing the grunt work of patternmaking and grading my own patterns. I found early on that the mathematical approach of sizing up did not always work and didn't take into account that when a person gets heavier they don't necessarily become taller, their arms don't grow, etc. Later on when I had my custom bridal business, the point was driven home time and again when I would start with a commercial pattern for a gown that according to the measurements on the pattern envelope SHOULD have fit the bride, but in reality needed umpteen additional alterations to make that so. It was a seriously eye-opening experience and one I took with me when it became time to write and grade patterns for knitwear.

Contrary to what the knitting public would like to believe, the possibility of buying a pattern (sewing or knitting) and having it fit everyone who makes it "as is" right out of the envelope is nil. That being said, writing a few fitting tips into patterns is a smart thing to do, it helps make a designer's pattern more useful to a wider audience and surely improves the bottom line.

One of my first jobs out of design school was as a designer for Frederick's of Hollywood. It's where I learned much of what I know about making and fitting lingerie. Some of the designs in my book Knitting Lingerie Style are taken directly from patterns that I drafted while I was there, most particularly the cover bodysuit. I have a box in my attic filled with brown paper patterns from that time; basic pieces and shapes that translate well into modern styles, and I referred to them often while doing that book.

JULIET BERNARD

Website: http://www.theknitter.co.uk

How did you get into this industry?

I studied Textiles at Manchester University and worked for a big Textile company called Courtaulds working in fashion and knitwear. I was lucky enough to work on projects with Jean Paul Gaultier, Paul Smith and John Galliano. I strayed from textiles for a few years, but never far until I re-met Patrick and Jane Gottelier from Artwork and worked on their PR for a year. Then I was taken on by Rowan to do their PR for nearly 4 years. I was approached by Future Publishing to help with the original proposal for The Knitter and later became the editor.

What do you wish you'd known going in?

How many amazingly inspiring people I would meet. I learn something new from every knitter I meet

Where do you see the industry heading?

I think there will inevitably be some consolidation but I don't think hand knitting will go out of fashion in the UK like it did in the 1960s and 1990s. The pride we have in our skills and the way knitters have passed on the pure joy of what we can do are too celebratory to fade away.

What traits make a designer stand out to you? Or, what separates a good designer from a GREAT one? Is it all creativity-based, or...?

A good designer reads the brief. Seriously, a great designer has a clear idea of how a yarn will knit up, what the fabric will be like and how their design will look on the body. Designing hand knits is not a 2-dimensional thing. Designers need to understand the impact that each choice they make will have. Great ones just *get* this.

When you launched The Knitter in 2009, what specific hole were you looking to bridge in the knitting magazine market and why?

There were a number of good knitting magazines in the UK but none that combined a sense of fashion and style with new or advanced techniques for the experienced knitter.

Tell me about your time with Rowan – what you learned there, how it prepared you for your current job, etc?

Working with Rowan was an amazing privilege and helped me to focus my attention on what knitters wanted but I think my earlier experience of fashion and trends have really helped as well

Are there differences between the US and UK knitting market or knitting cultures?

Technical ability. US Designers and knitters often look at knitting almost as a piece of engineering and the elegance with which they put together a design is sensational, often reclaiming techniques that started in the UK or Europe. British knitters are learning to be more fearless but seem to prefer the safety of a pattern. I love the way UK knitters put color together – sometimes delicate, provocative and inspirational.

Do you frequently work with designers from outside the UK?

We work with designers from all over the world and are very proud to do so. We need the yarns we use to be available in the UK but that's about the only stipulation.

How does The Knitter use the internet and social media, and why?

Digital communication has made a huge difference to how we communicate with knitters and Ravelry is quite amazing. Last year we raised £32,000 for Macmillan Cancer Support by communicating through our Ravelry fan group and various blogs. However we know that, in the UK there are still many knitters who don't use sites like Facebook or Ravelry.

What kinds of mistakes do you see designers making all the time (especially newer ones)?

They don't read the brief.

How can they stand out from the crowd, professionalism-wise?

Read the brief.

How long does it typically take from the time a designer submits a design to The Knitter for them to hear back from you? (positively or negatively) Do you forbid or discourage designers from submitting the same design to other magazines simultaneously?

I think it would help if you understood how we commission first and this will explain why for 3 answers I have put 'read the brief'. I work up to 2 years in advance looking at what is coming out of Pitti Filatti, Trend Union presentations, catwalk shows etc. Then I interpret these trends for hand knits – one trend per issue. I then put together a mood board for each trend. We work on 6 issues at a time (i.e. the entire Autumn Winter or Spring Summer), so I pull together 6 mood boards with briefing notes from our technical editor and these are all sent out to all the designers that we have contact with and approach us. This is a huge amount of work and I collaborate with my contacts from all over the industry to make our seasonal brief as inspirational as possible. It is my job to stimulate the designers and help them to be the best they can. We try to give the designers 1 month to pull together sketches and swatches. Then we go through them and make our selections – sounds easy, but it takes 3 of us 2 days just to make the preliminary selection. We are usually exhausted but exhilarated at all the fantastic patterns we will be bringing our knitters. We try to get back to the designers within the week if they have been successful. It may take just over a week if they haven't. Because our trends are so specific, I sincerely hope a designer would not submit the same design simultaneously to another magazine. We wouldn't consider that to be professional or indeed in their best interest either.

KIRA DULANEY

Website: http://www.kirakdesigns.com

Where do you see the industry heading?

I think that both knitting and crochet are heading towards a more fashionable place. I'm seeing many more designers bringing an up-to-the-minute stylishness to their patterns, and a more flattering, body-conscious fit. For a long time people knit and crocheted boxy drop-shoulder sweaters because they were simple to make and didn't interrupt stitch patterns, but these days the vast majority of patterns have fitted shoulders and that makes a huge difference in the way the sweater fits. I've also been a big champion of waist shaping, since it looks good on most women's figures whether they have a defined waist or not.

Ten years ago a lot of people were scared to adapt patterns for their particular gauge, size, or style, or to make their own patterns. These days there are so many great books on writing and adapting patterns that most knitters have at least tried it out. Ravelry and other websites have also expanded one's circle of crafters worldwide, so if you need an opinion on a yarn choice at 2 a.m., you can get dozens within just a few minutes.

When I started seriously getting into knitting and crocheting, few people I knew did both crafts, and there was even sometime a little animosity. Now it seems like many knitters know at least the basics of crochet and vice versa, which I think is wonderful. They are very different crafts, and even if you feel a strong affinity for one craft, you may find that a certain project just works better in the other one. When I'm writing patterns, I often use a crocheted edge on a knitted garment, both because it's a good choice for the design and because I want to get knitters to do at least a little crochet.

What do you wish someone had told you when you first started off as a designer? How did you get into the business?

I wish that I'd know about the concept of technical editors and test knitters. For my first patterns, I checked them myself and handed them to another knitter to look over, but of course it's impossible to really check your own work since you're so close to it, and a friend looking the pattern over doesn't have the skill or spend the time that a tech editor will.
I started knitting when I was young, making simple things and working mostly without patterns. In the meantime, I got a degree in costume design and worked in a variety of theaters. When I got back into knitting and crocheting in earnest, I found it impossible to follow a pattern as written. I'd change the gauge, work in the round instead of flat, swap out stitch patterns, add waist shaping, and by the time I was done my sweater didn't look much like the original. Eventually I started working up my own patterns, although I still changed them as I went. I was working a yarn shop at the time and customers would ask about my sweaters, but my patterns were a mess of scribbles and often I hadn't even taken notes on the changes I'd made mid-stream. After a couple years I decided that it was time to try my hand at publishing my own patterns, and sat down to figure out how.

Having taught classes and helped customers in the store where I worked helped me to write clear knitting patterns, but there was still a lot of work to be done to make sure that everything was correct, nothing was left out, and that there was a consistency through my pattern line. I started small, selling patterns only in the shop where I worked at first, then starting up my website, and eventually moving to wholesale, 3rd party websites like Patternfish, and then to a distributor. I've had patterns published by a variety of online and print publications along the way, but the majority of my patterns have been self-published.
Do you earn most of your income from straight up design work or do you do other things as well?

It's a mix of teaching and selling patterns. I like to say that my business is full-time work for a part-time income. The percentage that teaching brings in varies wildly throughout the year, but pattern sales stay pretty consistent. I make more from wholesale pattern sales to yarn shops than I do from direct-to-consumer online sales.

What role does the internet play in knit design work these days compared to other more "traditional" information sources? Do you see a special benefit in social media, for example? How do you use social media in your business?

I think that the internet help so much in terms of checking out available yarns, and being able to see what work well for. Ravelry in particular is incredibly helpful when I'm checking out yarns to use for a new design, since I can see what projects people have used a particular yarn for. It helps me see if the yarn works better knit or crochet, in cables or lace, or if a lot of people find it difficult to work with. It's also great as a designer to see what people thought of my patterns, and how their projects turned out. Through the forums on Ravelry I've had great conversations with other designers, learned a lot about other people's processes, answered questions about my patterns, and made some friends.

The only other social media website I'm on is Facebook, and I try to keep that limited to non-work things. I sometimes use it to let friends know when I have a pattern in a magazine, or when I'm teaching a class for beginners, but I try not to do much work-related stuff there. I'm steadfastly avoiding blogging and Twittering, because I'm just not witty enough.

What do you see as the most influential traits/activities when it comes to being a successful designer? What do great designers have in common, or have that sets them apart from lesser ones?

I think it's really a balance between somewhat opposing traits. Designers need to be creative, but also very organized and detail-oriented. They need to have strong opinions and be able to make decisions, but they also have to listen to tech editors, publication editors, test knitters, and customers. Designers also need to have a firm background in their chosen craft(s), which usually comes from working with other people's patterns for a while so they know how seamless raglan yokes work before they design their own.

What are your current career goals? How have they changed and why?

I'd love to actually make a living with my design work and teaching, which has been my goal for a couple years now. Every year I get closer and I think that it's within sight. I definitely want to write a book, but the prospect is a little scary since it's so far outside of what I've done so far.

What advice would you give a new designer?

New designers, there are so many resources for you. Join all the designer-oriented Ravelry groups and read through the archives. There are a few books out on the subject, and reading all of them will give you a clearer idea of the variety of ways in which designers work. Don't underestimate the value of a good technical editor. Don't sell your pattern for $1 because you're new, because that devalues all of our work – make sure they're well-written and price them in the range of other self-publishing designers.

You just did your first ever booth at a Stitches show, how did that go? Things like what you expected going in, what actually happened, what you sold/what kinds of reactions you got from face to face retail, would you recommend it to other designers?

Stitches was absolutely worth doing, but totally exhausting. The convention center was 40-70 minutes from my house, depending on traffic, so I drove back and forth every day. The concrete floor of the convention center made my feet ache after the first day, and by the end of the long weekend my back and legs were tired, too. I sold enough patterns to cover my expenses, but didn't make much of a profit, but I think that it was worth it anyway in terms of advertising and name recognition. I handed out a lot of business cards and fliers for my upcoming classes, and expected a bump in both online sales and class sign-ups. That did happen, especially with pattern sales, but neither bump was as large as I'd hoped. Still, considering the cost of advertising in knitting and crochet magazines, being at Stitches with all of my samples for people to look at and try on was absolutely worth the time I spent being there.

STEFANIE JAPEL

Website: http://www.glampyre.com

How did you become a designer? What do you wish you'd known about the industry going in?

For me, designing happened as an organic extension of what I was already doing in my knitting life. I learned to knit at a very young age (8) but I didn't learn to read patterns until I taught myself at about age 19. So knitting for me has always been an experiment. I learned early on how to shape and manipulate knit fabric and never had any fear with regard to the creative process in knitting. If my Barbie wanted a skirt, I just had to figure it out for myself.

So, when I started blogging in 1999, my knitting story was already very different from most of the other bloggers. I would just cast on and see where the yarn took me. It was these early blog posts about my creative process that really drew me into knit design as a profession. I'd post about a sweater I was making and people would ask for the pattern. I didn't actively pursue knit design until Knitty.com came onto the scene. It has always been such a welcoming, blogger-friendly venue that I really wanted to be featured. It was my early Knitty patterns that really launched what I see as my career in knitting.

As far as what I wish I had realized before jumping in with both feet...it's pretty basic, and will make me seem very naive, but I wish I had realized that it's a 'real' industry and as such is very money-driven. I'm not sure why it wasn't apparent even as an outsider, probably because for me it was initially a hobby. I quickly learned that everything is done to sell something...whether it's yarn, books, magazines, patterns, needles...whatever. I think that if I had realized this, it would have made it easier for me to get my rather abstract ideas into a more saleable format. For instance, I would have been more informed as to yarn choices for my self-published patterns and wouldn't have published them with samples knit in handspun or with any vintage or hard-to-find yarns.

Where do you see the industry headed?

I see the industry as being headed toward an increasingly online presence. I think that there will always be a need for the Brick and Mortar knitting store. Knitting is a tactile experience and we need to connect on a human level with (at least some of) the yarn that we buy. We also just crave the live feedback on our projects. However, I think that as we experience more and more of our education, our work, our family interactions online, the industry will evolve to provide similar functions online. For example, I'm already teaching knitting classes online, I do most of my business online, and I use Skype video conferencing to talk to far away business contacts for interviews, conference calls, etc.

Where do you earn most of your income these days?

This breakdown changes month to month for me, and depends on how my books are selling and whether I'm currently offering any classes online. Because I've just had a baby (two babies in 3 years, actually) I've more focused over the last months on online income and income from existing projects (rather than taking on too many new things.) So, I'd say probably 20% online pattern sales, 20% residual income from books, and 60% from teaching online.

What would you change about the industry if you could?

This is a really difficult question, because it's really hard to picture an idealized version of the industry. I don't know what I'd change.

What advice would you give to a new designer? or to one who's been around for a while but needs a jump start?

I think that it's important to constantly re-evaluate your approach to the business. If you feel stagnant, take a moment to look around and see what you might be doing (or not doing) that could be either blocking you or making your efforts feel forced instead of natural. For example, when I started in this business, I was young, single, and knitting really funky garments. I lived in a big city and had constant inspiration from streetwear, from club kids, from shop windows. I also lived in a cooler climate, so I actually had a need for tons of sweaters in my own wardrobe, so it was easy to think of a sweater that I'd want to wear, make it, and write up the pattern. NOW, I'm no longer (as) young, I'm married, I have 2 kids, I live in a small town in the middle of the desert. EVERYTHING about my lifestyle has changed. I've had to consciously allow those changes to affect my business. I still think about what I could use / wear and design for that, but my aesthetic is very different, I don't have a need for lots of new sweaters every season so I've started knitting smaller projects like scarves and shawls, I'm designing more for kids.

Basically, you have to go with the proverbial flow...allow your business to change as your life changes and look for ways to capitalize (both monetarily and in terms of ideas) on those changes. If you try too hard to stay the same, and to keep up with what you see as an ideal but one that doesn't really suit your own life...you won't be able to maintain...it'll be too much of a struggle.

For new designers: read the above and then find your niche. The reason that people read your blog is to learn more about YOU and to see what interesting things you're creating. If you just model yourself after someone else, you lose that special uniqueness that is really the only way to stand out when there are SO many blogs!

Also: Play nice. DON'T COPY. There are so many infinite ways to manipulate yarn. You really don't have to use another person's idea as a basis for yours. If you do, you need to find another profession!

How was the knitting culture different in Germany when you lived there compared to here? Did that influence you at all?

It was different in that not a lot of younger people knit. It was something that was big in the 80s for political reasons (the green party knit in parliament as a form of protest) and so the young people when I was there a few years ago really saw it as old-fashioned. Another difference was that the yarn stores seemed like storefronts for a single brand.

TANIS GRAY

Website: http://www.tanisknits.com

Tell me more about your (former) job as yarn editor for SoHo – what kind of responsibilities did you have, what sorts of things did you learn that might be useful to a designer, etc?

I loved working at SoHo Publishing. I was the Yarn Editor there for over 4 years and the co-editor of knit.1. Being a liaison between SoHo, the designers, the yarn companies and keeping everyone on schedule was no small task. I would sit with the Editor in Chief and we'd choose the garments that would be in the issue, then I'd draw up a sheet for everyone to have so we'd all be on the same page. I'd write up the yarn information sheet, order the yarn, contact the designers, get them everything they needed, hold their hand throughout the design process, get everything back in and prep it to be shot. Things that are useful for a designer to know are have a well written, typed pattern. I always say it's better to have too much info than too little and to let the pattern editors decide what needs to be there and what does not. Always do a gauge swatch and send that in with your finished garment.

What mistakes do you see designers making again and again, or what's your pet peeve in working with other designers when coordinating yarn for magazine work? (Inflexibility on yarn choice? Do designers need to realize magazines are going to make project yarn choices based on their advertisers and such? How are those decisions made?)

The mistakes I saw the most were poorly written patterns (sometimes no pattern at all!), garments not coming in looking like the submission and disorganized paperwork. People sometimes forget that this is a business transaction and we work in a professional environment. A hand written pattern on loose leaf paper covered in coffee stains is not acceptable! Being a designer as well and working in publishing, I've seen the industry from both sides. Yes, people can be very inflexible on yarns. Designers should know that the yarns chosen for them were chosen with purpose and yes, sometimes the yarn just isn't working and it's good to contact whom your working for and talk it through, but don't be fussy just to be fussy. We'd all like to work in 100% hand dyed cashmere, but sometimes you'll be sent cotton. Who knows, you may end up loving it and just never gave it a shot! So many people have sent me a "this yarn is never going to work and I hate it" email then at the end of the process when the deadline is around the corner I would get "the yarn turned out to be perfect and it's all I want to knit with now." Trust us. We know what we're doing. Yarns are chosen individually for each garment. Drape, color, fiber content, yardage, etc are all taken into account. Nothing is done on a whim.

Where do you see the handknitting industry heading?

A lot of people are self publishing and I think that's great. People can get disenchanted with their designs being rejected or just don't know how to go about submitting to large publications. I still think books and magazines will continue to be a large part of knitting publishing, but I like looking at both.

What do you wish someone had told you when you first started off as a designer? How did you get into the business?

I got into knitwear design purely for the fact that I was working at SoHo. I had always designed my own things growing up but never considered it a career or made the assumption that someone else' might like to knit what I had designed. Being around the amazing SoHo staff upped my knitting game significantly and I learned so many new skills and techniques that I may never had had the opportunity to otherwise. The advice I can give to designers is not to give up! Just because your design may have been rejected that doesn't mean you're a bad designer. Maybe the garment didn't fit in with the overall scheme, maybe there was something similar in the issue already, maybe it's not right for the season, etc. There are so many factors as to why a design gets turned down. Be persistent and keep your confidence up! Try again!

Do you earn most of your income from straight up design work or do you do other things as well?

I earn most of my income from designing, but I LOVE teaching knitting so I've found myself teaching more and more. I've also been doing books and self publishing. It's all sort of a melting pot. Each activity influences another so for example, I may get a great idea for something to teach while doing sketches for a submission, or may be teaching and get inspired by comments made in class about what they're looking for in a design. Living in DC and going to museums constantly also helps with daily inspiration.

What role does the internet play in knit design work these days compared to other more "traditional" information sources?

The internet is both a good and bad thing as far as I'm concerned for knitting design. You get a lot of people putting patterns up that are amazing and never would have been made available otherwise. On the other hand, the pattern market has become flooded with a lot of copycat or just not great design work. On the internet, anyone can put a design out there but if you hold a magazine or book in your hand, they were selected. Someone told me recently I had a "lot of street cred" because almost all of my work is for publication. Social media can also be a great thing. I enjoy Ravelry and seeing my students on it and checking out their progress, looking at new designs and designers and keeping in touch with knitting friends. I try to keep up on Facebook but I just cannot get behind Twitter. I am anti-Twitter.

What did you like to see in submissions (pattern and/or editorial) when you were co-editing knit.1 with Faith Hale? Do people generally follow the submission guidelines – or again, if they don't, what's the big pet peeve and what you wish people would/would not do?

knit.1 is gone, unfortunately. People for the most part seem to follow instructions, but the biggest mistake I saw while combing through piles and piles of submissions is the lack of presentation and lack of information. What yarn weight are you looking to design this in? A swatch alone isn't enough info, we need to see a full sketch. Many people wouldn't do something as basic as putting their name and email address on the submission, which makes it useless if we don't know who designed it. Also, you get one chance to make a first impression. Keep your submissions tidy and clearly written.

What do you see as the most influential traits/activities when it comes to being a successful designer? What do great designers have in common, or have that sets them apart from lesser ones?

My favorite thing about being a successful designer is going on Ravelry and seeing other people knitting one of my designs, or be on the subway and seeing someone reading a magazine that has one of my designs in it. To think that I designed something that people all over the world are making and talking about is mind-blowing. Great designers have many traits in common, I've noticed over the years. Most of my friends are successful designers and we're all pretty quiet people that keep to ourselves, organized, deadline driven, able to focus and get the job done, take criticism well, a lot of us love sci-fi (which is a nice way of saying most of us are giant nerds) and we like to sit around and knit together. We're normal people who always have knitting in our bags, no matter where we're going, knit during the movies, knit at meals, knit anywhere, anytime. We love our craft. There are a lot of people who are "Sunday designers" who dabble and that's great, but I think the defining line is that there are people who like it and then there are people like me who LOVE it and cannot imagine a day without knitting.

MARY BETH TEMPLE

Website: http://www.marybethtemple.com

Mary Beth and I had an interesting conversation about a number of topics that was less question-and-answer and more freeform chat...

First and foremost – I am not just a crochet designer – I have a bunch of knit patterns out too. Primarily a crochet designer, but not only a crochet designer.

As for current trends – I wish I knew!
I know several successful designers that have made a career out of specializing, and if I was passionate about one specific technique rather than both crafts as a whole, I might have gone that route. But I love it all, so I do it all, and gather my checks as they come.

The way I go about earning a decent living is to spread my designs out among several venues. There are so many income streams available to us, and while one designer can't be all things to all people, it makes good business sense to utilize as many income streams as you can, because each area may have its ebbs and flows of good times.

For example, I derive income from book advances and royalties for print, e-books, and audio, selling designs to magazines, selling designs to yarn companies, my independent pattern line which is available both in print and as downloads, and teaching both online and at conventions and yarn stores. Sometimes I focus more on one thing than another, and it often feels like I have a lot of balls in the air, but when royalties stink, there's a magazine fee coming in, or when I have a teaching lull I might get a check from a print distributor. My goal is to be getting paid by as many people as possible at all times.

The same sort of spreading out theory applies to my marketing/branding as well. Because while the overall knitting and crocheting market is large, there are so many different segments that sometimes it's like marketing to a completely different group of hobbyists. The customer who either doesn't live near an LYS or shops primarily at a big box or chain craft store is not necessarily going to want the same products as the person who goes to knit night in a high end indie store every week. So for the former customer, I have products that utilize mass market yarns and are available at the chain stores, for the latter, I use yarns that are available at the indie stores, where they can also pick up one of my patterns.

About self-publishing...Actually, I hate that word! I much prefer independent publishing. 'Self publishing', maybe because of all of the truly awful vanity press novels that are out in the world, still has a whiff of second-best about it so far as the terminology goes. There are many independently published books and patterns out there that are terrific and not second-best at all, so why tar them with that semantic brush?

Anyway, my biggest point is that there is no one right way to handle any part of this business. The smart designer will do some research, ask some friends or mentors, experiment, read books like this one, and a pattern of what works and what doesn't will emerge. Then you can capitalize on your strengths. But what works for me may not work for you and vice versa – each person/company is better at some things and worse at others. Figure out what you do best and do the hell out of it!

I would also advise keeping an eye on the big picture of your business as a whole. I have made a big push in recent months to keep a better eye on when rights to some of my earlier works become available to me. It is always easier to squeeze more money out of an existing piece than to start a new one, from scratch. When I started the pattern line I was focused on cranking out as many pieces as humanly possible, now I have names of pieces plugged into my calendar for the next 18 months, so that as soon as the rights revert, I can immediately release my indie version. I could wait until those rights revert, but planning ahead makes me waste less time in production.

How to capture the crocheter? Again, I hope my mix is doing it for me. I hope that the person who buys my mass market leaflet will be coaxed onto my web site or into the yarn store to try one of my indie patterns. I hope seeing my name over and over in all sorts of knitting and crocheting magazines will keep it in the forefront of his or her memory and s/he looks for more of my work. I hope that the person that buys my indie afghan or baby pattern – which is where many traditional stitchers focus their work – will entice that person to try a sweater or a shawl. My name is my brand, and I am ALWAYS pushing the connection between Mary Beth Temple and Hooked for Life. And if I can't drag that crocheter into the yarn store or onto my web site, perhaps I can convert a knitter or two along the way. I really hope one of the new trends in stitching is a breaking down of the perceived gap between crocheters and knitters.

As for internet marketing/social media. I have read over and over that I should be doing it all – blogging, posting on Ravelry.com, Twitter, Facebook, etc etc etc. And I tried, I really tried. But now I focus on what works for me, which is Twitter and podcasting.

As anyone who has ever met me in person can attest, I know how to talk. So doing Getting Loopy [*her podcast*] every week is a no-brainer for me – yes it takes time booking guests and arranging contests and what not, but when it's time to do the podcast, I am essentially sitting down and talking to my friends for 45 minutes a week, and that part isn't a chore at all. The side benefit is that I have learned so very much by chatting with industry people, just hearing so many different experiences can color my thinking, leading me to examine ideas in a new way.

For Twitter – I just find it easier to squeeze in 140 character blurts than to sit down to plan out a blog post with photos. I did finally break down and open a Facebook account, but haven't figure out how best to utilize it.

There has to be a balance – you have to be an ace marketer, but if you spend all of your time marketing you won't have any new products to bring out to the market, which will quickly make you yesterday's news!

And don't take anyone's advice as gospel, even mine. If I had listened to the conventional wisdom that indie crochet designers cant make money in print, I would be a whole lot poorer right now.

DEBBIE STOLLER

http://www.knithappens.com

I'm curious to know what things would you pass along to a newer designer from a branding perspective? How do you effectively brand yourself when you are building your career as a designer or as an author?

I learned most of the branding stuff when I was working at Nickelodeon And, before I started BUST and between graduate school figuring out what I wanted to be when I grew up, I accidentally ended up working at Nickelodeon, and that was part of MTV Networks. This was back in the early days where they talked a lot about brand, the brand. I didn't know what it meant. But at Nickelodeon the idea was that there was this bigger idea as to what all the shows were on Nickelodeon – that a kid would say, 'I want to watch Nickelodeon' instead of 'I want to watch this show or that show'. The idea of what that brand was, it was also all these behind the scene promises; ideas that went into everything that was on Nickelodeon, whether it was a show, or a promo, or whatever. Actually, that really made me think about Bust when we started it as a brand more than just as a magazine. That there were a set of ideas that went with it, so therefore we could do a magazine based on that set of ideas, or a website based on those ideas, or into the future we could do anything, books or t-shirts. Just an idea behind it. People who would read or see something with BUST on it would already have a sense or an idea of what that would mean beyond just a particular magazine. When I did the first Stitch 'N Bitch book I wasn't thinking of it as a brand at all, I was thinking of it was the kind of book I wanted to write and thinking about the audience for whom I was writing it. One thing I did learn was that I don't think so much in terms of things I want to make, but what kind of person it will appeal to, what kind of people may be into that.
So instead of saying this is what I want, you are thinking of the end user first.

Right, and what they might need or want. What don't they have yet.

Who was the end user when you did the first book? Were you thinking that you knew how to knit, had a family history of knitting, "I know a lot of people who want to learn how to knit so I'll write something for them"? Or, was it a little more complex than that?

I had been doing the group for years, so I was seeing the new younger people who wanted to knit. I was right there, every week, and from my own experience teaching and re-teaching knitting I saw how many important instructions were being left out of knitting manuals that were written by a designer who wasn't awesome at explaining something. So I was approached to do the book because I had been writing about knitting in BUST, the publisher asked if I knew anyone who would like to do a knitting book, and I said, "I would love to do that". I felt this need for a book that had patterns for people like me who want something simple but that are kind of interesting and fun. I want to write instructions that are completely clear, too. It was very much: what do people need that isn't there? What would I have liked when I was trying to teach myself?

Did you have your editor hat on when you gathered the patterns? Like sorting through and do they fit this book? Or was it 'let's find cool stuff'?

It is a mix, always. I have an idea of what kind of patterns I want to go in the book. So some of the patterns are good when they come in, and sometimes I'll see someone wearing something and ask them to write the pattern, and looking on the internet searching I'll come across stuff on Flickr or I'll be like wow, 'lets' work with this person to turn it into something for the book' I know this may come off to some people as a bunch of bullshit, but for me, I'm always going thru submissions and adding and subtracting until I feel it has a good balance of things. Not too many sweaters, not too many socks, or hats – just the right mix. Not too many blue things, or red things, I actually keep a database where I put up all the submissions and consider and weed away things until I can at leaf through the pages. I actually have this secret website, when I leaf through it has the pictures so I can see and get a feel it is coming together as a book. What to add, what to take away, and I do all of that before I assign anything.

Is it just like building a magazine, making sure you don't have too much of one thing or another? Do you think running a magazine of any kind gives you an eye for that, since having an 'editorial' eye is an acquired skill? Is it something you can cultivate?

Sometimes I'll ask for help. Like when I was working on the Son of Stitch 'N Bitch book I had an idea of the sort of things I would have liked. But I went and asked the men in my life to look at things, like what would they want to actually wear? Things I sometimes thought were really cool got knocked out, because they weren't interested. Sometimes I'll do that also when putting together something I'll ask girls at different ages with different tastes, let me know what you like, and I'll whittle it down. I think one thing that comes from magazine publishing is considering that audience and a clear idea of what it is they might want, plus what you want. That's important, I think. I'll close my eyes and make a picture…um, let's say someone that's familiar with your work; what would you expect to see when they go to your website? Like, even before they go to the website you can almost start to imagine what pieces need to be there. Rather than saying, 'well I know what I want to put on my website and I know what I want to tell people about me', think to yourself more about what they would expect to see on the website. What is useful for them rather than what's self-promotional for you.

Do you think of yourself as a designer?

I don't think of myself as a designer, I'm more of a teacher, and…facilitator and observer of knitting culture.

But in the end you really do need to consider the brand?

Yes. It is important to consider the sense of the brand, Designers who are doing well, you know what to expect from them and they don't make things willy-nilly. Their websites, their colors, their ads, patterns all are one piece and reflect a particular personality. Maybe they come up with something that's not quite their thing – so they might not include it because they'll say, 'well this isn't the sort of thing you'd expect from X,' **There has to be an aesthetic.**

VICKIE HOWELL

http://www.vickiehowell.com

How did hosting Knitty Gritty come about, and what did you learn there that helped your design career going forward?

Knitty Gritty was a gift from the universe. I used to work in the entertainment industry years and years ago. I stopped when I became a mom, and I put together a few side businesses – crafty web businesses just to keep my sanity as a creatively-driven person. At the time there weren't a lot of those sites (in 2001 or so): I had a handmade baby accessory site and a site that was vintage revamp. Then I started the first Stitch 'n Bitch group in L.A. – well, I know they've been around since the 50s, but this one was the first in L.A., and then one in Austin. The only reason this is relevant is because I created a logo for the Stitch 'n Bitch groups and I put it on the websites for these businesses I had. The producers of Knitty Gritty Googled the keywords I had attached, and that's how they found me. But I always wanted my own craft show. At that time I was in Austin and had totally removed myself from the L.A. industry thing, so it fell in my lap. The stars aligned because I was already making a trip to L.A., I could be there to audition, and I had my design up on Knitty – that guitar strap from ages ago – you know. So, it was just meant to be.

There was that two-year period where everything happened at once.

I really feel it was post-9/11 when everything started, because I think everyone was trying to comfort themselves. The industry really picked up after that.

New yarn stores and everything…

Yes, 2002-03 – that was when editors were practically passing out book deals. And now, you could have 10 books and that won't guarantee you'll get to do another one.

Tell me about the taping schedule for Knitty Gritty, those intense bursts. You were surrounded by designers…what were your impressions while actually doing the show?

It's funny, I did a season or two at a time, 3 shows a day for 2-6 weeks and then I'd come home. That was my indoctrination into the business. Ironically, knitting is the craft I had been doing for the least amount of time at that point. It just happens to be what took off professionally for me. I really feel like I had the best teachers at my fingertips. I learned a lot from that show; I really felt my job wasn't to be the supreme expert of needle arts – it was to be the facilitator of information. I wanted to get people excited and tell them what I did know, show them it was okay to learn more and get people to get creative. That's how I feel today. Obviously my level of expertise has risen, and I would call myself an expert now, but, I still consider that a secondary role to using my influence to get people to get creative.

It was a learn-on-the-job situation.

It really was baptism by fire, because at that point I had only been knitting for a few years.

With your own design work, you ended up doing books instead of the single pattern by single pattern model that's blossomed in the Ravelry era. What are the differences you see in the industry now?

I did feel like getting the show was a gift and I felt a responsibility to do as much as I could with this gift. I hadn't even shot any episodes yet: I pitched a book. And I had no idea! I had done VERY little designing. A purse here and there. But, that's how I do everything in life. And so, no, I didn't have anything to show anybody. But, I don't think back then it was expected in any sort of way.

Do you find yourself backtracking, i.e. "now I have to fill in what I don't have that others do"? Thinking "I have only X number of patterns I can sell."?

I have very few single patterns. I have tons of free patterns that are used as promotions. Because we need to value ourselves, I stopped doing free patterns on my own – meaning I when I offer them it's usually in conjunction with another job that I'm being paid for. A lot of that was me pushing this agenda to value craft, and then realizing I was being hypocritical. But for me, a free pattern is a great way to get people to your site. If you can keep them small so that they aren't labor intensive– baby legwarmers, techie cozies, or whatever –and put them in the same column as products, it isn't selling yourself short. Consider it as if you are a big firm – that would be your marketing budget. As independent designers, the currency for our marketing budget is our skill.

In other words, we don't have money for a national campaign but we have 2 hours for XYZ? So, when you observed designers, what traits stood out as 'that's the designer I want to be and that's the business I want to run'? In your recent book Craft Corps, *you also spoke to a lot of other types of crafters, too. What have you seen that you think you would like to maybe emulate or adapt for yourself?*

I think it was pieces of many people. I'm sort of odd in that my business is myself. I'm not pushing products – I am the product. I'm not trying to sell stuff I've made, or make a living designing garments. Mostly because it is nearly impossible to do, we are still today being paid what designers were paid in the 1980s. Because the particular craft we have chosen takes hours, you know, compared to say, sewing or jewelry, it doesn't even out. So, I think bits and pieces. Like, Jessica from Ravelry – she encourages everyone to charge at least something for their patterns even if it's only a dollar.

I really liked watching certain designers freeform, watching people's process. Since I didn't have formal schooling, I didn't have a reference. What was liberating for me is that because knitting and crocheting are oral traditions – and all education is secondary – there really is no single definitive way to do things. There are no standards really, or not many. So I have to say that was liberating – I am not working from the math out like Lily Chin, and that's okay because it isn't me. I had to find my own way, but that worked and I learned about licensing. Amy Butler is brilliant: she started by licensing the Country Living name for herself to put out patterns – not the other way around. And that's applicable to pretty much any creative business. We are in this whole new era where we're creating our own new American dream, I think that although Craft Corps focuses on craft & design, its underlying theme is the bigger-picture concept of creating new careers all because of the technological resources we now have.

So you as a product as opposed to the patterns as the product. But what happens when you're selling you as the product? Where does the money come? Licensing?

Frankly, if the product were making the money, I probably would have taken that road. The patterns, you really need ads, and 20 patterns to make a meager living doing that. So the money comes from different areas. You have to build your name for people to want to pay for it. I was fortunate to have a TV show, but that's not the only place people know me from, and I worked hard. It is writing columns and pitching columns – I'm constantly pitching myself. That's how you have to be. It comes from writing guest posts and making a decision you won't work for free anymore; even the big corporations want you to work for free for "exposure" – you have to see the value in yourself. For me it might be hitting a certain demographic, or maybe giving them expertise on something or some randomness they wouldn't get on their own. You have to be confident on what you are giving them, it is so easy to undervalue yourself in this industry.

It's difficult not to get excited about free yarn, but…

To me, free yarn landing on my doorstep means, "Oh crap, I am behind on work." I'm still totally in love with the yarn but no matter how gorgeous it is, free yarn symbolizes deadlines. So, the excitement of bartering time for yarn wears off.

The knitting industry is guiltier of using product as currency than other genres within the craft industry. For example, I write weekly posts for a major paint & glue company and they not only send me all of their products, but also pay me to make and write about projects with those products. It makes sense. By using companies' products in articles, books, television shows, etc – you're acting as a living, breathing ad for them. Even if you're just getting paid $25 to link to a company in a blog post, or list one of their projects in the materials list in a magazine, you're providing a service and should be paid for it.

It adds up and all the things combined add up to a living. A lot of designers think they are going to design all day and that will be it.

Unfortunately, at least right now, you can't. You have to have multiple jobs at once; I'm never doing fewer than 3 things at a time. I get to do what I love and pick up my kids from school, but I still work 60+ hours a week easily. I'm always working. That doesn't mean I don't ever stop, but until I crash at night there is something going on – pitching an idea, posting on Twitter or Facebook, writing a blog – and honestly I spend less time physically knitting or making things than I do all of my other jobs. One design, unless it is the design du jour, won't do much for you press-wise (and press is what helps build your brand). You can put less time into a thoughtful blog post, an article or contest to garner the necessary attention that leads to a pay check. It isn't everyone's gig, if you want to spend 8 hours a day knitting, then you'd better have back-to-back book deals lined up and an agent to negotiate high advances on them.

Effective self-promotion is the bottom line, otherwise you won't make it money wise?

Not if you want to remain self-employed. If you want to be an independent person then self-promotion is the key. It is a learned skill. The first bio I wrote, it might have been for Knitty Gritty, I felt so gratuitous and self-centered, and I had to get out of that mindset. Now I pimp myself 24/7!

BRETT BARA

http://www.crochettoday.com

How might submissions differ for your magazine compared to submitting to a knit-only magazine? What do you prefer to see in a submission?

I look for submissions that show that the designers really "gets" current style in terms of shaping or construction or color use. It's easy for crochet to look dated, so I work really hard to make it look as fresh as possible, and I'm always on the lookout for designers who get it. I also look for designers with strengths in particular areas – say lacework, tunisian crochet, crazy shaping. Sometimes those specialties are more important than aesthetic, because when I need a specific type of design, I love knowing that I have a designer on hand who can execute it well. If you have a specialty like that, tell me in your pitch! I also appreciate submissions that demonstrate that the designer is familiar with our content and our range of yarns; ideas that feel like they've been formulated specially for us are always appreciated. (Too often it feels like designers have a generic batch of designs they're pitching to one magazine after another, and I'd give more of MY time/consideration to pitches that feel like they were made with my magazine in mind. Feeling like I'm getting another magazine's cast-offs is a major turnoff.)

What I don't need is fancy binders, overly long presentations, or complete, fully-crocheted projects. Designers are way better off putting their time into the design concept, and keeping the presentation simple. A sketch is fine, an image pulled from current media (a fashion or home magazine, runway shot, or ad) is great too. A suggestion of what yarn to use often suffices; a swatch is fine but really not necessary unless the stitch is really unusual.

Do you create chart for the designers in-house or are they expected to supply them? What's your overall position on charting crochet vs. line by line instructions, and do you see that changing? Do you use or recommend any particular charting software, or...?

We create all of the stitch diagrams for our patterns and the designer is not expected to provide anything in that arena. For schematics or assembly diagrams, it's preferred that the designer submits a rough document for us to work from. A hand-drawn and scanned image is fine, or anything created in whatever software the designer uses. Our in-house staff usually recreates these to match our style so we don't need the designer to do much other than give us the important information. We are currently providing line-by-line instructions for EVERY pattern, and stitch diagrams for all patterns where it makes sense to use them. I think this balance is working well and I don't see it changing for us anytime soon.

How do designers submit for your magazine, and what types of submissions do you prefer?

Our editorial calendar and submission guidelines are at crochettoday.com/about. I really prefer digital submissions. We ask that designers wait six months after submitting before following up.

Even though there are more crocheters in the US than knitters, why do you think crochet hasn't gotten as much exposure until recently? Is that changing?

I don't know the answer to the age-old question of why crochet seems to be in the shadow of knitting, despite there being more crocheters. All I know is that our industry responds to demand like all others – and the best way crocheters can show their numbers is by buying crochet books and magazines, logging crochet projects on Ravelry, downloading free crochet patterns from yarn companies, starting crochet blogs, attending industry events, and otherwise being loud and proud about their hobby – and putting their crafting dollars directly toward their hobby, too. When you're at the craft store or the LYS, tell the managers that you love crochet and you want more crochet stuff! It all trickles down (or up) eventually. That said, I think it's kinda cool that crochet is sort of the scrappy underdog, and I don't have a problem with it. Who cares what everyone thinks about knitting vs. crochet? If you love what you do, just love it and have fun with it – why worry about how you compare to other hobbies? The best way to shine is to simply love what you are doing, without worrying about anything else.

Have you noticed that particular crochet trends seem to take off (such as amigurumi) and stay strong while others falter? Why is that? Do you see a movement towards more wearable crochet garments than in past years?

As with any subject matter I suppose, some trends have staying power while others are just a flash in the pan. I think the crochet trends that have really taken off are the ones that show what crochet does best: sculptural shapes like amigurumi, for example, are really just made for crochet. When we try to make crochet do what it's really not meant to do, those trends aren't as successful.

The same thing goes for more wearable crochet garments. Crochet certainly does some things better than others in terms of garments, and it's all about understanding that and using crochet to its best. And really the same is true for any technique or medium.

What can designers do to make your life easier as an editor?

One of the worst things a designer can do in my book is be high-maintenance. I really appreciate designers who work independently and know when to check in with me, and when not to. I do like to be involved in the design process of each of our projects, so I always want designers to check in with me at key moments so that I know we're on the same page. But calling very frequently or sending really long emails that feel like too much for me to digest – I prefer to avoid that. There are some designers who I avoid because I know it will take way too much of my time/energy to work with them. I prefer when designers take the reins, but just keep me in the loop. For example, if you're unsure about something in the design, send me the 2-3 options you're considering, and tell me which one you think is best and why. But don't send me 6 options and expect me to pick – that starts to feel like I'm doing your job for you, and I want YOU to do your job because you're better at it than I am! It also helps when possible to save up all your questions for one well-organized email, rather than a bunch of different questions at different times. It also really bugs me when designers whine or stress about tight deadlines. If you can accept a tight assignment great, and if you don't have time, don't accept. But please don't accept then freak out about it endlessly to me afterwards, or send passive-aggressive emails about how little time you have! Believe me, I'm just as stressed as you are about that tight deadline, and I want to know I can count on you to come through for me and to help the magazine come together in time!

Another no-no is blowing a deadline – there's a right way to do it, and a wrong way. If a designer gets into trouble with time, but if they contact me about it a week beforehand to come up with a plan B, I will always do everything I can do accommodate. But simply not sending the project on time, or giving all kinds of excuses at the 11th hour – that's not good. It's ALWAYS better to manage expectations by 'fessing up early that you need more time, rather than letting it go till the last minute. The former makes you look responsible and on-the-ball, while the latter gets you blacklisted.

What else can you tell really talented crocheters out there who want to break into the design business?

Honestly I really don't think this business is hard to break into if you are talented. Just put yourself out there and make yourself part of the community. It's easy to do, and free. Start a blog, even if you only update it occasionally when you have new work to show off. Create your own patterns from your designs and make them available for free or sell them in an Etsy shop. Post your stuff on Ravelry. Follow other designers on Twitter to get in the loop. And send submissions to magazines – if you can demonstrate that you're talented and up-to-date with trends, I will definitely notice your submission and I'll be happy to give you a try because I'm always looking for good new people!

AMY SINGER

http://www.knitty.com

How did Knitty get started? what was the original thought process behind the site, and how did you get it going?

I spent 20 years proofreading in the advertising industry. This is not as glamorous as it sounds. It's deadly dull, most of the time, and worst of all, the threat of losing your job is always present. The proofreader is the first to go up against the wall when the revolution comes [aka when money's tight, sack the proofreader]. Summer is the worst time: the whole industry is slow, so sitting there *not* reading anything becomes a real flag for your boss that maybe they could do without you.

Meanwhile, I'd gotten to edit a little, and found that I really liked it. I wanted to be an editor, so I signed up for a class in copyediting at a local college. But I also started to notice that there was a lot of online knitting content starting to appear on blogs, for free. A great pattern on this blog, a really detailed and informative tutorial on that blog over there. I wasn't the earliest of early web adopters but early enough. I'd had experience designing super-clean, simple websites in the late 90s. I'd been a typesetter in college, and a wannabe art director my whole proofreading career. (Ask my former coworkers. It drove them nuts).

One night in June, I was sitting on the couch and it occurred to me that I could take the content I'd been finding all over the web and compile it into a rather awesome online magazine. So I told my husband this. "What would I call it?" I asked him. "Knitty?" he said, almost instantly. A quick whois search found that the URL was available, and poof, a magazine was born. Of course, all the work came afterwards, but it was about that easy to decide I was going to do it.

I posted a call for submissions on my reasonably well-connected knitting blog – maybe there were a hundred of us back then? – with this text: "I have wanted to do this, in one form or another, for a quite a while now. And now I have. I've registered a domain name and am going to start up an on-line knitting magazine.. And I want all my knitbloggy friends to be my designers! In case you wondered, I have a background in web design, writing and editing and I'm ready for my part of this challenge...If you're interested in submitting designs for online publication, check out the FAQ. I'm insanely excited about this and hope you are, too. Please join me and spread the word. If all goes well, the first issue will be out by Labor Day."

The surprising thing was that people were into it immediately. There was very little "who says you're good enough to do this?" Or "why should we waste our time? How do we know you're really going to come through?" People took my at my word and submissions started flowing in. By September, we had a magazine and I realized I really liked doing this. So my let's-put-on-a-show first issue grew into a quarterly magazine. In November that same year, I was laid off (see? I told you) and though I had to get another job proofreading to pay the mortgage, I discovered that making Knitty was my dream job and I didn't want to stop.

When did you decide to transition to doing this full time and what informed that decision? Workload at Knitty vs day job, increasing revenue stream, what?

It never even occurred to me that I might be able to turn Knitty into my full-time job for the first few years. I was glad to have something to do that I loved, and it wasn't about the money. It made being a proofreader more tolerable, because I had something else to be proud of.

Things started to change when someone approached me about writing a knitting book that had already been picked up by HarperCollins. So I wrote the book. And then there was a tiny book tour which consisted of me, a rental car and a GPS, trying to find our way through the northeast US for a week. And then there was another book. And another. I was starting to build a reputation as an author as well as the editor of Knitty, and opportunities to travel and teach were starting to come in faster than I had vacation days to spend on them.

At the same time, ad revenues had finally reached a stage where quitting the day job was a possibility. There was an often opened Exit Strategy spreadsheet sitting on my computer, where I tried to crunch numbers to see if we could really survive without my full-time wage and health benefits.

One really important difference between Canada (where I live) and the US: in Canada, health care is paid for out of our taxes. Things like prescription drugs, eyeglasses and dental stuff – those are your own responsibility, and what I was relying on my day job to provide as part of my employment package. But when my gall bladder blew up a few years ago, it cost us nothing. OHIP (Ontario Health Insurance Plan) covered it all. If I had lived in the US, I'm not sure I ever would have been able to quit the day job.

We decided in April. I held my breath for a month or so, checking and re-checking the numbers to make sure I wasn't making a huge mistake, and immediately upon returning from TNNA in June, gave my notice to my employers. Terrifying and exciting all at the same time.

Where do you see the industry heading?

There's no question in my mind that the internet is the reason knitting's early 21st century popularity has grown to the exponential level it's currently enjoying. I think the internet will continue to be the means of spreading inspiration and support to knitters worldwide from now on.

There's a current shakeup in all areas of print publishing – newspapers and magazines in every industry are having to rework the way they do business in order to survive. Craft books are susceptible to the same pressure. I'm not sure where print will end up and what it might look like when it gets there, but I'm quite sure that independent online publishing (downloadable PDFs), whether in single-pattern or book form, will be a vibrant, growing area of the knitting and crafting world. I'll be interested to see if the projected move to notepad display computers (like the iPad or Kindle) actually happens for magazines. I think it's a great idea, but I also think nothing will ever replace paper.

What sort of conflicts did you have with the established industry when you first started going to things like TNNA, etc? Were they inflexible or disinterested in the online experience? (I know that even today there are a lot of LYS owners who think online stores aren't "real"...)

The first time I went to TNNA, it was 2004. I walked around and tried to explain what an online magazine was, and many people got the idea. I'm not sure if they were impressed or confused, but there was enough positive support that I didn't walk away crushed. When I went to my next TNNA in 2006, people knew me without introduction and I had to explain what Knitty was about only 1 in 10 introductions. I haven't met a lot of naysayers, though I'm sure they're out there.

As a designer yourself, where have your income streams come from?

Knitty allows me to stay in my house and feed the rabbits. Since most of my teaching happens when I'm away from home, the profit is mitigated by the costs of travel, but I'd say about 5% of my income is teaching.

What kinds of changes have you instituted over the years to keep Knitty ahead of the pack? (print friendliness, big girl-sizing friendliness...) You had such great success with the Big Girl Knits books, so why was there such an uproar when Knitty changed its sizing guidelines?
I don't remember an uproar. Did I miss it? I was pretty casual about adding larger sizes to our patterns at first, but with time and Jillian's guidance, we decided to officially institute CYC sizing on all patterns. It's more work for the designers, but the payoff is that the patterns are much closer to real size for more of our readers, and if they have to do math, it's not like they have to start with a 34" chest and try to make it fit a 3x body.

We did have a little kerfuffle when some small-minded fat-phobic readers noticed us proudly showing big-girls in knitwear and a rather legendary discussion in the KnittyBlog's comments with someone who thought big girls should not be seen nor heard. The great fun was watching the flood of unsolicited comments who supported including people of all size, and the woman (who ironically worked in a yarn shop and should have known better) eventually skulked away.

What do you see, wearing your editor hat, that you wish you didn't in submissions? i.e. do people not read and follow the guidelines? or what catches your eye and brings something forward into "great submission" category?

Most people do read the guidelines, which I really appreciate. Religious submissions come in from time to time despite our clear "Knitty is religion neutral, so nothing related to any religion will be published" note. Those are rejected outright. People who stick their images in the document with their pattern – that's frustrating. Pictures that are 5 MB each (huge!) – or the size of an avatar (aka tiny) – those slow down the evaluation process.

Overall, people spend a huge amount of time on their submissions and I'm so appreciative of that. The quality of work that comes in is really impressive. The last-minute quickie submissions, however, usually look like just that; the amount of thought behind a submission always shows in every aspect from how the pattern is written to the photographs to the e-mail that goes along with the submission.

The way to catch my attention is to have insanely great photographs, striking in every aspect from the location to the clothing that goes along with the knitted item. This assumes that the knitted item is also fabulous, but sometimes a great photo can make a simple piece of knitwear into a piece of art. There's nothing wrong with simple – in fact, it's likely more wearable, if we're talking about sweaters. A good photo can grab reader attention and make them see something that they might have skipped over, if the photo was merely mediocre.

The next best way – find a new way to do something and tell me about it in the e-mail. New construction methods or techniques are something I think we're becoming known for, and I'm really proud of the contributors who stretch their brains and then send the results to Knitty.

With the Knittyboard – how did that develop over time and help build not just a fanbase but a community?

That is entirely the result of our Knittyboard members and moderators. They want to be a loving, supportive, creative community, and that's the direction we took early on. Our "no religion; no politics" rule came about from feedback from people posting on the board in our first year. There have been some amazing stories of people supporting Knittyboard friends as they had to relocate across the world, or through a catastrophic illness. And of course, the happy celebrations when good things happen to our members, those are huge.

APPENDIX A

This is one version of the "classes I offer" list that I keep on hand to send to yarn stores or other event organizers who ask. I've cut all but one class description to save space, but the formatting should give you a general idea. I've also included comments, which are in italics.

Fiber classes with Shannon Okey

Start off with a quick explanation of who you are, what you do and why they should care. In my case, most people have heard of my books, so I make reference to them. It's also good to mention where you've taught in the past. Treat it like a resume: if you've only ever taught at your local yarn store, say something like "I have taught sock knitting and cabling classes at Sheep Pun Yarn Store in Your City and State for four years, averaging 10 students per session." instead.

Looking for an engaging teacher who will bring both new information and plenty of entertainment into your shop? Shannon Okey, author of a dozen knitting- and fiber-related books, is available for shop and show workshops, guild appearances, and private / semi-private lessons, not to mention workshops in her Cleveland, Ohio studio (knitgrrlstudio.com). She has taught in venues of all sizes, for clients ranging from the National Needle Arts Association (TNNA), Louet North America, the Original Sewing and Quilting Expo and Make Magazine's Maker Faire to knitting festivals, yarn shops and unusual locations such as the Holden Arboretum – where better to explore unusual plant yarns? – as well as a 1920s Kansas high school-turned-arts center.

Further biographical information for use in publicity and your class flyers is available at the end of this brochure, along with general terms and conditions, information on kits, rates, etc.

Want a specific class that isn't listed here, or a class that combines two or more of the subjects covered? Contact us for details. We can do custom classes with sufficient notice. Shannon's office aims to respond to all emails within 24 hours; phone messages may take longer depending on current teaching load and book deadlines.

Here's where you list the classes you teach. It's always a good idea to give maximum enrollment numbers so unscrupulous organizers don't have you teaching 50 people in a room for the same amount of money you'd make teaching 25. If the class can be taught in more than one session length (i.e. 3 hrs for the short version, 6 hrs for an all day version), say so. Materials lists are very important – have them ready so the organizer can either supply them or make sure students bring them to class. Or, if you can provide kits, say so. I prefer providing my own kits for certain classes that are materials-dependent so I can guarantee successful outcomes in class.

Nuno Felting

Max # of students: 25

Length of class: 3 hours

Materials fee: $20

Materials in kit: silk gauze fabric, fiber batts, shredded sari silk and yarn scraps, bubble wrap

Student supply list: beads, thread, floss, fabric pieces, yarn and fiber scraps or any other embellishments you might like, bath towel, scissors

Class description: Nuno felting is the art of forcing fiber through a fabric base to create a light, wearable felt with lots of drape that's suitable for use in garments, art quilts or anything else you can imagine. We will use silk gauze as the base fiber for this class – you can choose to experiment with several small pieces or make one large wrap/shawl/scarf.

Terms, conditions and general information

Don't omit this section under any circumstances, however you choose to word it. A professional expects to be adequately compensated for his or her services, and that is what you are providing. This is a starting point for negotiations, and reputable event organizers will realize this (or should, anyway). If they can only afford to pay you X per hour and you usually make Y, they'll tell you so – and you can decide if other factors involved (publicity, chance to travel somewhere you've wanted to visit, etc) makes it worth your time.

Pricing:

For classes with instructor-supplied kits, the charge is $75 per class hour. If you prefer to supply kit materials, per-class pricing minimums for 3-hour classes will apply, namely $300 per class for 1-10 students and $350 for 11-25. (Inquire for larger demos or lectures; Thrift Store Knitting, for example, is $175 when booked alongside other classes). You may need to send samples of the materials you plan to provide if the class is highly material-dependent, such as nuno felting or yarn painting. For full weekend or multi-day engagements, pricing is negotiable: please ask.

See what I did there on that last line? Heck, I should put it in bold. This gives store owners on a budget some wiggle room when it comes to figuring out what makes sense for them. Usually, it's silly to book someone to do just one class when there is a lot of traveling involved. This "pricing is negotiable" line indicates you are flexible, but only if it will be worth your time overall.

Travel and accommodations:

For classes more than 4 hours outside Cleveland, OH (enter zipcode 44107 into your mapping software of choice to calculate drivetimes to your shop), I prefer to fly unless other arrangements are made in advance. I do try to combine travel costs with other events whenever possible to minimize your expense, and will clear prices with you before finalizing arrangements. In the event a class is cancelled once tickets have been purchased, you will still be responsible for paying my travel costs invoice unless you are able to find another shop or guild in your area that will sponsor an alternative or replacement event.

Class sizes and classroom layout:

I am always willing to budge on class size if there's high enrollment, or teach a second session. U-shape table layouts are preferred when possible. Some classes require water or a water source; nuno felting and dyeing classes in particular, please give as much information as possible about your classroom space when inquiring so we can determine what's possible and how we can accomplish it.

Book signings:

Book signings of 1-2 hours can be added on to any class or classes. I prefer for shops to order books before I arrive and can provide any needed publisher information for ordering. If you want me to bring books to a non-driveable engagement, I ask that you pay for shipping them to/from my studio: this usually works best for guilds, shows and other groups without a retail presence.

About Shannon – biographical info for brochures:

Make it easy for the shop or event to promote you! 99% of the time they will directly cut and paste whatever you write, so if nothing else, make sure you have a short updated bio ready to go at all times.

Shannon Okey is the author of *Spin to Knit, Alt Fiber* and more than ten other fiber-related books. She is the former editor of monthly UK knitting magazine Yarn Forward, and previously wrote a column for knit.1 magazine in addition to her frequent contributions to other crafty publications. When she's not on the road, Shannon teaches at her business Knitgrrl Studio in Cleveland, Ohio. Named one of Vogue Knitting's six New Guard of Knitting in their 25th anniversary issue, she has appeared on Knitty Gritty, Uncommon Threads, Crafters Coast to Coast and other television programs. Visit her online at knitgrrl.com.

Need a photo of Shannon for your website? Here's one you can use: http://www.knitgrrl.com/images/shannon-okey.jpg

In addition to a standard headshot, it's a good idea to have images of your work, your classes or related materials ready to go.

For print resolution photos or any special media requests, please email admin@knitgrrl.com

Publicity:

Help them help you. Make it easy for the shop to promote your event. If you have books or patterns for sale, make sure the shop has them in stock before you arrive. Be sure to mention where you'll be teaching on your own website, Twitter, etc. People who are already following you know who you are, even if a store's particular customers don't. I've had a lot of class signups happen at out of town events because the person's friend/relative/knitting buddy told them I was coming to town and that they should sign up for my class.

I want scheduled classes to be a success as much as you do. Experience has taught me that coordinating publicity efforts is good for both of us, therefore I ask for the following:

- Make an announcement on your shop's website/Twitter/Facebook/etc as soon as we have confirmed the class or classes
- Announce events in newsletters or other shop communications
- Publicize the event with your local media: send press releases to all newspapers and TV stations. I will be happy to provide you with a boilerplate press release that you can customize with your shop information. Smaller local newspapers will often publish a release in its entirety – great PR for you, too!
- I will make myself available for as many interviews or media appearances as is feasible before and during the workshops.
- I will announce the events on both the knitgrrl.com events page and in my newsletter (when possible), and post information about your shop and classes on the news portion of my site.

**IF YOU LEARN ONE THING FROM THIS APPENDIX, MAKE IT THIS:
ALWAYS HAVE A SHORT (30-45 WORDS) BIO AND HEADSHOT READY TO SEND!**

Any other questions or concerns? Please let us know. We try to be accommodating whenever possible, but making requests as far in advance as possible optimizes your chances for booking. Thank you!

Shannon Okey
admin@knitgrrl.com
[phone number]
Knitgrrl Studio, [address]

APPENDIX B

Book proposal template

Most knitting book proposals are submitted directly to a publisher directly unless you have an agent. Even if you do have an agent, he or she typically won't write the proposal for you, but will tweak whatever you send in to meet the needs and focus of the publisher in question, to optimize your success. This is one reason to have an agent – he or she is keeping your interests in mind and presenting you in the best possible light to the publisher based on personal knowledge of their needs, wants, dislikes and more. I have used variants of this book proposal template ever since my first book, *Knitgrrl* (which was proposed to its publisher, Watson-Guptill, in spring 2004).

Explanations along the way will be in italics like this.

☆ **Overall book concept**

For Alt Fiber *(first pitched in 2005), I started with facts about not only the popularity of knitting, but also information on why a book about plant fiber yarns would be relevant and interesting.*

Knitting is clearly one of the fastest-growing crafts today. The percentage of women under the age of 45 who know how to knit and crochet doubled between 1996 and 2002, climbing from 9% to 18%, according to research sponsored by the Craft Yarn Council of America.

And although true wool allergies are rare, many are highly sensitive to the fiber. According to the International Wool Secretariat (aka the Woolmark Company), over 30% of American consumers report wool sensitivity. Still more choose not to wear or buy wool due to personal preference (vegans, for example). Multiply this by the number of knitters who want to make something for a friend in the above categories and you have a sizeable potential readership!

Remind the editor reading your proposal why your idea is important, relevant and will appeal to a variety of people.

Until recently, one was limited to knitting with cotton, perhaps linen. However, an explosion of new fiber alternatives has arrived on the market during the past few years, and many knitters haven't had a chance to try them yet. There's soy fiber, yarn made from bamboo, corn, even wood pulp. … There are many choices for the adventurous knitter.

Now we've further nailed down the group who will best enjoy this book (adventurous knitters), as we pique the editor's interest. "Wait, what? They can make yarn out of WHAT?"

☆   **Marketing assessment**

"But I want to talk about the yarn some more!" No. Not right now. Editors at major publishing houses are concerned with a short list of issues, among them "how will I get this past the marketing committee who helps decide which books get published." Make his or her job easier by doing some of the research! They'll need to know which titles are potentially competitors (if the field is too crowded with books on Specific Knitting Topic X, you're unlikely to sell another one…at least not right now), what sorts of coverage the topic is getting (when I first started pitching Alt Fiber, *maybe one of the major knitting magazines had mentioned soy fiber yarn, if that), and whether the title is likely to earn a profit.*

Although most of these fibers have been around for centuries (photo right; Henry Ford wearing one of the first-ever soy fiber suits), they were not commercially available as knitting materials until recently. There is a lack of books that specifically discuss wool alternatives other than cotton on the market.

What's new and fresh about this book? Give the editor something to hold onto…if you were pitching a topic in person, as I have in the past, I would bring samples of soy or bamboo fiber. But if you're limited to paper, go for figurative "hold onto" – anything cool or "wow!" you can show them that will stick in his or her mind is important. In this case, I used a photo of Ford's founder wearing a suit made out of soy nearly 100 years earlier.

- "Doing It Yourself: The Cool Kids Stick to Their Knitting," by Karen Holt. Publisher's Weekly, 24 May 2004.
- (Other relevant examples: aim for at least three)

Publisher's Weekly is a widely read industry publication – chances are good if a topic is getting a lot of press there, publishers are scrambling to find the Next Hot Thing *to publish, book-wise, on it.*

Recent knitting books targeted to the same demographic:

List books that have come out within the past 2 years that are closely related to your topic, or appeal to the same audience. Conversely, if nothing has been published about the topic in 20 years, make the case by showing that there isn't any competition, and this book can go on to be the leader in its category if accepted.

☆   **About YOUR NAME HERE.**

Who are you, and why should they care? Remember the concept of 'platform'? Here's where you explain yours. If you have solid, verifiable statistics of any kind, whether it's how many visitors come to your blog each month, or how many copies your last book sold, or… put it here. Here's one text chunk from a past proposal of mine:

Shannon has been writing in various capacities for over a decade. Her bestselling, award-winning books for "tweens," *Knitgrrl* and *Knitgrrl 2* (Watson-Guptill Publications, 2005 and 2006) teach beginning knitters through a series of patterns by fresh new designers. *Knitgrrl* sold 6000 copies in the period leading up to its release plus 2 months afterward without placement on the shelves of Barnes and Noble or Borders. Borders then decided to order over 3000 copies in its next sales cycle!

Shannon emphasizes both the DIY and community-centered aspects of knitting. The young adult division of the American Library Association took notice: they published an article by Shannon in their spring 2005 issue on starting a library knitting group to attract teen readers. Librarians have given the books consistently excellent reviews, including a starred review in Booklist, as have all the major knitting magazines. (See knitgrrl.com for clips).

Almost a year before publication, the Knitgrrl website (designed by Shannon) and mailing list boasted over 1100 subscribers! Notably, these two tween books also filled a large void in their market. Nearly all other knitting books for children are meant for a considerably younger age bracket, or are designed for parents who want to knit *for* their kids.

☆   **Photography / illustrations for book**

If you are capable of providing professional-quality photographs, charts, illustrations, etc for your own book, say so! Many a book has been sold based on its photography alone.

☆   **The patterns**

Sum up the patterns or the content (if it's not a pattern book) briefly. It's not a bad idea to add a line such as "Please note that patterns shown in this proposal are samples only, and the final list will be developed with publisher's input." Some editors like to have more control over the final pattern list than others, and it's stupid to look inflexible going in.

☆   **Table of Contents**

Here comes the good stuff. When I work with other designers who are developing book ideas, this is where I tell them to start – write the table of contents first! It's an excellent way to get all your thoughts down on paper (or computer screen) and figure out what order makes sense for the content, where patterns should go, which chapter might be a little information-heavy or need another pattern, etc.

CHAPTER ONE: Introduction and basics

- Introduction
- Short history and background of [subject]

Write a short introduction as if you were already doing the book. Get the editor interested in what you have to say – it's also a writing sample for them to judge how the end product may turn out, and it shows that you know your topic.

CHAPTER TWO: Whatever

- Break down the subject of the chapter into 2-5 key points each time, so an editor who's merely skimming can get a sense of the content without reading everything.
- *Hey, look! I'm the second key point!*
- *And I'm the third!*

If this is a chapter that has patterns in it, too, be sure to list them here, like this:

- Pattern name: a pattern that has these characteristics, such as…
- Rivulet: a cabled cardigan that flatters women of all sizes, by Shannon Okey

And here comes a brief paragraph about the other stuff in chapter 2.

Repeat the Chapter Two outline for as many chapters as possible. Then, look over the list and check to make sure it's sensible. Have you put a pattern into chapter 3 that uses a technique you don't discuss until chapter 5? Did you forget that you need to explain what that technique is, since no one's used it since the 18th century in Argentina? Go back and make sure everything is logical and will make sense to a reader with little to no subject matter expertise.

☆   **Backmatter / Guide**

Here's where you list the sorts of information that will go into the back of the book, such as appendices (like this one!). The publisher will create an index, so you don't need to list that, it's assumed.

- Where to buy
- Suggested websites
- Resource guides

And there you have it! Now get to work on a cover letter that's professional yet get the editor interested enough to read your proposal…and good luck!

RESOURCES

Books

These are some books that I have personally found useful, and it is by no means an exhaustive list. Everyone learns differently, and what makes perfect sense to one person may be less helpful to another. Consider this and the other resources listed here as a starting point.

Patternmaking For Fashion Design, Helen Joseph Armstrong. Designed more for those who work with wovens, but an invaluable resource on drape, sloper-making and other skills that professional knitwear designers can easily adapt for their own use.

9 Heads: A Guide To Drawing Fashion, Nancy Riegelman.

Note: both *Patternmaking for Fashion Design* and *9 Heads* are often used as a textbook in fashion schools, check nearby university bookstores for used copies if you can't find it for a reasonable price online.

Knitwear Design Workshop: The Comprehensive Guide to Handknits, Shirley Paden
Knitting from the Top, Barbara Walker.
Sweater Design in Plain English, Maggie Righetti.
Knitter's Handbook, Montse Stanley
Designing Knitwear, Debbie Newton
Knitting Without Tears, Elizabeth Zimmermann.
Big Girl Knits and *Big Girl Knits 2*, Amy Singer and Jillian Moreno. The frontmatter alone will save you hours of agony when working out appropriate grading for plus size womens' patterns.

Online tutorials and resources

Jenna Wilson's Thinking Beyond The Pattern archive: http://www.knitty.com/archiveTBP.php is an invaluable learning resource, particularly on sleeve cap shaping.

Jessica Fenlon's pattern writing series on Knitty.com

```
http://knitty.com/ISSUEspring04/FEATpatterns101.html
http://knitty.com/ISSUEsummer04/FEATpatterns102.html
http://knitty.com/ISSUEfall04/FEATpatterns103.html
```

A large number of links to various resources that may come in handy for you as a designer:

```
http://www.fibergypsy.com/Charts_and_Other_Helpful_Resources
```

Publicity, marketing and more

```
http://www.famefoundry.com
http://www.mashable.com
http://ittybiz.com*
```

* A word of warning before you click: Naomi Dunford, who writes IttyBiz, is personable, smart, entertaining to read...and she swears from time to time. If that offends, she might not be right for you. However, I've picked up more valuable chunks of wisdom from reading her site than you might gather from 1000 "Capital-B Business" books. Ours is a business with a lot of personality in it – don't be afraid to show yours! Also, inspiration and ideas can come from unlikely places.

Getting paid

```
http://www.paypal.com
http://checkout.google.com
http://www.E-junkie.com/?r=4470
https://www.payloadz.com
http://www.propay.com
https://squareup.com
```

If you opt for a full merchant account with a credit card processor, I've had nothing but great experiences with Merchant Warehouse (tell them Knitgrrl Studio sent you):

```
http://www.merchantwarehouse.com
```

Magazine submissions guidelines

Interweave submission guidelines:
```
http://www.interweaveknits.com/contact/guidelines.asp
```

Vogue direct submissions link:
```
http://www.vogueknitting.com/design_submissions.aspx
```
You can attach up to 3 additional files, they prefer JPGs or PDFs)

See also the frequently updated list at:
```
http://www.ravelry.com/wiki/pages/designerresources
```

Professional Organizations

The National Needlearts Association (TNNA):
   http://www.tnna.org
Association of Knitwear Designers:
   http://www.knitwear-designers.org
Crochet Guild of America:
   http://www.crochet.org
The Knitting Guild Association:
   http://www.tkga.com

Educational resources and opportunities

TKGA's Master Knitter program:
   http://www.tkga.com/mastersprogram.shtm

A variety of textile education links, links to relevant museums, etc:
   http://www.tex.in/education/education.html

Nottingham Trent University (UK):
   http://tinyurl.com/knitdesignBA

Canadian Guild of Knitters accreditation:
   http://www.cgknitters.ca/kap.htm

Fashion Institute of Technology (FIT) in New York City offers the Craft Yarn Council's Certified Instructor Program:
   http://www3.fitnyc.edu/continuinged/CPS/CraftYarnCouncil.htm

The Pratt Institute:
   http://www.pratt.edu

Parsons The New School for Design:
   http://www.newschool.edu/parsons

San Francisco's Academy of Art University:
   http://www.academyart.edu/fashion-school/bfa_program.html

The Fashion Institute of Design and Merchandising:
   http://fidm.edu/academics/majors/fashion-knitwear

The Rhode Island School of Design:
   http://www.risd.edu

Philadelphia University (formerly the College of Textiles):
http://www.philau.edu

Art Institute (Miami):
http://www.artinstitutes.edu/miami

Textile Museum (Toronto):
http://www.textilemuseum.ca

Textile Museum (Washington DC):
http://www.textilemuseum.org

Central St. Martins College of Art and Design in London:
http://www.csm.arts.ac.uk

Knit-1 in Brighton (UK) offers ultra-intensive design courses:
http://www.knitdesigncourses.com

Other Ravelry Groups/Resources

Budding Designers
Crochet Designers
Designers and Crafters Working Together
Indy Pattern Designers Resource
Self-publishing Knitters
The Testing Pool

Other places to read designer interviews

If you enjoy the interviews in this book, you'll find that there are many more available on various websites. Robin Hunter (http://knittingrobin.blogspot.com) has some excellent ones, with Teva Durham, Sally Melville and others.

Printing resources

http://www.48hourprint.com
If you want to do several hundred (250-500) pieces at once, this might be a good option for you – the per-piece price works out fairly low for full gloss, 100# paper.

http://www.vistaprint.com
Great for business cards and other promotional materials, but can take quite a long time to arrive if you don't pay for expedited shipping

More links that might interest you

```
http://www.kimwerker.com/2010/02/04/that-woo-woo-money-
thing
```

The inherent value of 'free' in building relationships online, from a craft-related perspective by Kim Werker, crochet author and former editor of Interweave Crochet.

```
http://makeandmeaning.com
```

On a related note, this website, with several high-visibility craft community visionaries at the helm, frequently hosts fascinating conversations about larger issues that tie in to things you should know about. The link above started off from a topic there.

```
http://techknitting.blogspot.com
```

"25 years of knitting tricks want out of my mind and into yours" says the tagline, and with good reason.

```
http://www.mimeo.com
```

They also do CD and DVD reproduction, if you would like to package a how-to CD with your pattern booklet or other items for sale, and you can customize booklets and other training materials for a specific yarn store or other customer

Take classes with the author

I teach many classes on topics related to this book (both in person and online) including how to publish, Designer 101, and others. At the time of publication, my online classes can be found at:

```
http://knitgrrl.ning.com
```

In the event this link is no longer valid, please visit my main site knitgrrl.com, send me an email or write to me care of the publishers. If you own a yarn store, I do still teach at shops and events throughout the year. Get in touch, I'd love to hear from you!

ACKNOWLEDGMENTS

Many thanks to all the designers and other industry professionals who took time from their busy schedules to answer my questions, make suggestions and otherwise help with the creation of this book. I'm listing in alphabetical order because I can't possibly rank them by level of thanks – they all contributed so much:

Adina Klein, Alexandra Virgiel, Amy Singer, Ann Shayne, Annie Modesitt, Brett Bara, Charlotte Quiggle, Debbie Stoller, Elizabeth Lovick, Janet Szabo, Jenna Wilson, Jillian Moreno, Joan McGowan-Michael, Josi Hannon Madera, Julie Turjoman, Juliet Bernard, Karin Strom, Kate Atherley, Kay Gardiner, Kira Dulaney, Lily Chin, Louisa Harding, Marnie MacLean, Mary Beth Temple, Melanie Falick, Melissa Wehrle, Miriam Felton, MK Carroll, Myra Wood, Nicky Epstein, Stefanie Japel, Tanis Gray, Tina Whitmore, Trisha Malcolm, Vickie Howell and Ysolda Teague.

Special thanks to the anonymous NYC agent, my own agent, and the lawyers, named and unnamed who checked over the legal bits, not to mention arts and crafts lawyer extraordinaire Tammy Browning-Smith.

To all the members of Stitch Cooperative (stitchcooperative.com) and its predecessor, the erstwhile Fiber League, and especially to Andi Smith of knitbrit.com: for always making me look good and being the best sounding board in the world.

To Tamas Jakab, and the furry contingent: Anežka, Spike and Giles, aka the ones who get neglected most when I'm in full-on writing mode. As ever, Tamas got drafted to help with the technical side of putting this together, and he created the cover design and typography. I love you all!

A *very* special thank you to Franklin Habit for his cover illustration.

To my InDesign gurus: Cinnamon Cooper and Stacie Ross, and to Kerrie Allman and the staff (both current and former) of KAL Media for being such wonderful colleagues during my tenure at Yarn Forward, and to our readers there, who taught me so much.

To Arabella Proffer – pattern model and friend – with whom I share a studio space and a penchant for getting into trouble. Her help on last minute interview transcriptions was appreciated more than she'll *ever* know.

And finally, to **YOU**! Thank you for reading, and I wish you the best of luck in your design career.

BIBLIO- AND BIOGRAPHY

Also by the author

Knitgrrl (Watson Guptill, 2005)
Knitgrrl 2 (Watson Guptill, 2006)
Spin to Knit (Interweave Press, 2006)
Felt Frenzy (with Heather Brack) (Interweave Press, 2007)
Crochet Style (Creative Homeowner, 2007)
Just Gifts (Potter Craft, 2007)
Just Socks (Potter Craft, 2007)
AlterNation (with Alexandra Underhill) (F+W/North Light, 2007)
The Pillow Book (Chronicle, 2008)
How to Knit in the Woods (Mountaineers, 2008)
Alt Fiber: 25 Projects for Knitting Green with Bamboo, Soy, Hemp, and More (Ten Speed Press, 2008)
Knitting For Dummies (editor, second edition) (Wiley/For Dummies, 2008)

About the author

Shannon Okey has published a dozen major-publisher books and is the former editor in chief of monthly UK-based print knitting magazine Yarn Forward. She previously wrote a column for knit.1 magazine, and has been a frequent contributor to many others, including CRAFT, Adorn, Vogue Knitting, SpinOff, knit.1, Interweave Felt, Sew Hip, Inside Crochet, and Yarn Market News (the business magazine of the yarn industry). Okey has appeared on numerous television shows, among them Knitty Gritty, Uncommon Threads, Crafters Coast to Coast, and Knitting Daily TV, and was named one of six "New Guard of Knitting" in Vogue Knitting's 25th anniversary issue. She has taught all over the world, even on the high seas (if you think spinning yarn is difficult, try it on a cruise ship that's rocking from side to side!), and has pushed innovation in the industry through online fiber arts instruction in association with her studio/shop Knitgrrl Studio.

You can find her online at **knitgrrl.com** and **knitgrrlstudio.com**
shannon@knitgrrl.com

ABOUT COOPERATIVE PRESS

partners in publishing

Cooperative Press (formerly *anezka media*) was founded in 2007 by Shannon Okey, a voracious reader as well as writer and editor, who had been doing freelance acquisitions work, introducing authors with projects she believed in to editors at various publishers.

Although working with traditional publishers can be very rewarding, there are some books that fly under their radar. They're too avant-garde, or the marketing department doesn't know how to sell them, or they don't think they'll sell 50,000 copies in a year.

5,000 or 50,000. Does the book matter to that 5,000? Then it should be published.

In 2009, Cooperative Press changed its named to reflect the relationships we have developed with authors working on books. We work *together* to put out the best quality books we can, and share in the proceeds accordingly.

Thank you for supporting independent publishers and authors.

☆   http://www.cooperativepress.com

rgne, TN USA
nuary 2011
659LV00005B/97-130/P